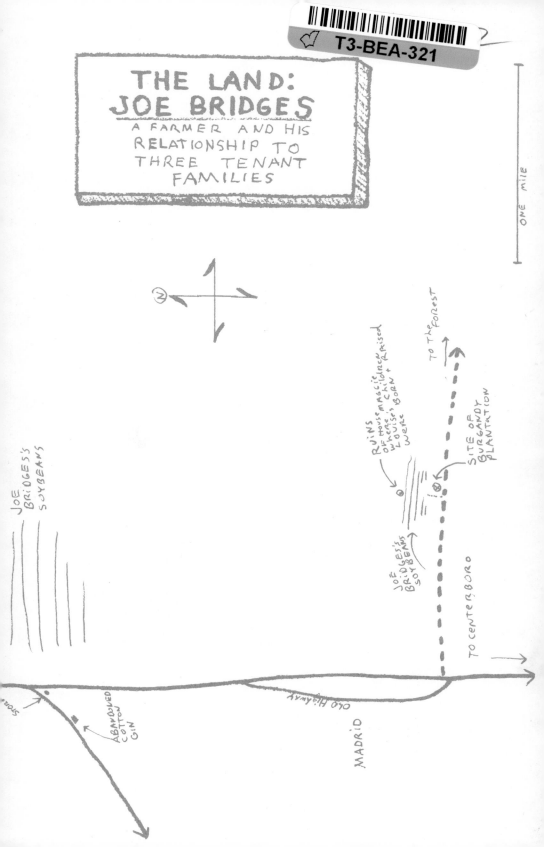

THE LAND:
JOE BRIDGES
A FARMER AND HIS
RELATIONSHIP TO
THREE TENANT
FAMILIES

ONE MILE

N

JOE BRIDGES'S SOYBEANS

Ruins of house, Maggie where children, Louise's born + raised were

SITE OF BURGANDY PLANTATION

TO THE FOREST

JOE BRIDGES'S SOYBEANS

TO CENTERBORO

ABANDONED COTTON GIN

STORE

OLD HIGHWAY

MADRID

AND THEIR CHILDREN AFTER THEM

PHOTO CAPTIONS ARE ON THE LAST PAGES OF THE BOOK.

PHOTOGRAPH BY WALKER EVANS

PHOTOGRAPH BY WALKER EVANS

4

PHOTOGRAPH BY WALKER EVANS

The Two I Love,
when ALL MY hart
MOM ANd Dad.
      Gertrude

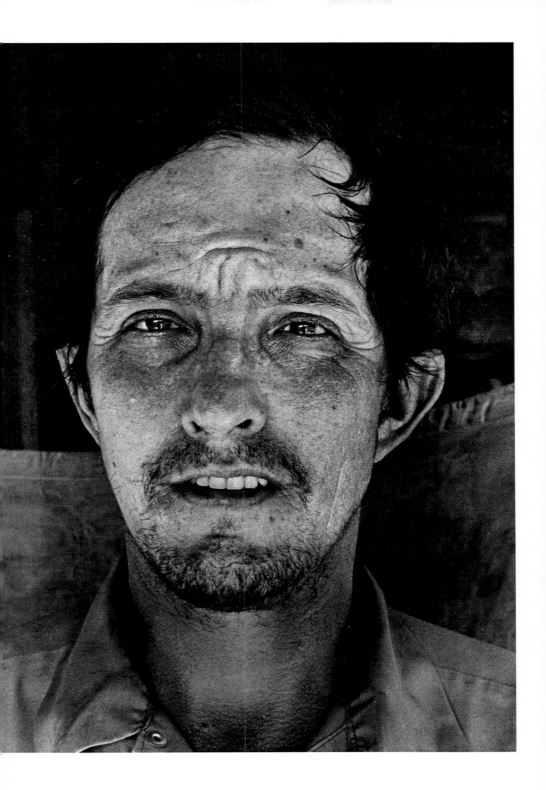

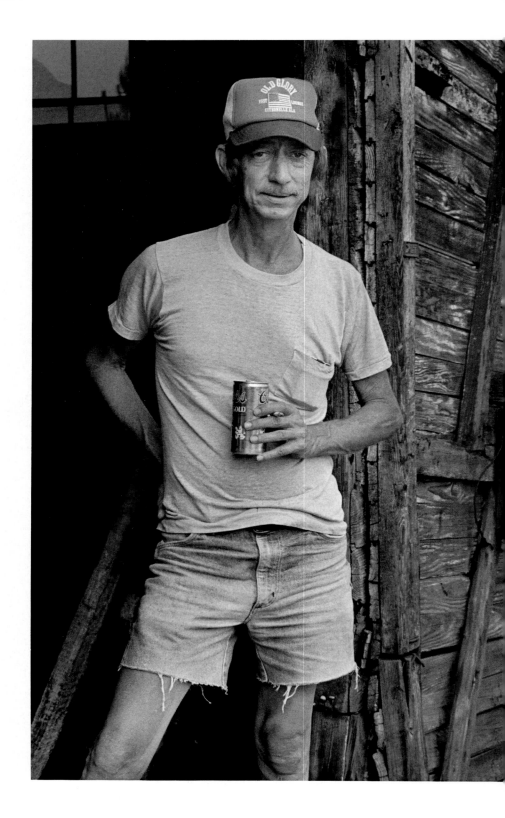

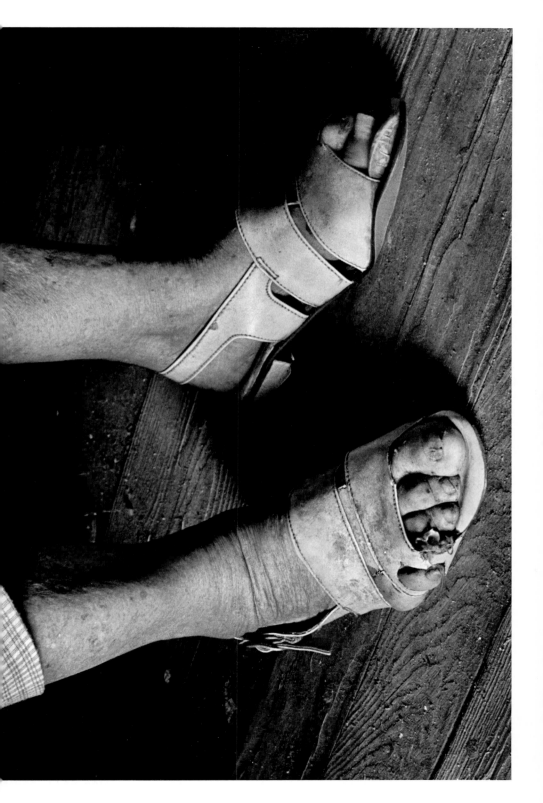

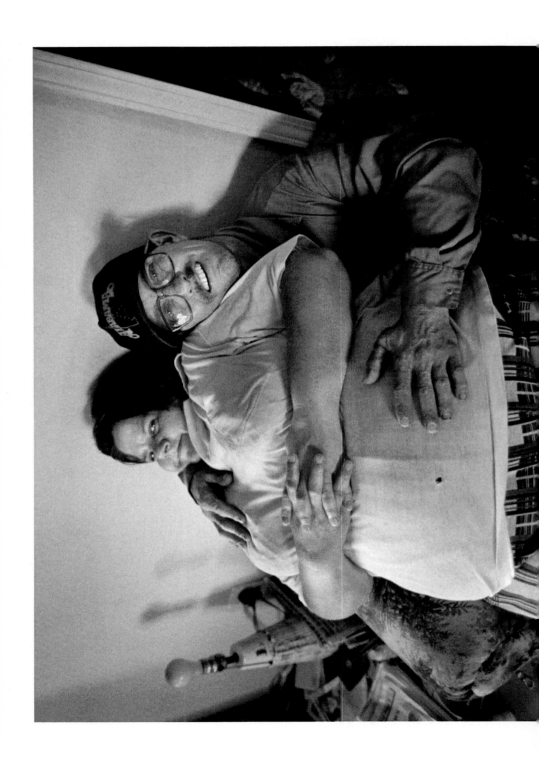

51

MAGGIE LOUISE

It was August 1936, and the parents of ten-year-old Maggie Louise had a visitor, a stranger, a writer from New York who had come with a photographer friend to do a story on sharecroppers. The visitor was James Agee, who, during his short stay in Alabama, would become much more than a stranger to Maggie Louise.

If Agee wanted to know something about what it meant to be an Alabama sharecropper, he had come at a good time of the year, when the Alabama sun is at its hottest, attacking any head left unprotected out in the field even for a moment, when your hair is quickly matted and wet through, as if you had just been swimming, sweat not just dripping into your eyes but washing down over your face.

In *Let Us Now Praise Famous Men,* the classic report of that visit, Agee tells us that Maggie Louise was vaguely aware that things weren't this miserable for ten-year-olds everywhere. He told her so himself, but she had learned it even earlier, from her favorite third-grade geography textbook, *Around the World with the Children.* The book talked about distant lands where most of the year was cold and snowy and even the hottest summer sun didn't make you sweat as you did in the Alabama summers. It told her about Ikwa, an Eskimo boy near her age, and his sister Too-kee. They wore thick furs, lived in a house made of ice, and played under a sun "so pale that we can look at it without blinking."

Still, such places must have seemed a little like cruel fiction to Maggie Louise in that late summer of 1936. All of her ten years had been dominated by that August Alabama sun. Its arrival meant the cotton was ready for harvest. She'd look out on fields bursting with cotton and not question what she would have to do next.

Before the sun cleared the top of the pine and hickory forest at the end of the field behind her house, she'd put on her handmade corn-shuck hat and start in on the rows. She'd stay out with her family all day, bent at the waist, hands ceaselessly moving, until the sun went down behind the trees on the other side of the cotton patch. Or, as they said, "from can to can't." She was an excellent picker, one of nine million sharecroppers in the ten southern cotton states. On a good day she'd fill her sack with 150 pounds. There were many adults who couldn't do that much upland cotton in a day.

A good picker's hands have to know the way past the sharp, thorny sheaths the low-lying cotton plant grows to protect the lint. They reach into the bur with all fingers, aim at a point deep in the five-celled chamber, and pull. Some come easy. Most don't. There can be no hesitation. Fingers have to move fast, as if snatching at flying bugs all day from a stooped position. For the worst two months of every cotton season, Maggie Louise's fingers were raw from going into burs as rough as splintered wood. The first days, they were simply red and sore. After a few weeks, they bled. Some older croppers soaked their hands in turpentine each night to soften them for the next day of picking. If you've ever lifted a fluffy plastic sack of the medicine-cabinet variety of cotton balls, you can easily imagine how many thousands of strokes it must have taken to make up those 150 pounds that Maggie Louise picked every day.

"They are used to it. Those people are different than us," the cotton buyers said of the sharecroppers. Maggie Louise didn't know about being different from other folks. She just did it. Because that's what you were supposed to do.

But that August was a little different from the prolonged sameness that made up the cotton seasons of a sharecropper's life. Agee filled Maggie Louise's head with exciting ideas, things she had never thought possible. He stretched and challenged her intellect, and as Maggie Louise came to like him more—after taking rides all over the county with him in his automobile, so much more exciting than her father's mule-drawn wagon—she began to wonder about the outside world, questioning whether there was more to life than cotton farming.

One night, Maggie Louise and Agee were sitting on the porch, her sister Gretchen later recalled from stories Maggie Louise told. The two rose to walk in the darkness among the chicory weeds growing in the packed earth behind the house. He lifted and perched her on the roof of the chicken coop that stood to his shoulders, her legs dangling over the planks, white and cracked as beached driftwood, so that she was looking down at him as they talked. Maggie Louise always spoke fondly of that moment to her sister. She looked down at this man who knew about so many things outside their county and asked him about eternity, the stars in the heavens. It was one of those clear Alabama nights, a sky weighing on them as if they were suspended at the bottom of a black ocean, the bright shimmerings of the Milky Way floating on the surface. Crickets and the call of distant whippoorwills were the only voices besides theirs. Maggie Louise questioned many things. Agee tried to explain. She wondered about her future. He later wrote she might get her wish and become a nurse or teacher, getting away from this life. He told her about city life in New York, and it all seemed wonderful.

Maggie Louise was full of expectations. Her grades were among the best in her school. Her parents supported her. It seemed the possibilities for her were as vast as the sky.

In the years that followed, she'd recall that night to friends. She'd speak warmly of Agee. He had confirmed for her that the world was bigger than Alabama cotton. She liked what he had said.

But she never did become a nurse or a teacher. That was okay, she decided. In her twenties, she was still picking cotton, and even that didn't seem so bad—she had her children and the love of a good man, and she could still dream, though on a lesser scale. She went from great expectations to hopes, entirely different matters, and then even those simple hopes never seemed to work out. Each passing year mocked the dreams she had dreamed with Agee, reducing her a little each year, so that at the end of each year the vacant spot inside her took up more and more of the space that defined her to herself. Maggie Louise finally discovered she could no longer aspire to anything, because the part of her that used to aspire was no longer there.

Thirty-five years after Agee encouraged her to go on in school and make something of herself, she reached a decision that seemed, to her, quite logical.

It came on an unusually warm February afternoon in 1971, when she, her mother, and her sister Gretchen went to the store together. Maggie Louise said there was something she had to get, according to Gretchen. The first store didn't have it. At the second, they all stood together outside at a pay phone, and Maggie Louise called her youngest brother, Sonny, in Georgia. He told her he was going to send her some money so she could fix her hair up real pretty, just the way she liked, and that he looked forward to her visit in the coming week. He told her he loved her. She cried, but didn't let on. She made it sound like laughter. The brother was happy to hear his sister laughing, he later said.

While her mother continued the conversation on the phone, Maggie Louise went into the store. She came out and was smiling. They had had what she wanted.

Once back home, Maggie Louise went into her room and closed the door. From her purse, she lifted a bottle, unscrewed the lid, tipped the bottle back, and calmly started drinking.

The bottle fell to the floor with a loud noise, and her sister and mother rushed into the room. They saw the skull-and-crossbones warning on the label and the words "rat poison." The active ingredient was arsenic.

Gretchen tried to force saltwater down her throat to make Maggie Louise vomit the poison. Maggie Louise clenched her teeth in refusal. They pushed her into the backseat of a car and rushed to the hospital. Maggie Louise cursed the doctors who tried to save her. She ripped the tubes from her arms.

"I don't wanna live," she said. "I wanna die. I've took all I can take."

The sister asked, "Maggie Louise! Why are you doing this?"

Maggie Louise never responded. She didn't have to. Some of them already knew.

By the time she drank the arsenic, cotton fields were a memory in most of the Old South. Maggie Louise's life had transcended the death of cotton, but not by much. Over her four and a half decades, she and most of the other nine million cotton tenants were forced off the land. The journey was harder for some than for others.

Maggie Louise stopped breathing just after midnight, February 21, 1971. Her last words were "Tell Mama I'm happy now."

They buried Maggie Louise at the edge of a hill, two miles up the road from where she had sat on the chicken coop that night and dreamed the stars.

The Legacy of
LET US NOW PRAISE FAMOUS MEN:
James Agee, Walker Evans,
and the Rise and Fall of Cotton in the South

AND THEIR CHILDREN AFTER THEM

Dale Maharidge and Michael Williamson
With a Foreword by Carl Mydans

Pantheon Books • New York

A portion of this work first appeared in the *Sacramento Bee Magazine,*
September 28, 1986.

Grateful acknowledgment is made to the following for permission to re-
print previously published material:

To Houghton Mifflin Company: Excerpts from *Let Us Now Praise Famous Men* by James Agee and Walker Evans. Copyright 1939 and 1940
by James Agee. Copyright 1941 by James Agee and Walker Evans.
Copyright renewed 1969 by Mia Fritsch Agee and Walker Evans. Reprinted by permission of Houghton Mifflin Company. To *The New York
Times:* Excerpts from "Rights Crisis Laid to Mechanization" by Austin
C. Wehrwein from the April 25, 1965, issue of *The New York Times.*
Copyright © 1965 by the New York Times Company. Reprinted by per-
mission. To *The Tennessean:* Excerpts from an article by Scott Osborne
from the March 1979 issue of *The Tennessean.* Reprinted by permission.
To the University of North Carolina Press: Excerpts from *The New Rev-
olution in the Cotton Economy: Mechanization and Its Consequences* by
James H. Street. Copyright 1957 by the University of North Carolina
Press. Reprinted by permission.

Photographs reproduced through the courtesy of the Farm Security Administration Files, Library of Congress.

Library of Congress Cataloging-in-Publication Data
Maharidge, Dale.
    And their children after them.

    1. Agee, James, 1909–1955. Let us now praise famous
men. 2. Cotton farmers—Alabama—History—20th century.
3. Farm tenancy—Alabama—History—20th century.
4. Alabama—Rural conditions. 5. Alabama—Description
and travel. 6. Agee, James, 1909–1955—Journeys—
Alabama. 7. Evans, Walker, 1903–1975. I. Williamson,
Michael. II. Title.
F326.A173M34   1989   976.1'06   88–43136
ISBN 0-394-57766-3

Manufactured in the United States of America
Book Design by Fearn Cutler
First Edition

CONTENTS

Foreword by Carl Mydans   *xi*

Preface *xv*

King Cotton *3*

1 9 3 6 – 1 9 4 0

Gudger *19*

Ricketts *33*

Woods *46*

Bridges *61*

Gaines *69*

1 9 4 0 – 1 9 6 0

Gudger *75*

Ricketts *97*

Woods   *108*
Bridges   *122*
Gaines   *124*

1 9 6 0 – 1 9 8 6

Gudger   *129*
Ricketts   *165*
Woods   *182*
Bridges   *204*
Gaines   *228*

Coda   *246*

Acknowledgments   *255*
Main Characters and Places   *257*
Photo Captions   *259*

FOREWORD

In the depths of the Great Depression when the Farm Security Administration was hastily established along with many other New Deal bodies such as the NRA, the WPA, and the CCC, the FSA was staffed with men and women who worked for the most part in rural areas among farmers and others who made their living off the land.

Usually these staffers were chosen for their familiarity with the region where they were sent to work, and most of them were native to those areas. Many had gone to school with the impoverished people they worked among, knew them from childhood, knew who had married whom and how they were faring in those hard times. They shared the same prejudices and the same suspicion of outsiders from the big cities.

But more than anything else they were knit together by language. They differed slightly in their speech from region to region, but within each they all talked the same way—not just using the same native words and phrases, but with the same particular lilt and swing. An outsider was marked at once by the way he talked.

There was, however, one exception to this careful selection of FSA field people. It was in the choice of FSA photographers to travel around the country to tell in pictures what the Depression had done to America.

None of us photographers came off the land. We all had roots in big cities and had college educations. But other than that, and our experience with the camera, there was no common link. We did not know each other very well. And because there were so few of us and we were not assigned to regions near each other, we rarely saw each other or came together to compare our experiences. Moreover, we were all distinct individuals with strongly held opinions and differing backgrounds. There was no sure way to predict how we would react to the plight of the people whom we were sent to photograph.

So the wonder is: How could all of us, with so many different views and personalities, produce such a powerful collection of images of America and Americans with such a common and unified impact? The answer lies in the presence and brilliance and drive of one man: Roy Stryker, whose vision of a documented story in pictures of the people and the land in those Depression years inspired us and propelled us all with the power of his dream.

He was a man of strong feelings and often unpredictable responses, but he was consumed by one central enthusiasm: he loved America and the people who made it what it was. And he sent us all out to record this vision, imbued by his excitement. He was a catalyst of such power that, for me, he was and still is the strongest single force in my life as a photographer. And sometimes, even now, some fifty years later, when I am looking through my cameras I still hear him talking to me.

Looking back on those years when I was taking pictures in those rural areas, I remember what I came to call the spell. When I was photographing people, especially when there were several talking or working together, I was continually aware that I and my cameras were an intrusion. And sometimes, when the possibility developed into that decisive moment that would record the essence of what I saw and felt, I would tense up nervously and keep my mouth closed for fear my outsider's voice and words might break the spell.

Through the years as I have looked at the pictures of the other

FSA photographers, I see in them also much of the quality that I have come to call the spell: the essence of a moment caught in those days in America in the thirties which so marks the FSA picture collection.

There are only three of us from Roy Stryker's original FSA staff left now: Jack Delano and Marion Post Walcott and I. And that is why I am so delighted—so moved—to find Michael Williamson and *his* pictures of America in this new book, with text by Dale Maharidge: *And Their Children After Them.* For he has shown very much the same eye and feeling that marked the pictures of the FSA photographers.

I first met Michael Williamson when I found myself shooting beside him in 1986 in the streets of Manila, covering the fall of Marcos, and there in the middle of that revolution he talked to me about how much the FSA photographers and their pictures had influenced his life. In fact he said that he and Dale Maharidge had been so influenced by the book that FSA photographer Walker Evans and writer James Agee had published in 1941, *Let Us Now Praise Famous Men,* that when this revolution in the Philippines was over he was going back to Alabama to finish the pictures for *his* book, bringing up to date wherever he could every picture Walker Evans had taken fifty years earlier for his *Famous Men* book.

And now, in their new book, *And Their Children After Them,* I see that Michael Williamson has done it. And as I look through his pictures I follow him in my mind's eye, working with his cameras among the very people we photographed half a century ago. And I see him strained and intent, careful not to intrude—not to break the spell. And looking back, I know that Roy Stryker would have welcomed him aboard.

Carl Mydans
January 3, 1989
New York

To J.A. and W.E.,
those of whom the record was made,
and those whose journey continues

PREFACE

For three years, Michael Williamson and I spent a considerable amount of time in the Deep South. We made many trips, the longest in July and August of 1986. By 1988, our work was finished. We were involved in an endeavor that seemed at the start odd, later foolish, but ultimately rewarding.

The product is this book. The idea was born in 1982, when Michael and I were finishing another project about the new poor, riding freight trains and visiting hobo jungles across America. In the middle of that undertaking, a friend gave me a book that had a familiar title but that I confess I had not yet read—James Agee's *Let Us Now Praise Famous Men,* with photographs by Walker Evans. It described the lives of three Alabama families who grew cotton as tenant farmers during the Depression and with whom Agee lived for a while in 1936.

Many in the general public know James Agee as the screenwriter of the Bogart-Hepburn-Huston film classic, *The African Queen,* and as the author of the Pulitzer Prize–winning novel *A Death in the Family.* After his death, Agee emerged as a major cult figure, and *Let Us Now Praise Famous Men,* which had had a short and unspectacular publishing history, was reissued, this time with phenomenal success. It may have become Agee's best-read work, at least among the most dedicated of the cultists, selling many tens of thousands of copies. As a consequence, those familiar with the work are generally surprised to learn the extent to which the book remains relatively unknown to much of the population.

In turn, I lent the book to Michael. One night, about one o'clock in the morning, he phoned to say he had just read some of it. He was quite excited. Agee had stayed with and collected information about the three families in the summer of 1936, and Michael thought it might make a good story for our newspaper to go back over the same ground on the fiftieth anniversary to learn what had happened to these people in the half century since Agee's visit.

The prospect was intriguing, but in the press of other projects I put it out of my mind. Over the next few years, I learned certain things that caused me to become as enthusiastic as Michael.

I found there had once been nine million cotton tenant farmers in the South; virtually all of them lived under the most brutal conditions, often not too much better off than slaves. They worked from sunup to sundown, raising cotton with their own strong backs and mules as their only help. These nine million workers added one billion dollars of wealth annually to the world economy. Yet most ended each year further in debt.

That their condition resembled that of slaves was no accident. The cotton tenant system was devised by plantation owners after Emancipation at the end of the Civil War. Unlike most food crops, cotton required a large pool of cheap, exploitable labor. Though certainly not nearly as brutal as slavery, tenantry became almost a form of indentured servitude.

My first trip to the South was made when I was a child, somewhere around 1967, when I traveled through the region with my parents. I remember seeing old black men selling watermelons from mule-drawn wagons. My mother told me they were sharecroppers.

As we drove away, I stared—fascinated by the shacks they lived in. That was my first image of the South, and, like most first images, it dominated my perception for a long time to come.

In the early 1980s, the time Michael and I first went to Alabama, I somehow assumed that a few of these sharecroppers were still around. But none were left. The last of them had vacated the land or died off more than a decade earlier when the cotton tenant system had gone through the last of its death rattles. There may still have been—in fact, there may yet be as I write this—a holdout family or two that still plow with mules or pick cotton by hand the old way, but if so we were unable to find them in our wide travels throughout the region. The only cotton handpicked these days is for a special and rare grade called Sea Island cotton. The vast majority of today's cotton crop is planted and harvested by machine, just like corn or wheat. Agricultural mechanization has belatedly freed cotton from its notorious history as a crop of exploitation.

Neither did I know then that of today's domestic cotton crop relatively little is raised in the old Cotton Belt. Texas and California combined have nearly six million acres in production, almost double the current acreage in eight of the old-time cotton states combined, according to the Cotton Council. Most of the cotton still raised in the Southeast is grown in Mississippi. Alabama now has just one-third of a million acres devoted to cotton; in 1936, it had two and one-third million. Most of the onetime cotton lands have become a wilderness covered with pine trees. Yet the dominant image of the South retained by many Americans is that of a cotton region.

Cotton, as it was once grown, vanished for myriad reasons: synthetic fibers replaced cotton as king of the market for lightweight, easy-care fabrics; imports encroached on what was left of the cotton market; boll weevils chased production westward. Most important, however, may have been these two: in the 1950s and 1960s cotton-picking machines finally displaced strong backs and tough hands; and the advent of the civil rights movement changed the social mind-set of southern blacks, liberating them from field labor. Market competition drove down prices and the boll weevil decreased yield, but the social, economic, and psychological servitude built into the old system would have commanded the tenants to stay put and work the land, at whatever reduced profit, had machines and the civil rights movement not combined to free them.

The old cotton empire of the rural South was slow to die. By the 1950s, when the wealth of postwar prosperity had begun to filter down, many whites were able to give up tenant farming, leaving mostly blacks in their place. For those who hung on, the 1960s further elevated expectations and showed blacks and whites alike that they could really have better lives.

Seldom in our nation's history have so many people in so wide a region had their lives so dramatically altered by so definitive a technological change. The demise of cotton transformed millions of lives in the Old South, but I found little written about the death of this system; as it was happening, newspapers and magazines either wrote nothing about it or ran occasional and mostly inconsequential short pieces. The story of the people who went through this transition has been largely ignored.

Later, fractions of the story were recorded. The movement of black sharecroppers to the North has been documented. Many books and researchers have studied the urban impact on blacks who fled the South, a great number from the imprisonment of tenant farming. I could find little said about the actual system itself, the whites under it, or the postcotton rural South. Most people think of blacks when tenant farming is mentioned, because blacks were the last to do it in large numbers. But whites were actually a majority of tenants in 1936, and for years before and afterward. So if this book seems to focus on whites, it is because of their long-dominant position in tenant farming, because it was with three white families that Agee lived, and because we were attracted to the project by curiosity about what had happened to these three families. But we've tried not to ignore the existence of black tenant farmers. We visited a black family of ex-tenants during our several years of research for this book, to explore the special experience of at least this one family.

I also will not delve into the history of the Civil War, Reconstruction, or the civil rights movement, which all had important roles in the birth, life, and death of tenant farming, for these great events have been better covered elsewhere.

If we understand the death of cotton, we understand many things about modern America. Agee and Evans's book was about a seemingly eternal system that oppressed millions. If we now count the children born to the nine million tenants in 1936, we find several dozen millions in our nation who are first-generation casualties of the debilitating mind-set of that system. The problem of these disenfranchised masses, both black and white, has never been fully dealt with. Our project is about what has happened to a few of these millions since that system perished.

Of course, on the surface, it seemed fascinating to find out what happened to the lives with which Agee had become so intimately entwined. There were, however, larger questions I thought might be answered at the same time.

Long before I became acquainted with *Let Us Now Praise Famous Men,* I had read *The Grapes of Wrath,* John Steinbeck's famous work that chronicled a fictional Depression-era family of Dust Bowl cotton farmers who fled to California. Being somewhat a student of the so-called underclass of society, I always wondered what would have happened if the Joad family had been real. Would Rose of Sharon have married a career man and had children who went to college in the prosperous 1950s and grew up to become professionals? Or would she and Steinbeck's other characters have lived out their lives in some backwater county of California's Central Valley, on the edge of bleakness, where a number of their kind did indeed end up? Was there even more to learn about poverty from following the generations to come than Steinbeck had taught us in his snapshot of this one family?

Agee's three families, and a few others we found, were a window on this past and could perhaps provide some clues.

. ii .

By the first day of this project, we'd come to suspect it was jinxed. More than once, we almost abandoned it.

We'd spent the early part of that first day at the home of Margaret Ricketts and were reeling from horrors, too numerous to fit here, that we discovered and that we'll describe later. That night, we had to cover a civil rights meeting in Cherokee City for our newspaper. It was a fiery gathering that ended late, and I was sick from heat, lack of sleep, and confusion.

Michael was driving. A mist sat in the road's low spots, too thick for the lights to cut. We accidentally struck a stray dog that had leapt into our path. It wandered off, wounded, and we didn't know its fate; with a considerable amount of anguish, we drove on. The next sight to emerge from the night's mist was a sign on a Baptist church alongside the road. It announced, "The key to happiness is a clear conscience."

Soon we were in Centerboro, a town we'd later come to despise. We made a wrong turn and found ourselves driving up the old main street for the first time, the town's center that had been bypassed by the modern road that led to our hotel.

Michael shouted, slamming the brakes. He pulled out our copy of *Let Us Now Praise Famous Men,* turned to one of Evans's pictures, and studied it. His memory had served him correctly. We'd stumbled onto the same street that appeared in the photograph. We ran up and down it into the night, book in hand, searching for the very window in which Evans stood and from which he took the picture.

We reached the courthouse and saw, right in front, that we were beneath the very same Civil War statue under which Agee had first met the men of the three families he lived with. Its identity was confirmed by another Evans picture, and even though it was one in the morning, the discovery caused us to holler and read aloud from the book.

Our jubilation was halted by a serious voice in command. It belonged to the sheriff, who emerged from the shadow of a magnolia, and we froze, afraid of being shot by this southern sheriff in a nowhere town on a hot night. I blurted out our business, and he relaxed. Sheriff Carver exhibited two bars sawed from his jail by prisoners who had just tried to escape—he thought we were accomplices. Reporters often find one utterly unbelievable moment that seems to happen in the pursuit of so many stories, and this was ours for the Alabama project. Sheriff Carver, a bone-faced man, invited us inside, telling us what he knew about the three families; his knowledge was considerable. He lit a cigarette and told us they still sing a song about Ivy Woods, and he smiled, blowing smoke—biggest whore in the county, he said, legendary even by modern-whore standards. We begged him to sing the song. He said he was up for reelection and couldn't do that. We promised off-the-record confidence. Again he smiled, smoking away, feet on his desk, the air growing thick. Three o'clock came, and we had to go. Still, the sheriff had not sung. Maybe next year, he said, when ya'll come back.

Sheriff Carver easily won reelection. He is as popular as he is representative of the character of Centerboro—curious and friendly, but friendly only to the point of cordial neighborliness, beyond which the code of small-town suspicion takes over.

The sheriff never did sing us his song. But that was okay. That day set the tone for the many to follow. In later trips, we became intimately involved in numerous lives, to the point that we felt like visiting family.

At other times, we were almost archaeologists. We seldom passed shacks, abandoned schools, or empty plantation mansions without stopping to dig through rubble. We looked for and found many documents and records that told of the cotton days. We searched for every trace. On Hobe's Hill, where most of the people I write about once lived, the jungle of vines and brush was so thick we had to crawl on hands and knees for two days seeking the remains of the Gudger house. Later, a few miles distant, I found the house their daughter Maggie Louise last lived in, in 1958, the last year she farmed cotton. Maggie Louise and her family were the final occupants, and thirty years later the vine-covered dwelling still contained Maggie Louise's shoes and other objects. It was, for us, something like locating the log cabin, still intact, of Abraham Lincoln, complete with a few of his schoolbooks. I brought back from Alabama several large boxes of torn wallpaper, scraps of leather, rat-chewed letters, books, documents, waste from dumps.

. *iii* .

There are three reasons why I described our work as odd, even foolish.

First, it should be noted this undertaking was marked by difficulties. On one level, it was a simple act of journalism, an exercise in investigative research, work we had been trained to do. This implies indifference, and no word could be less accurate in characterizing our attitude. Agee remarked that he and Evans were "spies," that they had been sent forth to learn of their subjects by infiltrating their lives in a somewhat secretive manner. It seems to me Agee also sometimes felt he was a figurative rapist. And now we were returning to the scene of the crime, so to speak, coconspirators in the eyes of some, not just to inquire of the deed but to demand seconds, reopening old memories of private things they'd been induced to yield to Agee, probing new ones.

As will be explained later, a few wanted nothing to do with us. But most of the 128 survivors and offspring of the original 22 family members were quite willing to tell their stories. As for those who desired to be left alone, we honored their wishes and stayed far away. To respect the privacy of all, we, like Agee, chose not to use the real names of any characters and of most places. We used the same pseudonyms he gave the families and small towns. To the people born after 1936, we gave new names.

The second reason I termed this a foolish endeavor has to do with the nature of American society. Books about the poor, as the syndicated columnist Bob Greene said of our first book, do not exactly fly off the shelves into readers' hands—especially not in the 1980s, if ever. Telling people about the troubles of others is not a way to get rich. We are fortunate to have found a publisher willing to print our findings. In the unlikely event that any profits beyond our expenses come our way, we will set up a trust fund that will receive a majority of our royalties. We desire a perpetual endowment that can be used to educate the children of the descendants of the tenant families written about here. We hope in this manner to give something back to those who have been so gracious to us. If readers are interested in how this works out, or have any other thoughts on this or any other matters included here, we invite correspondence to the authors in care of the publisher.

Third, there is the thorny problem that we'll be criticized by some for following two legends of journalism. When beginning this, I was not aware of the cultlike status of Agee. Evans, one of the top Farm Security Administration photographers, is equally revered in other circles. While this book is in no way intended to imitate, parody, or otherwise denigrate the work of Agee and Evans, there may be those who will be upset that we seem to be tampering with, or exploiting, *Let Us Now Praise Famous Men.*

A conscious decision was made to treat Agee and Evans as characters as important as the families they lived with and reported on. Their actions, their style, and even their motives must thus be open to comment. This book certainly starts from the study on which *Let Us Now Praise Famous Men* is based, but its purpose and scope are different. Agee, beyond being a journalist, was a poet; I am not. Agee's study not only was a report of a major period of our history but became itself an important event in that history. My effort is offered as the report of a journalist who struggled to retain his detachment. At the risk of being accused of oversimplifying the differences between the two works, I offer that I saw my proper role as standing back and observing and that Agee saw his as jumping in and experiencing.

I believe the two works can coexist.

. *iv* .

I should mention the source of our title, which was given to us in a roundabout way by James Agee. It comes from Ecclesiasticus, the same biblical chapter in which he found the name for his book.

As for the pictures, in keeping with the form and spirit of our predecessors, they're meant as a separate but equal statement to the text. Michael has with his camera taken an approach somewhat different from mine. I believe this does not detract, but instead adds to the fullness of the work.

All dates, ages, and events are tied to 1986, unless otherwise noted.

We were not the first to seek out these people; certainly we won't be the last. A few magazine writers and filmmakers who preceded us have provided insight into the lives of people now dead or reclusive, and their work is occasionally quoted.

A technical note: A sharecropper can be called a tenant farmer, but all tenant farmers were not sharecroppers. I may occasionally use the term "sharecropper" and "tenant farmer" interchangeably. There is an important difference, as will be shown, but the two words have entered the language as to mean the same thing to most Americans.

This is a book about how people change. It is about how some do not. It is about how some persevere, only to end staring at hands worn from a lifetime of labor, realizing nothing—an absolute definition of defeat. It is about others, who, through hard work and hope, have achieved varying degrees of success, along with an understanding of who they are and where they came from. It is about a group of men and women who long ago told us something about America that we, as a society, do not readily want to face, and who today have something else to tell us about ourselves.

Unlike that of a novel, the story of these families is not static.

The lives Agee wrote about had already changed by the time their book was published in 1941. Some things we found have certainly changed as you read this. People continue to evolve. The final word of this book is not a conclusion. It is a story without end. We hope the reader approaches it with this in mind.

Dale Maharidge
Sacramento
February 14, 1989

AND THEIR CHILDREN AFTER THEM

KING COTTON

If we could fly backward on the Magic Carpet of Time to the city of Babylon in the days of King Nebuchadnezzar, many strange sights would greet our eyes.

On a sight-seeing tour we would want to see the hanging gardens and other unusual marvels of this rich and noted metropolis about which we have read in history.

But in ancient Babylon nothing that we might see would be so economically significant as the stocks of rare merchandise offered for sale by the traders.

Perhaps there would be jewels; exquisite pieces of handicraft would catch our attention; and there would be beautiful, delicate, fascinating pieces of cloth the like of which the world had never seen. It is this cloth with which we are concerned.

Where did these matchless pieces of cloth come from? By whom were they made? . . .

Although it is not known exactly where the treasured fabrics of the ancient traders were first made, it is more than likely that they came from India. . . .

We know that reference is made to cotton cloth as early as 1500 B.C. In fact, from 1500 B.C. until an equal number of years after the beginning of the Christian Era, India was the center of the cotton industry. . . .

Writers describe the cloth purchased in ancient India as being "so fine you could hardly feel it in your hand." Is it any wonder that poetic authors of the Orient spoke of these fine fabrics as "webs of woven wind"?

—from *'Round the World with Cotton,* a textbook published in 1941 by the U.S. Department of Agriculture for schoolchildren, discovered in 1988 amid debris on the floor of an abandoned school east of Centerboro, Alabama.

. *i* .

Cotton is a member of the mallow family, genus *Gossypium.* It is a beautiful plant, rich green and vaguely purple in color, with oddly star-shaped leaves, each with three to five lobes. There are twenty species of the genus, some of which grow to heights of over eighteen feet, though a range of one to seven feet is more common. The plant produces a white flower that is fertile only a few hours, then turns color and falls away, the fruit maturing into a green pod the size of a golf ball. This pod, or boll, dries as it grows and after about two hundred days splits open along four or five lines, each section containing eight to ten seeds. At this stage the pod is called a bur. The seeds are protected by lint, in an arrangement similar in a way to that of the fluffy dandelion head, except that the cotton fibers are long, strong, and securely wrapped in the chambers.

Cotton has hundreds of uses beyond being material for clothes—from the seed is squeezed oil for food, paint, and cosmetics, and the fiber is used for paper, explosives, and linoleum. Early on, cotton was referred to as "white gold."

Cotton was an American fabric long before Europeans arrived—woven cotton has been found in Utah cliff dwellings and in excavations in Mexico dating to 2400 B.C.; Columbus found it being cultivated in the West Indies when he landed. Cytogenetical studies have shown that the cotton of today is a cross between old- and new-world species.

Cotton was native to all temperate continents except Europe; it was introduced to Europe by the army of Alexander the Great in 300 B.C. In the 1600s, the English began weaving cotton, at first as a home cottage industry, and soon transformed the use of the fiber as far as modern man is concerned. In 1767, the British inventor James Hargreaves created the "jenny," a machine that could spin yarn cheaply and in large quantities, replacing home spinning wheels. A few years later, two other British inventors devised the "water frame" and the "mule," which further mechanized the spinning process. The appearance of the "power loom" in the late 1780s similarly mechanized the weaving process. These inventions spurred the Industrial Revolution, which had begun around 1760, and gave rise to a new industry and a new type of exploited factory laborer in Britain.

But common people still wore linen or wool, for no matter how cruelly effective the production of the fabric became, cotton goods remained costlier than those made from other fibers, because the raw material was still expensive. The bottleneck limiting wide, popular use was the difficulty in separating the seed from the fibers; without this "cleaning" the cotton was unusable. It took one long day for one person to deseed by hand four pounds of cotton and produce one pound of clean cotton for the new British machines.

That's where Eli Whitney came along and changed the course of American history—economic, political, and sociological. After graduating from Yale College in 1792, he took up an offer to tutor the children of a rich family in Savannah, Georgia. On the boat journey to that job, he met Mrs. Nathanael Greene. When the tutoring job didn't pan out, he began working at Mrs. Greene's Mulberry Grove plantation. The story goes that three planters visiting Mulberry Grove one night in January 1793 got to talking about how much they wished they could grow more cotton, for that region of the South was perfect for its cultivation. The problem was that producing cotton was made so uneconomical by the deseeding process that most planters grew tobacco, rice, and indigo, instead. Whitney, who had a knack for inventing, began work in Mrs. Greene's basement and, with some advice from his patron, came up with a device that used two rollers to remove the seed from the cotton. With his machine, one person could clean in one day an amount of fiber that used to take fifty workers. At the end of 1793, Whitney joined in partnership with Mr. Miller, Mrs. Greene's new husband, to produce the device they called a cotton gin.

"Miller and Whitney, as the firm was called, made a mistake often made by young men," reported another children's textbook found on the floor of the Centerboro school, *Great Inventors and Their Inventions,* published in 1918. "They wanted to make a lot of money, and they wanted to make it quickly." This desire to make fast money led to others' stealing the basic idea and not paying royalties for its use.

In the end, though the two never made the big money they envisioned, the cotton gin placed the United States at the forefront of technology in the production of cotton. Had the machine been invented elsewhere, the United States might never have been thrust into its role as the world's number-one supplier of cotton, a position of dominance that lasted well over a century.

"By reason of his invention, the United States is to-day the greatest cotton producing country in the world," said the textbook in 1918. It added:

> Production of cotton in the South increased by leaps and bounds. In 1792, the year before the invention of the cotton gin, there were raised and sent out of the United States 138,000 pounds of cotton. In 1793, about 487,000 pounds were exported. In 1794, about 1,000,000, and in 1800, about 17,000,000 pounds.

. *ii* .

Before the advent of the cotton gin, much of what is now known as the Deep South was frontier land, settled and worked by veterans of the Revolutionary War. Some were German, but a majority were Scotch-Irish. They moved into the South as the Indians were driven out, setting up farms on amazingly fertile lands. According to one report, forty thousand people from Ireland had moved into the Carolinas by 1760. In educational background or customs, they were not much different from the settlers who went into the Ohio territory in the North. They cleared land, planted crops, and would not have been expected to evolve a society much different from the one established by their northern counterparts.

But cotton could not be grown in the North. In the United States, it can be grown only in a region sixteen hundred miles east to west by roughly three hundred north to south, starting in southeastern Virginia and reaching to western Texas. It can also be grown in Arizona and California, but these regions were not yet a meaningful part of American culture or commerce. The South, with its established ability to produce cotton, a commodity valued throughout Europe, suddenly grew in importance to the young country. To say that near-mania took over is not to overstate the haste with which the big-money men moved into the lands of the South occupied by the Scotch-Irish. The quest to grow cotton was the South's gold rush.

Cotton was a curious crop, however. It demanded long hours of heavy labor at the start and the end of the season, labor that could be idle at all other times. The Anglo-Saxon busy-hands ethic was not geared for that. It was quickly recognized that an exploitable labor pool would be necessary for cotton cultivation—the work of slaves.

By bidding up the price of fertile land, by intimidation, and by controlling the new gins and thereby strangling attempts of small farmers to market their cotton, these money men drove the frontier settlers from the most fertile bottomland and established themselves as the beneficiaries of the new plantation system. A few of the original settlers were able to cross over and become plantation owners themselves. Others took the profits from the sale of their land and left the South. But most were forced by these changes, over which they had little control, to leave the fertile bottomland and resettle their families on far less desirable lands in the shale hills. This migration created a new breed of American and a special American society that would survive for more than a century, the community of white southerners that came to intrigue James Agee and Walker Evans.

Frederick Law Olmsted, who traveled throughout the South observing life in the 1850s, gave this view of a typical region resettled by the big planters in his book *The Cotton Kingdom:*

> Suppose it to be of twenty square miles, with a population of six hundred, all told, and with an ordinarily convenient access by river navigation to market. The whole of the available cotton land in this case will probably be owned by three or four men.

Cotton growing started near the coasts. In Alabama, when cotton first entered the state, the big-money men set up plantations near the gulf, and the Scotch-Irish moved inland. *Alabama: A Guide to the Deep South,* written under the Work Projects Administration, stated,

> Dispossessed small farmers were among the first settlers in the lowland Black Belt. When it was discovered that Black Belt cotton grew to great size and fruitfulness, wealthy planters began moving in from the Gulf Coast. So much land was planted to cotton that corn, other staple farm products, and work animals had to be imported.

The Black Belt, so named not after the skin color of its residents but after the rich soil, saw a typical forced movement of these poor whites.

No one knows exactly how many of these Scotch-Irish were forced off their land by spreading plantations, but at a minimum they numbered in the many thousands. One estimate put their number at one million. It is clear that the lives of these descendants of the original Scotch-Irish southern frontier settlers quickly degenerated into a relentless struggle for survival. Despite all their hard work, they could barely grow enough food on the inferior mineral soil in the hill country across the South to feed themselves, much less produce a surplus to sell. In time, in other ways as well, the quality of their lives spiraled down, as the wealth of the new cotton barons in the lowlands increased.

This period was studied by the *Presbyterian Banner,* a newspaper printed in Pittsburgh. In a booklet entitled *The Mountain Whites,* published in 1893, this process was described.

> In 1792 [sic] Whitney invented the cotton gin. Cotton lands became more valuable. Those . . . trying to hold their lands had to sell out; and thus an increased number had to betake themselves to the mountains.
>
> The present generation is greatly deteriorated, industriously, socially, mentally, morally and religiously, as compared with their enlightened and heroic ancestors of 1775–1782. The present conditions of these people is directly traceable to slavery; for, in making the slave the planter's blacksmith, carpenter, wheelwright, and man-of-all-work, slavery shut every avenue of honest employment

against the working white man and drove him to the mountains or the barren sand hills. . . .

The first generation of children were much more illiterate than their parents. Each succeeding generation was more illiterate than the preceding one.

The establishment of a southern cotton culture was well under way by the time of the War of 1812. When the war closed the British market for cotton, many planters may have wished they hadn't invested everything in a one-crop livelihood. After the war, however, demand not only caught up to prewar consumption but rose to unprecedented levels. With these record demands for cotton came new demands for slave labor. In 1820, the people of Alabama numbered 125,000, and 31 percent were slaves. By 1830, the number of Alabamians had grown to 300,000, and 38 percent were slaves. Production continued to increase geometrically—it doubled between 1849 and 1859.

Reasons for the regression of the poor whites included more than the infertility of the land. Isolation was also a factor. The hills were closed to the outside world, for the roads were poor to nonexistent. And the schools were substandard. Public schools were ridiculed by big planters, who hired tutors to educate their own children. The poor whites came to be called "sand-hillers" and "clay eaters," scorned not only by the new plantation lords but even by house slaves.

A northern traveler in this period, quoted by a Mr. Gilmore in *Among the Pines,* had this conversation with his black guide:

> "Are there many of these poor whites around Georgetown?"
>
> "Not many 'round Georgetown, sar, but great many in de upcountry har, and dey'm all 'like—pore and no account; none ob 'em kin read, and dey all eat clay."
>
> "Eat clay!" I said; "What do you mean by that?"
>
> "Didn't you see, massa, how yaller all dem wimmin war? Dat's 'cause dey eat clay. De little children begin 'fore dey kin walk, and dey eat it till dey die; dey chaw it like 'backer. It makes all dar stumacs big, like as you seed 'em. It'm mighty onhealfy."

According to another contemporary observer, quoted by Paul H. Buck in an article that first appeared in the *American Historical Review,* these people by the middle 1850s were "lank, lean, angular, and bony, with flaming red, or flaxen, or sandy, or carroty-colored hair, sallow complexion, awkward manners, and a natural stupidity or dullness of intellect that almost surpasses belief."

Many characterizations of hill whites from this period are similarly brutal. It was not until 1902 that a medical basis was found—a disease caused by hookworms—for a pattern of behavior that critics ascribed to innate stupidity. Dr. Charles Wardell Stiles, who discovered the illness, said the clay eating was due to an abnormal appetite created by the hookworm parasite, which also robbed its victims of energy and made them anemic. The disease was called the "poor man's malady," for the worm was found to prey only on people with inadequate diets and bad housing.

This disease and others—combined with the mind-numbing anguish of being unable to find a productive role in a society dominated by the master-slave relationship—served to reduce the mountain whites over several generations into a class that was rendered immobile and listless.

Those who profited from the commerce of cotton, seeing only a gleaming future in the fiber, tended to discourage new industry in the South. Apparently they were unwilling to encourage nonagricultural job opportunities for white laborers that could easily turn into temptation or encouragement for blacks to flee slavery.

Regarding this failure to do any planning for these white hill people, Buck says, "The planter justified his neglect by declaring the poor whites irresponsible, lazy, and dishonest, attributes rendering them valueless as laborers. This contempt of their capabilities was shared by the middle classes and the slaves."

To complete this paradox, these impoverished whites supported the institution of slavery. Olmsted remarked, "From childhood, the one thing in their condition which has made life valuable to the mass of whites has been that the niggers are yet their inferiors." Olmsted was told by one hill white, "I wish there warn't no niggers here. They are a great cuss to this country, I expect." Another man said, "Now suppose they was free, you see they'd all think themselves just as good as we."

Meanwhile, as the sixth decade of the displacement of the whites from their land neared, cotton cultivation continued to spread. In 1858, Senator James Henry Hammond of South Carolina said in the senate chambers, "You dare not make war on cotton. No power on earth dares to make war on it. Cotton is King."

Of course, the Civil War forever changed what the South had seen as an unchangeable world.

The close of the war left the South and the cotton culture in ruins. Land lay unplowed, unused, empty of value. Southern farmland, worth $226 million before the war, had shrunk in value to $78 million by 1870. The cotton system was in shambles with Emancipation. Those blacks who could leave the South did so. Others left plantations to try to find work in southern cities and towns rebuilding the destroyed infrastructure. Cotton, abandoned through want of labor and lack of capital to underwrite new production methods, seemed defeated.

There was much talk among planters about how they would rebuild their farms. The first problem to be addressed was the new relationship they would have to establish with potential farm workers, who were expected to come almost exclusively from the ranks of the former slaves, now all freedmen. In a series of letters that appeared in 1869 in *The Southern Cultivator,* a David Dickson of Georgia proposed a new contractual basis. A copy of this book was discovered in 1986 in the attic of an abandoned plantation mansion east of Centerboro, Alabama. Dickson said,

> The best method of hiring, I consider to be . . . a contract setting forth the duties of each party. The policy of managing freedmen is, to act firmly, and truly, and honestly with them, and require them to do the same; and as a good stimulus to do this, never pay them more than half wages till the end of the time for which they contracted to work. On plantations of any considerable size, the actual necessaries should be kept, and sold to the freedmen at a profit sufficient to pay risk and interest on the money. The rent of the land should be one-third of all the crops gathered; another third should pay for the horse-power, machinery and tools. The laborer should have one-third. In hiring laborers, a man should never allow less than fifty percent profit on the labor, for he is taking the risk.

Soon after the end of the war, proposals such as these became incorporated into what came to be known as the tenant-farm, or sharecropping, system. But if Dickson thought only in terms of the use of black laborers to pick the cotton of the South, others were starting to look elsewhere. Some were calling for immigration from Europe to fill the new labor needs; still others began to look with more interest at the hill whites.

In support of the idea of employing the hill whites, Robert Somers, in *The Southern States since the War, 1870–71,* noted that the hill whites had produced a little bit of cotton on their inferior lands for years and had some knowledge of the crop. In attempting to advance his idea of turning to white labor, Somers, reflecting as well as playing on the racism of many planters, suggested that blacks were being treated like royalty and guarded by "agitations extending from Washington." Others claimed that many blacks working for wages wanted the right to take their earned cash wages and leave a crop in the middle of a season. Of the whites, Somers said,

> These small hill farmers come down occasionally into the plain, looking for land to rent or buy; and it is not improbable that many of the better and more industrious class of families in "the mountains" will eventually come down altogether, and help to renovate the waste places, and build up the agricultural prosperity of the Valley. The negro, all in all, is the best labourer in the cotton fields the south is ever likely to have; but if the resources of the plantations are to be developed, and cotton is to be produced with profit at such a price as the world will give for it, the labour of the negro must be largely reinforced by the labour of white men. . . .

By 1877, a little more than a decade after the end of the war, cotton production once again equaled what it had been in 1861. Later, Rupert B. Vance, in *The Human Geography of the South,* said of the evolving sharecropping system,

> In what must have been an era of primitive barter, a system was arrived at whereby labor was secured without money wages and land without money rent. Up and down the Cotton Belt southern states after 1865 vied with one another in passing crop lien laws. Accepted as the temporary salvation of a wrecked economic structure, the system has increasingly set the mode for southern agriculture. . . . The crop lien system was developed to readjust the Negro to cotton production on terms more fitting a modern economy than slavery. Its success was so great as to be disastrous. Congregated on its original fringes, the unpropertied poor white farmers poured into the new scheme and helped to make temporary expediency a permanent arrangement.

Quite simply, and with no small bit of irony, the hill whites flocked into tenantry in far greater numbers than even Somers could have expected, working for the descendants of those same men who had forced their forefathers off the land decades earlier. John W. Johnston, a U.S. senator from Virginia, saw tenant farming as salvation for these lower-class whites. His article "The Emancipation of the Southern Whites and Its Effect on Both Races," published in the *Manufacturers' Record,* quotes the following figures on the changing racial makeup of tenant farmers in the years after the war.

YEAR	WHITE	COLORED
1880	44.0%	56.0%
1884	48.4%	51.6%
1885	50.2%	49.9%

Johnston claimed that the whites who replaced blacks were more productive. He said, "The emancipation of the whites will make the South great, rich and prosperous."

The numbers of whites continued to increase after the turn of the century, said *The Collapse of Cotton Tenancy,* a book published in 1935 by the University of North Carolina Press. It found,

> In the decade from 1920 to 1930, white tenants in the cotton states increased by 200,000 families—approximately a million persons. During the same decade Negro tenants decreased by 2,000 families as a result of mass movements to the cities.

James H. Street, in his book *The New Revolution in the Cotton Economy,* saw the system as not much different from slavery:

> The arrangement between planter and tenant took the form of an enforceable contract, though it was rarely reduced to writing. The legal device which was most frequently used to prevent the cropper from leaving his crop in mid-season, and when desirable, to prevent him from moving to another farm after the annual settlement was reached, was systematic indebtedness. Some of these arrangements were scarcely distinguishable from peonage, and they were often reinforced by the complicity of local law enforcement officers. Several states adopted "alienation of labor" laws which were designed to protect landlords from having their labor hired away from them by other farmers. . . . Farm hands who were attracted to new jobs by such offers were subject to forcible return by peace officers.

By the turn of the century, the system had firmly established its order. There came to be three types of tenant farmers.

The first kind of tenant paid the owner straight rent for the use of the land and kept the entire crop he grew, in an arrangement much like that of farmers who lease land these days. This type was relatively uncommon.

The second group included those who worked on what were called "thirds" and "fourths." These tenants had to provide their own mules and farm implements, as well as their labor. In a typical arrangement, in exchange for use of the owner's land, the tenant family might give over to the landlord one-fourth the corn they grew, one-third of the cotton. Out of the remaining share of the crop, they'd owe the landowner for most of the cost of seed and fertilizer, plus interest. They'd also owe on rations money advanced, plus interest as high as 40 percent. Often, they were not advanced cash but instead had to purchase their rations at a company store. This oppressive debt and the strict enforcement of lien laws ensured that tenants would stay through harvest and be there to work the next season. And this was not a job through which a man alone might support a family. Entire households were expected to work, children starting around the age of six or seven.

Sharecroppers were the third and lowest kind of tenant farmer. (The word "sharecropper" is sometimes used generically, to describe all of tenant farming, but we'll try to restrict it to this one subset of tenant farmers.) Unlike those who worked thirds or fourths, sharecroppers didn't own their own mules or tools. All they had to offer was their backs. The owners provided the "furnish"—land, tools, and mules. In return, the sharecroppers had to give over a much greater proportion of the crop than tenants did—half their corn and cotton, an additional amount to cover their portion of the fertilizer, and an average of 40 percent interest. For this reason, they were also called half-croppers, or said to be working on "halvers." Bad years, or bad luck, could mean no credit, which in turn meant disaster for the farm family.

The boll weevil, a worm that eats developing bolls of cotton, threatened the tenant system around the turn of the century. For a while, it seemed that this little worm might be able to achieve what even Emancipation had not—finally do in cotton. The people of Enterprise, Alabama, erected a monument to the boll weevil, "which had freed them from the tyranny of cotton." But the optimism was premature—the weevil was soon controlled, and cotton survived.

The environment in which this tenant system existed was described by Robert H. Montgomery as a "whole miserable panorama of unpainted shacks, rain-gullied fields, straggling fences, rattletrap Fords, dirt, poverty, disease, drudgery, and monotony that stretches for a thousand miles across the cotton belt."

The Great Depression exacerbated an already bad situation, as falling prices made it impossible for farmers to get out of debt with the sale of their crops. It seemed the only people making money were not the landlords but the town merchants and bankers. By 1936, blacks were driven to utter despair, and whites outnumbered them five to three on tenant farms. In that same year, there were nearly twice as many tenant farmers raising cotton as there had been slaves in 1860.

In an address to Congress in the middle of the Depression, President Franklin D. Roosevelt said:

> Half a century ago one of every four farmers was a tenant. Today, two of every five are tenants. While aggravated by the Depression, the tenancy problem is the accumulated result of generations of unthinking exploitation of our agricultural resources, both land and people.

. *iii* .

In the spring of 1936, the situation of tenant farmers caught the eyes of some New York editors at *Fortune* magazine, part of the Time-Life magazine empire of Henry Luce. These editors thought their readers might be interested in a "sociological" article on the situation. They chose to send James Agee, a twenty-seven-year-old writer who had graduated from Harvard College and had since been with *Fortune* three and a half years. He was a little strange, fiery—but ideally suited, it seemed, for the task.

Agee, however, was on a leave in Florida, trying to salvage a tortured marriage and rethink his future. He had been contemplating quitting *Fortune,* where, according to his later biographer Laurence Bergreen, he had been dealt "mind-numbing assignments" on such subjects as butter, orchids, and colonial Williamsburg. Agee was a poet—he had just published a book of verse—and these were not topics to excite him. He was filled with worry that he'd never become a "great writer."

On his return in mid-May from that five-month Florida trip, he learned of the tenant-farmer assignment. According to his friend Robert Fitzgerald in his 1968 book, he was "swallowing with excitement . . . stunned, exalted, scared clean through and felt like impregnating every woman on the fifty-second floor."

Picked to photograph the project was Walker Evans. Evans came from a wealthy Chicago family and had been taking pictures for eight years. At the time, he worked for the Resettlement Administration, later to become the Farm Security Administration, which hired photographers to illustrate the effects of the Depression and promote President Roosevelt's New Deal. He also did free-lance work for *Fortune.* Agee was the more outgoing of the two. The awkward-looking photographer, thirty-three, was much more reserved.

"Best break I ever had on *Fortune,*" Agee wrote on Thursday, June 18, 1936, to a priest who had taught him in his native Tennessee. "Feel terrific responsibility toward story; considerable doubts of my ability to bring it off; considerable more of *Fortune*'s ultimate willingness to use it. . . ."

On that note, Agee and Evans headed south on Saturday afternoon, June 20. They reportedly went first to Oklahoma, where they found no sharecroppers of the kind they wanted. They then turned east, back toward Alabama.

1 9 3 6 – 1 9 4 0

GUDGER

. i .

It's unclear what exactly James Agee and Walker Evans did those first weeks in Alabama before they found the three tenant families—the Gudgers, the Rickettses, and the Woodses—whose lives they would observe and describe.

It is certain that they had narrowed their focus to what is known as the Black Belt of Alabama. This region and the Mississippi Delta were the two most important cotton areas of the South, but of these two, the Black Belt had more of what they had been sent to find—white tenant farmers.

To help them find subjects, Agee had contacted a landowner and New Deal executive named Harmon. Harmon did try to help, taking Agee and Walker to a number of plantations. But his efforts were of little assistance.

At least one of these visits was not only unproductive but painful. Agee writes with some disgust of an occasion when Harmon took them to a plantation where the landlord interrupted a family reunion of some black sharecroppers and had them sing for the embarrassed journalists, while the landowner stood by with his fly down, scratching his scrotum.

Once it was clear that Harmon did not understand what they were after, Agee and Evans went off on their own, but they did not find immediate success. Years later, Harmon recalled to filmmaker Mort Jordan that some days after they left him, Agee's anxious and puzzled editor at *Fortune* telephoned asking if Harmon knew where his writer was. Harmon had to respond that he had no idea.

In fact, Agee and Evans were getting desperate on their own and needed no prodding from an editor. They had used up nearly the entire month they had been allotted and had still failed to interview anyone they thought fit for the study. Agee guessed that he probably had around two hundred unpromising encounters, or at least it seemed that way.

Finally, one afternoon they came to the courthouse in Centerboro and saw three men gathered at the base of the Civil War statue out front—George Gudger and two of his relatives, Bud Woods and Fred Ricketts. Woods was Gudger's father-in-law. Ricketts was married to Woods's half sister. The three farmed near each other, about fifteen miles north of town.

They had come to Centerboro, the county seat, to seek government relief or, if that was not available, then relief work. Their debts were high, and the cotton crop wasn't expected to bring in much. But by the time Agee and Evans arrived, the three farmers had already been told that they did not qualify either for straight relief or for relief work, because technically, as tenant farmers, they were employed. They were ruminating on their rejection as Agee and Evans tentatively approached. When Evans told them he worked for the government as a Resettlement Administration photographer, Ricketts and Woods heard the word "government" and jumped to the conclusion that he might be someone who could help them solve their problem.

It's not known if the journalists did anything to correct this misconception. All Agee reports is that small talk was made and that the three men invited Agee and Evans to come back with them to

Hobe's Hill, where the men lived with their families. Though Agee's account does not say so, it appears that the two journalists drove the three farmers home that day to the house of Fred Ricketts; George Gudger's ten-year-old daughter, Maggie Louise, came later, with her two brothers.

For Evans the photographer, the scene was apparently irresistible. Some of the more memorable shots from *Let Us Now Praise Famous Men* were those taken that day against the backdrop of the Ricketts shack. Though the two men did not linger at the Ricketts house after Evans had taken his photographs, their actions in the days that followed suggested that neither could put the day out of his mind.

Indeed, they came back often, driving up Hobe's Hill, talking to Bud Woods. Agee described how a father-son relationship soon developed with this man. Agee asked if he could pay room and board and live with the Woods family. Woods declined, saying he couldn't trust two young men with his wife.

In the middle of this, Agee writes that he and Evans, exhausted and eager to talk to people who weren't tenant farmers, decided to drive to Birmingham. Evans also wanted to develop some negatives. The two decided, furthermore, that they each needed some time alone. Agee left Walker in the Birmingham hotel and drove back toward Cherokee City. Agee wrote about how badly he needed sex, but he drove by a whore they'd seen. His desires then led elsewhere, drawing him back to Hobe's Hill.

But when he got to the hill, it was not to the Ricketts shack that he headed. Of the people he'd met the first day, it was two of the Gudgers—George and ten-year-old Maggie Louise—who had left the strongest impression on him. Both seemed more intelligent than the others, and both had been more talkative. His problem was that he didn't know precisely where they lived. As he drove up the Hobe's Hill road, a Ricketts child spotted his car and flagged him down, and then Fred Ricketts directed him up a small branch road.

The Gudgers—George and Annie Mae—worked twenty acres of land at the end of that remote muddy road, hardly better than a trail, passable to mules but just barely to cars. The twenty acres sat at the top of a small rise on the south of Hobe's Hill. It supported eleven acres of cotton, nine of corn. It was not good ground for growing either crop.

Geographically, Hobe's Hill is a low plateau at the southern end of the Appalachian Mountains, the final thrust of that great chain into the plains of central Alabama. It is about seventeen miles north of Centerboro and about a seven-mile drive south of Cookstown, the town serving the northern end of the county.

The Gudgers' portion of this hill was a lonely place—their house sat two miles from the main road and half a mile from its nearest neighbor. The neighbors to the north included Annie Mae's father, Bud Woods, and his family, and Woods's half sister, Sadie Ricketts, her husband, Fred, and their kids.

The counties north of Hobe's Hill were much higher and still wild, home to many of the "hill whites" and "clay eaters" who had fled to the high ground when the big cotton growers took over the fertile lowlands more than a century earlier. The Woodses and Gudgers knew something of at least one of these hill whites—a man with a long white beard that came to his waist. Bud Woods described to his children how when this man rode his horse, the beard bounced and blew in the wind. This is the last image Bud Woods had of his father. Some time in the 1880s, when Bud was about eight years old, the man with the long white beard rode that horse out of their mountain town and never came back.

As for George Gudger, Agee said his father had once owned land, but lost it. There is no family memory of how it was lost.

No one knows for certain what other ethnic backgrounds were brought together in 1924 with the marriage of Annie Mae Woods and George Gudger. The Gudger children and grandchildren knew only that there were a variety of Scottish, Irish, and English names among their grandparents and great-grandparents, and at least one relative believed there was also some Indian blood mixed in from pioneer days. (In some notes Agee said Annie Mae had traces of a Scottish accent.) A more precise accounting of the roots of the Woodses and the Gudgers is not possible. Alabama, always a little behind the rest of the nation in these matters, did not start keeping birth certificates until 1908. By 1936 the Woodses and Gudgers had been in Alabama a long time. According to Emma, Bud Woods's daughter and Annie Mae Gudger's younger sister, family memory has it that some time soon after the white-bearded man rode off in the 1880s, members of the family came down out of the mountains to work cotton in the vicinity of Hobe's Hill.

That day in August as Agee followed the trail to the Gudger house, a fierce storm threatened. Agee described the trail as a "broken little road," requiring some skill behind the wheel to negotiate. As he neared, a wind had kicked up, and just as he arrived, it brought one of those hard Alabama rains, a "gray roar" with "water like trays that bursts four inches wide in a slapping of hands." There was also plenty of thunder and lightning. George Gudger opened the door to him and invited Agee inside the dark bedroom where the rest of the family was gathered. Storms were feared in the Gudger family, and Annie Mae was curled in fright on the bed.

Agee was fascinated with their house, which he was seeing for the first time, and he describes the strong emotions awakened in him as he stood inside the dark, lamp-lit bedroom trying to adjust his eyes to the lack of daylight.

Maggie Louise sat in a hardback chair, holding her baby brother, Squinchy, and her eyes fell upon Agee. There was something about the eyes of Maggie Louise that caught him the first time they met. They were "temperatureless, keen, serene and wise and pure gray eyes," Agee said, and they seemed to look everywhere and see into things. To look into the eyes of Maggie Louise was "scary as hell, and even more mysterious than frightening," said Agee. She knew she'd like him and he her.

Agee would live with the Gudgers for about three weeks from that night on, sleeping in the room adjacent to this one, trying not simply to record what life was like for the Gudgers but to live it as a part of their family. This was not an agreed-upon plan, but when he left that night after the storm, he crashed his car nearby, in either a quasi-suicidal frenzy or a subconsciously planned accident, and walked back up the mud-soaked road asking to stay.

There were those in the county who thought the Gudgers were crazy even to talk with these strangers, let alone let one live with them in their house. "I saw him come in—he was a bum!" remembered a woman who was twenty-eight when Agee strode down the streets of Cookstown. Fifty years later, her voice still had a sharp edge when she spoke of that time. Word had spread around town of the Yankees nosing around, and that had set off a campaign of whispers. The Civil War was still fresh in the minds of many—some old-timers had lived through Reconstruction, and hate toward northerners was strong. At best, the people in the county seat of Centerboro said to each other, these two northerners had come down to make fun of impoverished southerners, to "low-rate" them, in local parlance. Some even said they were Russian spies, sent to make America look bad.

Others had more practical worries—this part of Alabama was a major moonshine center, and many thought the strangers were agents poking around in search of stills. Though forbidding alcohol in his own home, George Gudger was one of those who ran a still. He ran it with some other men back in the remote woods of Hobe's Hill to pick up extra money. If Agee knew about the still, he never mentioned it.

But the Gudgers did let Agee stay, and in the days and nights that followed, Agee pieced together the special story of these lives and surrendered to the poet in him the job of describing the personal aspects of their struggle, while the journalist's eye recorded the economic facts. Agee's description of the Gudger house would be incredibly detailed.

It was a typical sharecropper structure, of split design—the house had an open hallway runing down the center, so the house was cut in half by a corridor, with "weatherboard facing one another in walls six feet apart." This kind of home was known locally as a "dog-run" house, for a dog could run through it, in the front and out the back. More important, the wind could run through and cool the house on hot nights. It was of "expanded crate construction" and the roof leaked in the front rooms of each half, and the holes in the walls were so vast they let in too much wind, so those rooms were left uninhabited. "The floors are made of wide planks, between some of which the daylighted earth is visible." It was surrounded by outbuildings—a barn, a chicken coop, a smokehouse, a garden.

The house, like the coops, was constructed "out of the cheapest available pine lumber," which had never been painted, and lacked insulation. Only a "skin of one thickness" of boards separated the family from the rain and wind, and, Agee said, "there are screens for no windows but one, in the rear bedroom." Closing the shutters kept out the weather, but not the summer heat and the mosquitoes. Most windows were anything but square, and only one contained glass. It was Annie Mae's eternal frustration that no matter how much she swept and fussed, she could never get the house pretty.

Yet this was hardly the worst sharecropper house around. In fact, it was only eight years old, younger certainly, and in better condition, than the many tenant homes that dated to slave times.

Cotton was the sole business of the central Alabama county where they lived. It was the primary business of the state—64 percent of all farmers were tenants just like them, according to the 1935 report of the President's Committee on Farm Tenancy. The Gudgers were among the nine hundred thousand Alabama men, women, and children who grew cotton in 1936.

Economically, the Gudgers were half-croppers. To be a half-cropper was to be one of the least-advantaged tenant farmers. This group was largely black; though the majority of tenant farmers in the South were white, two and a half million of the four million sharecroppers were black, according to an article in the magazine *Southern Exposure*.

Because of this, the Gudgers were looked down on by some of their fellow whites. "None of these people has any sense, nor any initiative. If they did, they wouldn't be farming on shares" was how Agee described the attitude of the townsmen to those on half shares. Clearly, to be on halves meant you were just working to survive, if you were lucky.

For the Gudgers, it hadn't started out that way.

Agee had studied a picture that hung over the fireplace of their Hobe's Hill home. In that photograph, Annie Mae's mother, Lulla, was standing with Emma, Annie Mae's sister. Not long after that picture was taken, Annie Mae married George Gudger. He and Annie Mae were married April 17, 1924, according to courthouse records. Their first child, Maggie Louise, was born February 2, 1926. Annie Mae was eighteen, George twenty-two. Three sons followed Maggie Louise, and one daughter, but the daughter died at birth. Agee believed that George and Annie Mae lived for the children.

They began married life with hope and a will to work hard, but Agee found a metaphor for their altered lives in a hat that was crushed in a table drawer. He said,

> It is of such a particular splendor that I am fairly sure it was her wedding hat, made for her, perhaps as a surprise, by her mother.

She was sixteen then; her skin would have been white, and clear of wrinkles, her body and its postures and her eyes even more pure than they are today . . . she was such a poem as no human being shall touch.

The passage of a dozen years had changed everything, though at first, Gudger told Agee, it looked as if he might succeed. In Gudger's best year he cleared $125. "He felt exceedingly hopeful and bought a mule." With a mule, you could get off the halvers and go on thirds. Then you could save more money and, with some good crops, maybe in a few years, buy land. Then you'd owe nothing to any man. Perhaps when Maggie Louise reached her teen years they'd be among the landed people and she'd have a secure future. "But," Agee wrote, "when his landlord warned him of how he was coming out the next year, he sold it [the mule]." From then on, no matter how hard Gudger worked, he was working not only against weather and the usual vicissitudes of farming but also against the system itself. Unless you had a fair landlord the chances of escape were not good.

Gudger's problem was described in *The Collapse of Cotton Tenancy*, published in 1935:

The industrious and thrifty tenant is sought by the landlord. The very qualities which might normally lead a tenant to attain the position of renter, and eventually of owner, are just the ones which make him a permanent asset as a cropper. Landlords, thus, are most concerned with maintaining the system that furnishes them labor and that keeps this labor under their control, that is, in the tenancy class.

But the Gudgers never learned whether or not in the normal course of events they might have prevailed and worked their way out of the trap of tenancy, for another problem, one over which they had absolutely no control, soon doomed them. That problem was the onset of the Great Depression. By the late 1930s, the cotton market had long since collapsed and the government had moved to control it.

. iii .

When Maggie Louise was six, the Gudgers were half-cropping for sixty-three-year-old T. Hudson Margraves. Margraves lived in a big house in Cookstown; he and his brother had title to twenty-six hundred acres in the county. He also owned the store at which his tenants bought their supplies and rations.

In 1934, George Gudger went eight dollars into debt to Margraves. The next year, Gudger went twelve dollars into debt. Margraves would advance them no more money, only food, the value of which he would deduct from the proceeds of the next crop.

Each Saturday, Annie Mae would dress up in a print dress and go by mule into Cookstown, seven miles away, to Margraves's store. She would later tell a reporter from the *Tennessean* magazine who visited her in 1978, "They'd cut us down at the mercantile—just give us enough to live on every month. We'd get twenty-five pounds of flour, eight pounds of lard and some green coffee. Every year, them Margraves would strip us out of everything."

In the cotton-tenant South, most people ate what was called the 3-M diet—meat (salt pork), meal, molasses. They weren't allowed to have a large garden, because it would have taken away from space for planting cotton and because landlords understood that tending it would compete for their limited energy.

The tenants didn't have much, but many landlords saw it differently. To sum up their attitude, Agee quotes an unnamed landlord: "Tell you the honest truth, they owe us a big debt. Now you just tell me, if you can, what would all those folks be doing if it wasn't for us?"

Agee sensed turmoil in this family, indicated by a few notions he loosely attached to the Gudgers: "How were we caught?; What, what is it has happened?; What is it has been happening that we are living the way we are?; There's so much work it seems like you never see the end of it; . . . How was it we were caught?"

The Gudgers changed landlords for the 1936 season, hoping a new landlord would be better. That was how they moved onto Chester Boles's place on Hobe's Hill. Boles owned part of the hill, and the Margraves brothers controlled most of the rest. Right off, however, George Gudger had to borrow fifteen dollars from Boles to get through the winter. By the time Agee came along, midway through the cotton year, the money situation was even worse. Agee reported,

"Gudger—a family of six—lives on ten dollars a month rations money during four months of the year. He has lived on eight, and on six."

At the end of the 1936 season, the Alabama cotton crop was worth 87 million hard-times dollars, according to the *Handbook of Alabama Agriculture.* If you take that figure and divide it by the total number of farm families, you get an average of $435 produced by each Alabama family who farmed that year.

The Gudgers saw none of their share. They went further into debt.

Despite their impoverished heritage, George Gudger held his head up, and Agee was to write as much about the strength of character of these people as about their economic hardships. In particular, he wrote about the tenacity of George Gudger and Annie Mae and the aspirations of the young Maggie Louise.

George said it would get better. His family would just have to work harder and do more. Times would improve; they would get a little ahead. The Bible told him that, and he lived by the Book. He indoctrinated his children with this belief. Annie Mae had to keep her hair long, at his wish, and was forbidden to wear any makeup. No one could drink alcohol. Everyone in his house was expected to submit to dark-to-dark work, relatives said years later. As soon as Maggie Louise could walk, she had to contribute. Kids became adults quickly.

Maggie Louise was trained to thin the plants, called "chopping," and to weed, spread soda, dust arsenic to kill the worms and weevils, and be ready in late August, when picking time neared.

Agee described the whitening fields, the "enlarged bolls . . . streaked a rusty green, then bronze, and are split and splayed open each in a loose vomit of cotton." The process begins slowly, Agee said, but in "a space of two or three days . . . a whole field seems to be crackling open at once." Experienced tenants, said Agee, would then wait more days, so that picking was worth the effort. Maggie Louise took well to her teachings and became an expert at cotton. "Louise is an extraordinarily steady and quick worker for her age; she can pick a hundred and fifty pounds in a day," Agee said. Her industry and ability made her parents proud.

George was a quiet man, though he'd grow angry if his children weren't working hard, his children later said. But he didn't expect any of them to push as hard as he did—George was always first out and last in from the fields. Sometimes, he'd come in late and his children would all be in one room, scattered on pallets laid upon the floor, sweating from the heat that never lessened into the humid nights. George would sprinkle water on the floor and softly pace, waving his hat to create a breeze and lift the moisture to help cool them until they were lulled asleep, said several of his children.

The Gudgers had to depend on each other. Though things seemed dismal, they would not sink into living like some other half-croppers. Annie Mae felt the pressure of her mother's upbringing, Agee said, dressing the family by reaching to buy "materials of a 'higher' class." Agee was struck by the fact that though she had "exceedingly little money" she had "an intense determination to hold her family's clothing within a certain level of respectability."

Each of the children had to keep scrubbed like city kids—every night before going to bed, Annie Mae required them to wash their feet in cold water before stepping into their bed pads.

When Agee stayed at their home, he slept in the inferior front room. Maggie Louise slept with her brothers and parents in one room at the rear. That room had the screen on the window. It contained two iron beds, and the children slept on pallets laid on the floor. At night, Annie Mae and George lay on one of the iron beds, and Agee speculated that if they made love, it had to be done with the utmost care so that the children wouldn't hear. They would lie still in the last moments before sleep, Annie Mae clutching George's sun-reddened body, characterized by Agee as tight and already shrinking at thirty years from the load of work, hers already wrinkled at twenty-seven.

. iv .

September came, and the picking season blended with the start of school. As usual, Maggie Louise started late to school, Agee said, because of the need to finish gathering the crop. It was hard, beyond the normal vagaries of learning, for her to go to school even after all the cotton was in and the fields were shiny beneath the winter rains.

Those frequent rains made it difficult. In dry weather, she had to walk three-quarters of a mile down the dirt lane to catch the bus when it sidetracked up the Hobe's Hill road. In wet weather, the mud made it impossible for the bus to go that far, and she had to walk "a mile and a half in clay which in stretches is knee-deep on a child" to catch the bus on the main graveled road to Cookstown. Agee made much of these difficulties and felt it might hamper her chances.

In the 1935–36 school year, Maggie Louise had missed fifty-three days, much of it on account of bad weather, Agee learned from looking at her report cards. Most of the missed days were in March and April, the wettest months and the ones that demanded a lot of work to plant the cotton. Even though Maggie Louise had some of the best grades in her class, she missed a critical examination, was not given a chance to retake it, and so "had to take the whole year over."

In spite of the handicaps, Agee said, "Her father and much more particularly her mother is excited over her brightness and hopeful of it: they intend to make every conceivable effort by which she may continue not only through the grades but clear through high school. She wants to become a teacher, and quite possibly she will; or a trained nurse; and again quite possibly she will."

Agee found her a "magical" person—"one of the stronger persons" he had ever known.

Many landlords, however, didn't want children in school as they grew older. They wanted them on the farms they owned to help their parents grow more cotton. The general attitude among the leaders of their county was that the tenant children were born "incapable" of learning. As a result, Alabama schools were among the poorest in the nation. The children were educated accordingly, learning little, remaining ignorant, creating a never-ending cycle of defeat.

The worth of school for children versus their worth as creatures of work became an issue when Alabama passed a law limiting children to working an eight-hour day. In 1894, the act was repealed. By the 1930s, Alabama had started to pass child-labor laws similar to those passed in other states thirty years earlier. Under Alabama law, no child under fourteen could be employed, with an exemption for "agriculture or domestic service." There was a provision that said children under fourteen couldn't be employed in those two areas unless they had completed the sixth grade or had been in school more than 120 days. But it was routinely ignored. As if this weren't enough, problems were compounded when the state of Alabama reduced allocations for schools by 10 percent. Many schools would have closed, according to *Alabama: A Guide to the Deep*

South, a Work Projects Administration book, except that teachers taught for months for little or no pay.

Annie Mae went to school, but learned most from her mother. Agee reported that Annie Mae could "read, write, spell, and handle simple arithmetic," unlike many barely literate tenants. Many could only sign their own name. George Gudger never made it past the second grade and could do little more than scrawl his signature on a document. Annie Mae taught Maggie Louise just as her mother had educated her. For this reason, Maggie Louise was not totally crippled by all that was negative about the educational system.

Landowners like Margraves and Boles, though, had little doubt their own children would inherit the land and become landlords to Maggie Louise and the children she would bear. Annie Mae prayed that wouldn't come to pass. She felt that her children, especially Maggie Louise, would have things better. She had to believe that. Before he left, Annie Mae said years later, Agee told her she might not live to see it, but that it would happen. But as for now, Annie Mae could barely think about the future. "I'm so tired it don't seem like I ever could get rest enough," Agee reported as her sentiments. "I'm as tired when I get up in the morning as I am when I lay down at night. I tell you I won't be sorry when I die. I wouldn't be sorry this minute if it wasn't for Louise and Squinchy here."

The time Agee spent with the Gudgers in 1936 was intense emotionally. Annie Mae later said he left, seemed gone forever, but came back after a week, to say good-bye. His final visit was in 1937. Of course, Agee didn't know what happened to them as 1940 neared. Left to the future were his two predictions for the Gudgers: that Maggie Louise would reach success and that her baby brother, so sickly, would die in youth.

Fed up with Boles, the worn land, and its hard mineral soil, the Gudgers worked off their debt and left the Boles place before the start of the 1938 season and headed down to a farm near the river, working shares for another landlord they hoped would be better, their children said. Tenants were constantly moving to find the ideal landlord. Landlords were always seeking ideal tenants. It seemed every cropper worked for every owner at one time or another. Annie Mae gave birth to another girl, Gretchen, in 1938, and life continued the same for them on that farm.

The Gudger home on Hobe's Hill was next occupied by a man everyone nearby called Pretty Boy, because he was so ugly. His wife and child moved in to work on the shares for Boles. These black sharecroppers had no better luck on the harsh and barren land. In 1939, Pretty Boy rode a mule wagon to Cherokee City to seek relief help to keep his family from starving. On his return, where the branch road met the main highway at the bottom of Hobe's Hill, he stepped off the wagon, was struck by a car, and was killed.

At the Gudgers' new tenant farm, a young man started coming around to see Maggie Louise. His name was Abraham Jones. He'd known the family for a long time. He was seven when Maggie Louise was born. He later described how he'd wait in the woods at the end of the cotton rows and how, when she was finished picking in the harvest season, they'd run off together.

George Gudger did not like that boy.

RICKETTS

. i .

Growing cotton didn't require particular brilliance—just care, patience, dedication, and endurance in the face of long hours of tedious and often painful work. To get people to do such work, antebellum planters and, later, landowners had two choices—either hold out the prospect of a clear and sure reward at the end of the line or create a credible threat of terrible consequences should the work not be completed.

Rather than change the basis of their control and offer a more humane incentive to the cotton worker, some landowners devoted decades of their lives to finding a replacement for people. In 1820, an imaginative if not too practical Louisiana planter imported a shipload of Brazilian monkeys with the idea that he'd train them to pick cotton and put an end to his labor difficulties. The monkeys, however, acted as monkeys would and got little picking done.

Some visionaries invested their hopes in machines. In September 1850, the first patent was issued on a mechanical cotton picker, but it proved a failure. No machine seemed able to solve the special problems of harvesting cotton. Crops like corn and wheat were mechanized, but cotton, because of its peculiar nature, seemed to defy the advance of technology. In 1936, the Bureau of Agricultural Economics said it took thirty-seven hours of labor to raise an acre of corn, twenty for wheat, fifteen for oats, but eighty-five for cotton. "Cotton's hitherto successful defiance of the [cotton-picking] machine has kept the cost of production extremely high and has drafted women and children to work in the field," wrote Rupert B. Vance, in *The Human Geography of the South* (1932).

Cotton treated some of these people as nothing more than trained human monkeys.

Margaret Ricketts was born into such a family.

Like the patriarch of the Woods family, her father, Fred Garvrin Ricketts, was born, in 1872, into one of the white hill families that generations earlier had been displaced by slavery, driven up into the northern mountains of Alabama, where they settled in the coal country of Northfork County, living, as Agee said, in "shacks on shale, rigid as corn on a cob." The Rickettses were of Scotch-Irish descent, tracing their roots first to Scotland, later to Ireland, according to Margaret's recollection. To this day, the residents of Northfork County have a reputation among central Alabamians for zaniness. If a crime is committed and it turns out that the perpetrator is from Northfork County, Birmingham people roll their eyes knowingly. Old man Ricketts also had Miller blood in him, Agee said, referring to a long-ago notorious family, and that apparently made things worse for all the Ricketts people to follow.

At some unknown point, Fred Ricketts decided to come down out of the hills and settle in the Hobe's Hill area. He then married Sadie, the half sister of Bud Woods, who was the father of Annie Mae Gudger. Margaret Ricketts, born in 1916, was the first child of Fred and Sadie Ricketts to survive. But all the family hope that Agee described as having attended the birth of Margaret's second cousin, Maggie Louise Gudger, ten years later, in 1926, he found absent from the Ricketts family.

The Rickettses never expected Margaret to finish school. On the contrary, Fred encouraged her to drop out. She quit in fifth grade, she told Agee, "because her eyes hurt her so badly every time she studied books." It seems, from reconstructing that period many years later, that Fred applauded the decision, for books didn't help raise cotton or bring in money. Cutting off dreams meant cutting off options, and this meant that she would in fact devote her life to cotton. Everyone expected Margaret to mule farm the next sixty or so years until she died.

Margaret had "forgotten a good deal how to read," Agee said. But she learned to farm. By the cotton harvest of 1936, when Agee met her, Margaret had grown into something less than an attractive woman. Agee described her sister Paralee wearing a dress that she had seen "no sense to wash" in a year. She had "manure-stained feet and legs." But he said that Margaret looked worse, and she "was a year and a whole world more hopeless." She hardly ever bathed. This is how Agee found everyone in the Ricketts family. The odors at the Ricketts house were "hard to get used to or even hard to bear," he said, and the family had "a deliberated or cult-like acquisition of dirtiness." Their yard was littered with debris, and the interior of the house had "absorbed smoke and grease and dirt into a rich dark patina," Agee wrote; the kitchen work area was so covered in filth that it was as "thick and filming as sprayed soil."

Fifty years later, Agee's observations about the family's sanitary habits were confirmed by the recollections of others.

The son of a Centerboro merchant remembered an incident in which his father said to Fred Ricketts, "Mr. Fred, I can see by the egg on your mustache what you ate this morning."

"That wuz frm br'kfast a week ago," Ricketts answered.

A former neighbor recalls Sadie Ricketts's telling her, "The worst thing for children is for 'em to wear drawers 'n' atake a bath." Decades later, the neighbor was still baffled.

Another neighbor repeated a story that has become part of the Ricketts legend. A doctor went to deliver one of the Ricketts children back in the 1920s, and he asked for a bar of soap to wash up before he examined Sadie. Fred said they had none. Worried about such unsanitary conditions, the doctor returned after the delivery and gave them a bar of soap and a lecture on the health benefits of cleanliness. A year and a half later, the doctor came back to deliver

another child. He asked for soap. Fred Ricketts smiled and produced the same unwrapped bar of soap the doctor had brought after
the last birth. Fred Ricketts, according to Agee, felt that "It is foolish
to waste money that can be eaten with on soap when any fool
knows there is nothing cleaner than water."

The whole county heard these stories.

All of Margaret's six brothers and sisters were brought up this
way, and most were quiet about it. "The Ricketts are spoken of
disapprovingly, even so far away as the county courthouse, as 'problem' children," Agee wrote. In school, "they are always fighting and
sassing back," said Agee, and their attendance record was "extremely bad." He said they always got into fights because of the
peasantlike clothes they wore.

> They come of a family which is marked and poor even among the
> poor whites, and are looked down on even by most levels of the
> tenant class. They are uncommonly sensitive, open, trusting, easily
> hurt, and amazed by meanness and by cruelty, and their ostracism
> is of a sort to inspire savage loyalty among them.

Margaret had vague dreams, but hers were not at all like those
of Maggie Louise Gudger. Margaret, it was apparent years later,
didn't look at the stars and wonder about her future. She knew what
it would be.

Agee speculated that her dreams were "of a husband, and
strong land." But by 1936, although already twenty years old, she
still had not engaged in any of the precourting activities young
people of that time and place did; she was putting all that off. "Margaret has already the mannerisms and much of the psychic balance
of a middle-aged woman of the middle class in the north," Agee
said. He added that girls, "by the time they are eighteen, if they are
unmarried, . . . are drifted towards the spinster class, a trouble to
their parents, an embarrassment to court and be seen with, a dry
agony to themselves."

Family problems may have had a lot to do with her remaining
home. Sadie was chronically sick from pellagra, a disease caused by
poor nutrition, and Fred couldn't afford to lose Margaret's labor in
the field.

Margaret later would brag of her manlike strength and energy.
She was the first up in the morning, stoking the stove and cooking

breakfast by lamplight, then starting a full day of field work. She was proud she could handle a double team of mules, even turning the big steel plow at the row ends and wrestling it free of dirt clods.

In August 1936, Margaret's only concern was about getting through each day's work on the way to getting the crop harvested, looking forward each day only to the time when the sun would drop and she could head into their house on Hobe's Hill, about half a mile across the fields and a forested ravine from the Gudger house.

The differences between the Gudger and the Ricketts homes intrigued Agee. The Ricketts home, he observed, now more run-down than that of the Gudgers, was "built as an ordinary lower-middle-class frame house." In the beginning, the house belonged not to a mere tenant but to Mr. Hobe himself, the man who owned most of the land on this hill. According to Agee, T. Hudson Margraves probably was the one who foreclosed on Hobe and who in 1932 rented the Hobe house to Fred Ricketts.

Though the Rickettses lived as badly as half-croppers, they were in fact doing better than the Gudgers in some respects. They owned two mules and farm tools and thus worked on thirds and fourths, rather than on halves.

Ricketts averaged six bales of cotton, earning some fifty-four dollars a year, Fred told Agee.

"Years ago," Agee wrote,

> the Ricketts were, relatively speaking, almost prosperous. Besides their cotton farming they had ten cows and sold the milk, and they lived near a good stream and had all the fish they wanted. Ricketts went $400 into debt on a fine young pair of mules. One of the mules died before it had made its first crop; the other died the year after; against his fear, amounting to full horror, of sinking to the half-crop level where nothing is owned, Ricketts went into debt for other, inferior mules; his cows went one by one into debts and desperate exchanges and by sickness; he got congestive chills; his wife got pellagra; a number of his children died; he got appendicitis and lay for days on end under the ice cap; his wife's pellagra got into her brain; for ten consecutive years now . . . they have not cleared or had any hope of clearing a cent at the end of the year.

Bad luck always had a way of striking down any advances of the Rickettses.

. *ii* .

If Agee was attracted to the intelligent and voluble George Gudger and his family, he was put off, if not repelled, by the dullness of Fred Ricketts. But he clearly sensed that Ricketts believed that Agee had the ability to see through other men's pretensions, including his own. This is not to say that Fred gave even a minute's thought to the fact that Agee also had the talent to put those observations into well-chosen words that would reveal to a country who Fred was.

In his first descriptions of Ricketts at the steps of the Confederate statue in Centerboro, Agee wrote of Fred,

> . . . you did the talking, and the loudest laughing at your own hyperboles, stripping to the roots of the lips your shattered teeth, . . . the glittering of laughter in your eyes, a fear that was saying, "o lord god please for once, just for once, don't let this man laugh at me up his sleeve, or do me any meanness or harm."

Fred gave five words for each given, and Agee said Ricketts had "flashing, foxy, crazy eyes," watching for Agee's "true intentions, which he feared."

More than with either Bud Woods or George Gudger, Agee sensed that Fred Ricketts was seeking Agee's approval and did not want Agee to speak harshly of him for the way he and his family lived.

To make sure that Agee did not see him as someone with whom educated people could trifle without cost, Ricketts told Agee about a time when he was in school and the teacher told him the earth spun on an axle. Ricketts challenged the teacher, arguing that if that were so, everyone in hell would be trying to chop the axle and destroy the earth. The earth was still here, so it had to be false. Ricketts summed up his triumph for Agee: "Teacher never did bring up nothn bout no axles after that. No sir, she never did bring up nothin about no durn axles after that. No sir-ree, she shore never did brang up nufn about no dad blame axles attah dayut."

When the three men left the courthouse on the day of their first meeting with Agee and Walker Evans, it was to the Ricketts house that they returned. Fred's was the closest of their three homes to a road that a car could easily reach. The Ricketts children saw them coming and ran scared into the woods. They "started out from behind bushes and hid behind one another and flirted at us and ridiculed us like young wild animals," Agee wrote, fascinated with this primitive display.

Evans saw a good picture.

The Ricketts children were in retreat through the brush, heading up the road, when Ricketts called them back with shouts and threats, Margaret recalled later. They emerged with reluctance. Margaret took in the groceries they'd bought. Then Fred ordered the family to stand before Evans's camera. Agee wrote that Sadie Ricketts looked at her husband with eyes "wild with fury and shame and fear," but Agee felt she obeyed the man because "a wife does as she is told and keeps quiet about it."

Evans didn't talk with them. He didn't even talk down to them. He talked at them, as if they were objects, Margaret said later. In interviews he gave in the 1960s and 1970s, Evans seldom referred to any of the people he had photographed in 1936 as people, but always as "rich" material. This was nothing new. Evans mentioned in a later interview that he was "shy" and didn't like to photograph anyone. A study of many interviews with him showed he considered himself an artist. He preferred to shoot barns and buildings. Usually, when he photographed people, it was done in secret. In New York subways, he later took pictures with a hidden camera. In other places, he used a "side-angle" camera that could take pictures at right angles, so the subjects thought he was shooting in another direction. The first pictures of the three men at the courthouse were taken with such a camera. This way, he escaped having to face them with what he was doing.

Fifty years later, Margaret recalled the arrival of Agee and Evans and seemed not to have forgotten a detail. Paralee, the second oldest of the Rickettses' offspring, at age nineteen, she remembered, didn't want to cooperate with all this, in spite of her father's demands to please the photographer. She was forced to, but rebelled by keeping her eyes closed while the picture of their family was being made. A study of that picture reveals that terror filled the eyes of the smaller children.

"Those men wore monkey suits and talked funny," Margaret said when she was older. In fact, she'd never before really seen anyone from outside the area, so once her own initial terror subsided her natural sense of adventure took over and she grew more and more curious. The strangers soon became a source of great amusement. Margaret came to like Agee, who seemed friendly, but recoiled from Evans and his indifference to them as people and his obvious loathing for the way they lived.

That Evans wanted nothing to do with any of these tenants is clear. While Agee grew closer to the farmers, Evans preferred to spend most of his nights in a hotel in town, even after Agee started living with the Gudgers. Evans stayed some nights, but not many, said family members who are old enough to remember.

Agee favored the Gudgers. He came around less frequently to the Rickettses and wrote that he didn't really want to see more of them. Once in a while, he did show up, such as the time he and Evans came to play a game of "poison oak," a form of tag played by southern children. During their play, one of them—it is not clear who—accidentally knocked down four-year-old Clair Bell, the youngest child of the Rickettses. Her head struck a rock supporting the front porch.

That day Clair Bell went into a coma, an event Agee's literature vérité did not encompass. Indeed, it seems that neither Agee nor Evans ever told anyone of the incident. That it had indeed occurred came out in an interview fifty years later with someone who was there that day. Before leaving to go back to New York, Agee came back one more night. He brought with him a tea set as a present for the injured child, assuming that if she died they would place it on her grave as an ornament, which was the local custom.

As Agee was saying his good-byes, wondering how he'd write his *Fortune* article and describe the poverty he had witnessed on Hobe's Hill, an event over in the Mississippi Delta threatened to rock the cotton South.

. *iii* .

It was August 31, 1936.

Hundreds of curious people were gathered that day at the Delta Experiment Station in Stoneville, Mississippi, to watch a demonstration by John D. and Mack Rust, two brothers who were about to unveil an invention they billed as the first practical cotton-picking machine.

The brothers were the sons of a man who had fought in the Civil War on the side of the South and, after the defeat, had moved to Necessity, Texas, to raise cotton. The boys worked with their father, much as the Gudger and Ricketts children labored with their parents. While out in the fields picking cotton, John Rust continually complained. It had to be the worst job in the whole world, he said to his brother. A picker on poor land could do only about a hundred pounds a day, and it took fifteen hundred pounds of seed cotton to gin down to a standard five-hundred-pound bale. He fantasized about inventing a machine that would forever end the grueling task.

The Rust brothers' parents died when John was sixteen. John began living as a migrant farmhand, picking and chopping cotton. On the side, he took a mail-order course in engineering, which he completed in 1924. Then he set out to realize his dream of developing a cotton picker.

He faced numerous problems that had defeated dozens of other inventors before him. Cotton bolls do not all ripen at the same time, for instance, and most fields must be picked three or four times over a two-month period. A machine would have to pick ripe bolls without destroying the plants, so that they could be gleaned later. It would also have to pull the lint from the boll without crushing the delicate shell and adding waste material that would destroy the cotton for ginning, the post-harvest process that removes the seeds. On top of this, a successful machine would have to pick cotton lower than a man's knee in Georgia, cotton that was bushy and head tall in the Delta, and cotton on skeletonlike plants in Texas.

Men had tried suction tubes, threshers, and other fanciful Rube Goldberg devices, and none really worked.

One night, while lying in bed, John remembered how cotton clung to his fingers in the early morning dew. Water attracted the fiber. That was the secret! He sprung to his feet, got a nail, wet it, and applied it to some cotton in the medicine cabinet. It held the cotton, and the fiber fell off after the moisture was absorbed. He wrote down the plans for a machine using moistened steel spindles that would brush the plants and reach into the bolls to pluck the lint, which would quickly fall off and be collected. They were different from the barbed spindles others had tried that would not release the cotton.

Success, however, eluded him as years went by. He built models with the help of tens of thousands of dollars borrowed from family and friends. His wife divorced him, and he conducted his experiments in his sister's garage. None of the prototypes worked as well as he hoped, but finally, in 1936, he felt he could invite the public to witness his completed machine. That device was preceded by four-teen hundred patents on other machines that had ultimately failed. International Harvester itself had spent three million dollars over the preceding forty years on doomed designs.

Reporters came from all over to see this machine that day in August 1936. While skeptical spectators stood in the hot sun and drank endless sodas, the machine set out and picked four hundred pounds of cotton in an hour, as much as one average man could pick in four days.

Exclamations of amazement came from the plantation owners in their white shoes and hats, and from the bankers, ginners, dealers, and government men. One writer said the invention of such a device was akin to the discovery of a perpetual-motion machine.

"Now we won't have to beg for help to pick cotton," W. H. Hutchins, a grower who watched, told *Time* magazine.

Excitement quickly turned to fear and scorn. Some said the machine added a lot of trash to the cotton, and others wondered if such a device could be commercially manufactured. The Rust machine would not chop, hoe, or plant. People were still needed for that, so what good would it do to have a machine that picked when you still needed manpower standing by to plant and grow the next crop?

Within weeks, the *Memphis Commercial-Appeal* printed a cartoon of a black man with an empty cotton sack. The man was saying, "If it does my work—whose work am I going to do?" The *Jackson Daily News* suggested the machine be sunk in the Mississippi River. A prominent political boss in Tennessee predicted his state would pass a law against mechanical pickers.

The Luddites were having a field day, but *'Round the World with Cotton* opined,

> The trend in all production processes in the United States—both agricultural and industrial—has been toward the universal use of power and machinery. . . . If not used in cotton production, ultimately those who grow the crop will be laboring under a handicap from which all other large classes of workers have been liberated.

Some saw the machine as capable of freeing farm laborers not so much from that most noxious of farm chores as from the tyranny of their bosses.

Professor W. E. Ayres, the head of the government experiment station, said to John Rust, "I sincerely hope that you can arrange to market your machine shortly. Lincoln emancipated the southern Negro. It remains for cotton-harvesting machinery to emancipate the southern cotton [tenant] planter."

An article in *Reader's Digest* predicted the death of sharecropping within two years. Sharecroppers, the magazine said, "do not realize that their narrow little world of corn and cotton and sow belly is already tottering."

Liberals viewed the machine as salvation—with it, the South could be transformed from an alien and feudal society into one that might finally join the rest of America.

. *iv* .

The death of the cotton-tenant-farmer system sounded painless to these optimists. But John Rust knew different. During his migrant days, he'd become associated with the agrarian socialist movement, and he had a deep interest in the plight of the working man. Rust was aware how dangerous his machine was to the nine million tenant farmers of the South. He pictured hundreds of thousands of landless farmers crowding like war refugees into the cities or being left starving and forgotten on the land. Cotton work might be horrible and repressive, but it was the only work some of these people had. He didn't know Fred Ricketts, but Ricketts was the kind of man Rust had in mind. What would Ricketts do if the picking of cotton were suddenly mechanized? Rust knew about the character of men like Margraves, Ricketts's landlord. That kind of landlord would embrace the machine and discard Ricketts, not thinking twice of the family's fate.

"We are not willing that this should happen," Rust declared in an interview. "How can we prevent it?"

The question seemed to have two possible answers.

First, the Rust brothers refused to sell their invention to a large company to merchandise. They could have become rich instantly doing so but feared that a corporation would market it to large growers, who would outcompete and destroy small farms. Rather, they would try to develop a smaller version of the picker that the little farmer could afford and that would help the little farmer compete better. This, of course, is the opposite of what normally happens when new farm equipment is invented and introduced.

Their second idea was to lease rather than sell the machines, and to do so to large growers under restrictive rules. Those rules required the lessee to pay his workers minimum wages, to set a maximum number of work hours for all adult workers, and to eliminate child labor altogether.

They had other ideas, according to James H. Street in his 1957 book, *The New Revolution in the Cotton Economy: Mechanization and Its Consequences:*

> Community farming projects organized as cooperatives aroused considerable interest during the thirties. . . . The Rust brothers made their machine rather freely available to such communities, in the hope that a cooperative pattern would emerge which would make possible the collective ownership and operation of farm machines too large and expensive for widespread individual ownership.

Unfortunately, most of these collectives failed. Still, it is possible that at least for a limited period of time—that is, until someone else developed a machine that could do what theirs did—the Rusts might have been able to get some large planters to agree to their terms, had they not been hampered by serious design flaws in their machine. In constant use, the machines broke down more times than they worked and, when compared to the cost of cheap labor, were not economical. Under real farm conditions, the machine did not work well enough to make any significant dent. The skeptics seemed right. No machines were bought under the rules they imposed. In fact, in the years following the introduction of the Rust cotton picker, more tenants were employed than ever before in the history of cotton farming. This increase was due to forces unrelated to the machine. Families sought to return to the land to escape the Depression, reversing what had been an outflow to the cities. That trend created an even greater pool of willing and cheap labor for landlords looking for tenant farmers. Given this kind of labor market, it is not surprising that, as one writer estimated, it took between nine and fourteen dollars to cover all costs of raising a bale of cotton by hand and, under ideal conditions, about thirteen dollars by machine.

The cotton system was also facing other problems besides the threat of a machine that seemed to have so many bugs. *'Round the World with Cotton* said,

> For almost 100 years following the invention of the cotton gin by Eli Whitney, the United States was the only nation produc-

ing any significant quantity of cotton for export. . . . There was no other important source of supply.

By the year 1891–92, the United States was producing three times as much cotton as all other countries of the world combined. Twenty-five years after this date, in 1916–17, we were still growing three-fifths of all the world's cotton.

But in the year 1933–34, the combined crop of foreign countries exceeded that of the United States.

Never again would the United States dominate. The export market was destined to continue shrinking and with it the pool of farmers who grew the cotton.

There was another threat to those dependent on cotton for their meager livelihood. An artificially produced fiber, not in common use, but something that showed promise as a substitute yarn for clothing, had just been developed. It was called rayon.

The Rickettses ended the 1930s still farming by mule and hand on the thirds and fourths on top of Hobe's Hill for Margraves. Left to the coming years was a prediction by Agee that these children would "draw their future remembrance, and their future sorrow, from this place," and that most applied to the future of Margaret.

Margraves wasn't about to buy any silly machines. The growers in the county believed that the old ways were the best ways, which neither would nor should end.

As for the Rust brothers, they went back to their shop and tried to perfect the machine, holding to their dream that their machine would improve not only the picking of cotton but also the lives of the men and women who picked it.

WOODS

In the last days of the three intense weeks Agee spent on Hobe's Hill, his thoughts were very much focused on one woman in particular— Emma, daughter of Bud and Lulla Woods and sister of Annie Mae Gudger. He was physically attracted to her and wrote about this attraction with little embarrassment, indeed with a certain pride of conquest in winning over her affections. Like Agee, Emma was about to leave Hobe's Hill in September 1936 and did not seem likely to return.

Agee wrote about her in part to illustrate further what he called the "iron anguish" of the lot of women as daughters, wives, and mothers of tenant farmers. He described the work of a cotton tenant woman as one that "will be persisted in in nearly every day to come in all the rest of her life." This "accumulated weight," he wrote, will take a toll not only on her body, but be part of "her mind and of her heart and of her being. . . . The woman is the servant of the day, and of immediate life, and the man is the servant of the year, and of the basis and boundaries of life, and is their ruler."

Emma was about eight years younger than her sister Annie Mae and so had been a small child in 1924 when Annie Mae married George Gudger. The Woods household that remained after Annie Mae's marriage comprised father and mother—Bud and Lulla Woods—Emma, and Emma's two brothers—one older, who soon left home, and one younger, Clayton. The bond between the two remaining Woods women—Emma and Lulla—grew strong in the few years they had remaining together.

Bud Woods didn't value book learning, but Lulla encouraged Emma to sing, read, write, and believe in dreams, as she had with Annie Mae.

Emma recalls looking forward to school with a passion that fully equaled her distaste for the boredom of field work and for the life of uninterrupted hard labor she seemed destined for. "I was real good in school and I realy liked to go," Emma wrote of her youth many years later. After turning sixty, she began to keep a secret diary in a calendar datebook given to her as a birthday gift by a grandson. Each night, alone in her room, lying across her bed, she added more of her life story in her crabbed writing, both recounting recent events and putting down moments from her youth called up by memory.

"I was going to be a nurce when I finished school," another entry tells us; "that was always my dream." The diary records many of the familiar details of a country childhood: the three-mile walk to school, her mother tying strings around her pencils and then putting the strings around Emma's neck so that she wouldn't lose too many ("they was hard to get"), her brother Clayton having trouble keeping up with her on their walks to school because she "was just a tome boy," and their being chased on the way to school by an old gray mule, so she and Clayton would be late for class and then in punishment be kept after school ("we would have to stay in that afternoon and some time it would be dark when we got home").

Other entries tell of more troubled memories:

> When I was just 13 years old my mother died and left us.
> Dady, Clayton and myself. Oh I can rember that day. You see she

was in the hospitle. It dont seem like that she was there many days. I know me and Clayton went to see her once. That is all I rember. But she know us that day and we was so glad for we just knew she was better and would soon be back at home with us. But that didnt happen. She died. And left us. Clayton 10 and me 13. Poor old dady. There he was left with two little children and a big field of cotton to gather.

Thus were Emma's dreams snuffed out at 11:30 the night of June 7, 1929, when Lulla Woods, then aged fifty, succumbed to liver cancer. After that, Emma remembers, her father worked hard to keep the family afloat. "Dady was a real cotton farmer," she wrote with pride.

Of course, Bud Woods was not the only victim of this turn of fate or even the worst affected. Emma, just thirteen, was suddenly expected to take over the duties of the woman of the house. It was nothing like the situation a suburban child of today might face— there were no microwaves, dishwashers, or washing machines.

I had to do all the cooking and washing on a old wooden rub bord. I can rember I would just cry and rub them close and pray for the Lord to come and get me and carry me where mama was. I didnt know how to do any thing and I needed her so bad. And I havent for got yet that no one came in to help me and teach me how to do any thing.

When I would get throu then I had to go to the field and help dady and Clayton pick cotton.

Still, there was not one word of criticism for her father, and as heavy as the burdens were, there were memories as well of a family of love. "That poor dady of mine done his best," she remembers, and

he was always kind. And I know now that his poor old heart was so heavy. And I know he felt so alone. And didnt know what to do. He did not make fun of nothing I tryed to do. I dont see how he ate the food I cooked and worked as hard as he did. I can see him now siting on his cotton sack eating the slop I cooked. He didnt stop long enough to come to the house and eat and rest a little while. He ate in the field and went right on picking cotton.

It was at this time, when the family needed him so much, that Emma's older brother "got in some kind of truble" and had to leave home. Emma and Clayton went into the field daily to help, but there just weren't the hands or the strength to do all the work. "We never had any more Christmas. We didnt have any thing but one another. We just worked hard from year to year." There are also ominous notes: "But I know dady was lonsom. Now I can look back and see we was a pitiful 3. Me, dady and Clayton."

This was the time that Emma was forced to quit school. She doesn't set out the details of the decision, if indeed she recalls them. She merely says, "I dont gess he could send us to school any more. I just know we didnt go any more. I had passed into the 6th grade. I wanted to be a nurce so bad but that didnt work."

Boys were attracted to Emma by this time, and she already had plenty of suitors. She fended them off, not willing to enter matrimony so young. Annie Mae was already married and had a child of her own—Maggie Louise—by the time their mother died. Annie Mae had waited until she was sixteen to wed George, not really young for an Alabama country girl of that period, but Lulla had wanted Emma to wait even longer, and Emma was not going to violate her mother's wishes.

But it soon became difficult for her to remain at home. Bud Woods was lonely, and his desire for a wife caused the family problems. Emma recalls,

> . . . in 3 years after mama died dady married again and he married a woman that didnt suite our famly. You see I wouldnt stay with him after he married this woman that he had tote me aganst all my life. But I loved my dady. So then I set in to seprate him + her. I liked to done it to one time but then they fixed things up and stayed together.

The woman of Emma's scorn was Ivy Pritchart, just the kind of woman Bud had long held up to his daughter as a model of what every decent girl had to avoid becoming. Annie Mae apparently came to share Emma's sentiments, for when Agee arrived in 1936 he observed that neither could stand Bud Woods's second wife. This was more than the usual resentment of children toward their father's second wife. When Agee asked about her among the townsmen, he heard her described as "one of the worst whores in this whole part of the country." The only one thought worse was her mother, Miss Molly, of whom the men of the area sang a song when they were alone and snickering, a song that recounted her exploits. The women, mother and daughter, were described as "about the lowest trash you can find."

Until the lonely Bud Woods came into their lives, Ivy and Miss Molly lived back in the swamp. The man Ivy had lived with had died, and Bud Woods courted her. After they married on December 9, 1931, they first lived back in the swamp; then he moved Ivy, Miss Molly, and Ivy's eight-year-old daughter, Pearl, into his three-room shack on Hobe's Hill. An older daughter of Ivy's was given away to a family in Cherokee City. Emma was fifteen years old when her family was expanded.

Little Pearl was sexual beyond her years, according to Agee, and aggressive. She delighted in throwing rocks at the black children who came to fetch the warm, fever-laden water from the communal spring at the bottom of the hill behind their house. Like many poor white families in the Cotton Belt, the Woodses were racist toward blacks, who were equally poor, if not poorer. The Woodses attributed the feverish qualities of the water to the nearby black family that lived in the hollow, somehow believing that the blacks were contaminating it simply with their use. The black children were forced to come for the water when they were least expected by Pearl.

Pearl also hated Bud Woods. She felt he was responsible for forcing her mother to give away her older sister. In 1933, soon after the marriage, Ivy had a son, who was called Buddy. Ivy became pregnant again and gave birth to Ellen, who was twenty months old in the late summer of 1936. Pearl became jealous of her new sister. Ivy was again pregnant when Agee was visiting. That child was not due until 1937. That Bud Woods was having so many children troubled his daughters. Emma and Annie Mae felt he should not have started a new family at his age.

He was fifty-nine, not terribly old for a city man, but ancient considering the labor required of a one-mule tenant farmer. In 1936, Woods worked on thirds and fourths for Margraves, who owned the land on both sides of the Hobe's Hill road. In many ways, Woods had it tougher than the families of his stepsister Sadie Ricketts, whose house was in sight of his, and his daughter Annie Mae, who lived nearby. He seemed smarter than Fred Ricketts, but didn't have a large number of children of working age to help him, as Ricketts had.

The last really good year Woods had had was during the First World War, when cotton prices were at record highs and he had the help of Annie Mae and his older boy. With the onset of the Depression years, and the loss of Annie Mae and this older boy, he generally wound up clearing $50 or less annually. But he was strong for a man his age and worked extra hard, and this allowed him to end even these bad years in the black, though often just barely. In 1935, he told Agee, he had made $150, a considerable feat; one study found that in the crop year 1935 only one out of ten tenant farmers in one southern county had made any money at all.

The achievement is even more noteworthy because by 1935 Woods had long since lost the help of Emma, who had decided she did not want to live in his Hobe's Hill house any longer. The quarters were too close with that woman. To get away, Emma at first went half a mile through the forest and fields to live with Annie Mae and George Gudger.

Though Emma got away from her stepmother, she did not escape her other nemesis, field work. "I started staying with my sister and her husbun," she writes in her diary. "And he was a hard working man and he belived in every body working from day light till dark and that is what we done. I was so tird of the way I was living. Work work. That was all any body wanted with me."

Emma saw few options. The only proper states for a tenant-farm woman were too young to be married, about to be married, and married. A woman worked for her parents until some time into her teens, when she had to do what she could to find a man whom she could bear serving as wife, and then went to work for her new husband. In the South of the 1930s, a woman could not simply go off and live alone without local tongues painting her as a whore or spinster—a whore being someone who had put herself under the suspicion of having slept with a man not her husband; a spinster, a woman who had too little womanly appeal to attract any man and had to live on the largess of her family. The only way a woman might hope to live alone with some respect was to have a job. Emma's dilemma was that the only careers open to women at that time and in that place were in nursing or education, fields closed to her because of her limited formal schooling. What was left to her was to cook for, clean up after, and in other ways serve men—her husband, her sons, and any other men, friends or kin, who happened to be with her husband—laboring in the kitchen while the men ate, cleaning up while they sat on the porch and relaxed after dinner. For all the love between George and Annie Mae, this is the way it went even at the Gudgers'.

Emma didn't oppose marriage. She wanted love, though she had little idea what the word might mean, and simply accepted service as the price women paid for it. The social pressure to accept these roles as they were was extreme.

At the same time, Emma went through that tumultuous period of sexual awakening that all teenagers go through, and she was even more vulnerable than most because of her basically romantic disposition. She was "young and loved to sing"; when she wasn't "talking and laughing," she was singing. She also reports, "All the time I was realy lonly still surching for something. I didnt know what." She met a boy named Wilson Sharps, and in reporting this episode, the diary of a sixty-year-old woman becomes almost schoolgirlish in its entries:

> We was so happy when we was together. And had so mutch fun. You know I bet me and him was realy in love. And didnt have sence enough to know it. Some nights we would set in the middle of the road till mid night and after and try to count the stars and make wishes by the stars.

She said, "He didnt think I would marry Lonnie." Lonnie, the man she would indeed marry, was twenty years older than she. He was divorced and was pushing her to marry him. She may have been using Lonnie to play a lover's game with Wilson Sharps, a game that went wrong. Or she may simply have been no match for the older man.

> [Lonnie] began to talk to me about marrying him. I didnt want to . . . but any way I had ben tought that you was not soposed to marry any one that had ben married. And had a living wife or husbun. So I told him that but he went an showed me where it would be alright in the sight of God for me and him to get married.
> But any way he got the lisens and came after me and I ran away when I saw him coming. I went about 3 miles to Mrs. Sharps hous. That was Wilson mother. I stayed all the rest of the day and I got a curl of Wilsons hair and tide a string arond it and put it arond my neck. I did not tell him what I was up aganst tho, so it was about dark when I came back home. I thought he would be gone. I knowed that I would have.

Lonnie was there waiting, and he finally persuaded her. They married on February 20, 1934. Emma's diary tells us nothing of the ceremony, not a word about what she wore or who attended. Compare this with the way that Annie Mae had kept the very hat she had worn on her wedding day, as well as with the way that her family had shared her joy. Emma remembers only,

> I didnt know what love was really. I was like the old bo wevle. I was just looking for a home. But any way I failed on that. He carried me to his mothers house. I just couldnt stay there. . . . I stayed with him 3 weeks and ran away. Well to make a long story short we was married over 3 years and I stayed with him 7 weeks in the 3 years.

Lonnie was unemployed most of that time. He eventually got a job as a carpenter in Cherokee City, about twenty-five miles north of Cookstown. By July of 1936, Lonnie insisted on reclaiming his wife. Though Annie Mae did not like Lonnie, the counsel Emma seems to have gotten from her family was that she'd have to live with her husband. Emma agreed to go along, without ever quite knowing why.

Lonnie decided to leave Alabama, probably, Agee said, to get Emma away from George and Annie Mae Gudger, "so near a home she can return to." Lonnie had met an older man, a Mr. Jacobson, who persuaded him he should take Emma and go do what they called "bull farming." Jacobson told Lonnie he would set him up on a bull farm on a plantation in the red hills of Mississippi. Emma thought Jacobson had too much influence on her husband. "He was old but he made Lonnie think that money growed on trees in Stonewall Mississippi," Emma wrote of him.

Before leaving, Emma decided to return to Hobe's Hill and see her sister one last time before she left to go so far away. In seven days, Lonnie would come down with Mr. Jacobson to pick her up. Emma writes, "So I went to stay a week with her befor I left and that is when I met them to men that has wrote books about us and of the south."

. ii .

Emma was now twenty, and the two men, of course, were Agee and Evans, who had arrived to do their story on tenant farmers just a few weeks before Emma came back for her final visit. Agee was taken with this peasant woman and became quite fond of her. "She is a big girl, almost as big as her sister is wiry, though she is not at all fat," Agee wrote; "her build is rather that of a young queen of a child's magic story. . . ." He saw Emma as "a big child, sexual beyond propriety to its years." She looked younger than she acted. In fact, he got her age wrong, believing she was 18 when she was really two years older.

Agee seemed frustrated that the role of a cotton-tenant woman had been thrust upon Emma. His sexual longing for her grew in intensity, and he described great sexual tensions within the group, himself, Evans, and the family. Agee said it appeared George wanted to make love to Emma, his sister-in-law, and wrote, "If only Emma could spend her last few days alive having a gigantic good time in bed, with George, a kind of man she is best used to, and with Walker and with me. . . ."

There were flirtations, but they appeared not to set Emma's heart aflutter. She disliked Evans. She saw him as a cold, rude bore and avoided him. Years later she said there were never any thoughts between her and George. She considered Agee cute and admits that she did secretly wonder what it would have been like to become involved with him. "If only I could stay around longer," she said in an interview, admitting years later to feelings she had never told anyone about. But it could never have been. We have to remember that as all the world has changed since 1936 in regard to sexual mores, so too has Emma changed. Reasonable as such feelings may seem today, this was a fantasy impossible to talk about with her family at the time, certainly impossible to act upon. And contrary to Agee's belief that there was a kind of man she was "best used to," she had probably experienced sex only a few times. But though shyness and religious constraints prohibited the thoughts from going beyond fantasy, she flirted back with gusto and loved every minute of it. And Agee, who had all the women, monied and refined, whom he wanted in New York, could not have this peasant girl who enticed and teased him.

Like a scorned lover, Agee found his competition in the form of her husband not worthy of the pure heart he'd won. "He is jealous and mean to her and suspicious of her," he wrote. "He has given her no pretty dresses nor the money to buy cloth to make them. Every minute he is in the house he keeps his eye right on her as if she was up to something, and when he goes out, which is as seldom as he can, he locks her in. . . ." Whenever Emma left him in the early days, Agee pointed out, Lonnie would come down to Hobe's Hill, "begging, and crying" for her to come back, and the only reason she ever went back to him was that she hated the woman who had married her father.

Emma's final week on Hobe's Hill went too fast. Agee watched Emma begin "withdrawing into rooms with her sister and crying a good deal." She sank into a deepening depression two days before Lonnie was to come back with Mr. Jacobson and his truck loaded with their furniture. Annie Mae was "strong against her going, all that distance, to a man who leaves her behind and then just sends for her." She'd miss the company of Emma.

In the middle of all this emotion and sexuality, real or imagined, there was another secret interaction between the Gudgers, Emma, James Agee, and Walker Evans. One day, when the family was out working, Agee stayed behind. He wanted to learn more about them, so for several hours he rifled through all their drawers. He had a "cold beating" in his "solar plexus," tight with apprehension, and he listened for their early return, yet still he probed the bedroom and every nook, replacing all papers and things as he found them. When they did come home, he hurried to the porch and sat writing notes, as if nothing had occurred. "It is not going to be easy to look into their eyes," he wrote of the moment.

What Agee didn't know was that Emma, too, was curious.

The same week Agee did his snooping, Emma did hers. One day, when Agee was out driving with Evans and Maggie Louise, Emma decided she'd find out more about the tall stranger and his rude friend. She went into the front room, where George and Annie Mae had put up Agee and Evans. Their things were a mess and strewn in piles. Emma dove into them.

"Look—aren't these the biggest and floppiest pajamas you ever seen?" Emma said to Annie Mae, who stood outside the door, hands to her face in horror.

"Emma, you'd better come out of there!" Annie Mae warned her.

Emma laughed and ignored her sister's worries. She donned Agee's pajama bottoms and came prancing out. Annie Mae almost fainted. "What if they come back?" said Annie Mae. Emma went back in and got down to business—she wanted to see what Agee had been writing about them. She pulled out his notebooks, but found the writing so tight she couldn't read it. Frustrated, she carefully replaced everything so that he wouldn't find out.

There was also money lying around in plain sight.

"I'll bet they're trying to test us," said Emma. Each day the money was left out, and none was touched. There is no indication that Agee and Evans had indeed left money out as temptation; it is more likely that they had done so out of sloppiness. Nor is there any evidence that he ever suspected that Emma had gone through his things.

As much as the writer had been prepared to learn about the tenants, Emma, at least, was as curious to know more about him. The two cultures were locked in intrigue. Agee didn't want to look like a big-city Harvard intellectual, which he was. That would have turned them off. While Agee was in Alabama, his accent "veered towards country-southern," Evans later wrote, suggesting, "I may say he got away with this to the farm families and to himself." Agee did not do this with malicious intent—he truly liked these people who would become his story—but because he wanted them to like and trust him and not see him in the same, bad light he saw those who had sent him.

The families played along with this game, prepared for their own part to let him believe they were something they weren't. Agee was convinced, or convinced himself, that he was seeing them for what they really were, that they could not hide themselves from him, but at least in some respects they proved smarter than he admitted. There was a lot they didn't show and he never learned.

Each side thought it understood the other, but time proved that neither side was as right as it deemed itself. And so they spied on each other, put on false faces, the North meeting the South, each side unaware of the comic farce it was acting out with the other.

. *iii* .

Soon, the morning came for Emma to leave.

There was no conversation at breakfast that day. Everyone was depressed. Agee was out on the porch. Emma came up to him. She paused. It was hard for her to say what she wanted to tell him. She stumbled over her words. She said it was easy to be around him.

Emma said it was like being around her own people, that they didn't have to worry about what he thought of them, that they could act natural, that all of them cared for him a great deal, and she wished they never had to part.

Their eyes met for a time that went beyond comfort. Emma stood three feet from him and listened. "I went on to say," Agee writes, "that whatever might happen to her or that she might do in all her life I wished her the best luck anyone could think of, and not ever to forget it, that nobody has a right to be unhappy."

Half an hour later, Agee was driving Emma, Annie Mae, Bud Woods, Maggie Louise, and some of the other children down the dirt road off Hobe's Hill, to Gallatin's.

It had been decided that Emma would meet Lonnie at the house of Gallatin, her oldest brother, aged thirty-six, about seven miles away in Cookstown.

Gallatin had met Agee once before. He had little use for the writer.

Agee told everyone he and Evans had chanced upon the Gudger, Ricketts, and Woods families by accident when the three men had gone together to seek relief help in Centerboro. But in fact Gallatin had pointed Agee in their direction some days before that first meeting. Agee was not interested in Gallatin. "You're above average," Gallatin recalls Agee saying.

"They didn't want anything to do with me," says Gallatin. "I told him where daddy and his family lived. I told them they would be average. Daddy was poor enough for them. I was making a living. They didn't want to talk to anybody who was making a living."

And so now Agee was unexpectedly meeting this brother once again, forced to be an uninvited guest on his property. The brother served Agee weak lemonade without any ice and never took his eye off him.

Finally, Emma was helped into the truck and Lonnie drove off with her. The truck, laden with household goods and an iron bed, crawled down the dirt road and vanished.

"I dont believe I went," Emma writes. "I thought I would never see sister again."

Agee believed that, too. He felt Emma was doomed to "years on years of her cold, hopeless nights" with Lonnie.

Bud Woods went home to his shack on Hobe's Hill. Agee left to go back to New York.

. iv .

After Emma left, things turned even worse for Woods. He did not end the 1936 crop year in the black, as he'd been able to do in the early years of the Depression. He was sick, and the doctor told him not to do the hard work, but Woods persisted. He carried over a big debt into the 1937 season, which also ended in disaster.

By that winter, just six months or so after Agee left, the Woods family was starving. Margraves, the landlord, had decided he was not going to furnish any more credit.

Cut off by the landlord, the Woodses could not get government relief help. In the eyes of state and federal law, Woods was technically employed and therefore ineligible.

Those were the rules. There had been a move to help tenant farmers, but after the 1936 election, southern Democrats—who until then had supported the New Deal and whose support continued to be important in Congress, especially in the Senate, where southerners held many important committee chairmanships—turned President Roosevelt down when he tried to institute reforms to extend relief to tenant farmers. Southern politicians, acting at the behest of cotton landlords, blocked efforts to add tenants to the welfare or unemployment rolls.

In 1935, the authors of *The Collapse of Cotton Tenancy* said the landlords had important reasons for their opposition:

> The share tenant's situation is the impossible one of being forced by the inadequacies of the present system, on the one hand, to seek relief as the only means of keeping alive; and, on the other hand, of having this relief opposed by the landlord because it may spoil him as a tenant, if and when he can be used again. There are other fears back of the landlord's attitude: the fear that the tenant will be removed from the influence of the landowner and learn that he is not entirely dependent on him; and the fear that the relief will raise the standard of living to the extent that bargaining on the old basis will be difficult.

An old joke told among tenants illustrates just how dependent on the landlord the tenant was. A tenant takes five bales of cotton to the gin. The landlord comes over and weighs it. He carefully looks it over this way and that. After some serious head scratching—figuring what the tenant owes him for rent, fertilizer, and so on, and what price the cotton would bring—he tells the tenant they break exactly even for the year. The tenant's eyes widen happily at that news. He still has one more bale at home that he hadn't been able to fit on his wagon, he tells the landlord. "Shucks," says the landlord. "Now I'll have to figure it all over again so we can come out even."

With welfare, a tenant could have told his landlord he wouldn't work for a year to end up in debt or just to break even. Some landowners privately admitted that if a decent and fair wage were paid for all labor, cotton could not be economically grown in the South.

Because of such attitudes, and the politics they controlled, the Woodses had no one to turn to. One might wonder about his family, but the code among tenant farmers, it seems, as among all those who live on the edge of survival, was that each man had to look after his own immediate family first, and in hard times there was seldom anything left after that for other kin.

Joe Bridges, Sr., heard about the Woodses' plight. It bothered him, and unlike Bud's kin, he wasn't right on the edge. Bridges owned six hundred acres at the bottom of Hobe's Hill and had six families sharecropping for him. He didn't need any more croppers, especially in a depressed cotton market, but he felt compelled to help the Woods family.

Bridges and a hand drove a wagon up the muddy road. It was a rainy December afternoon, and the family had gone without food for three days. Ellen was barely three years old, and Ivy was holding Marion, their baby boy less than one year old. Bridges and the hand found the family wasted and quiet. There wasn't much to load. They owned a rusted-out wood-burning stove that had to be carefully lifted for fear of its falling apart. A homemade table, nail kegs used as chairs, an iron bed, a mirror, a Civil War sword that belonged to some relative of Mrs. Woods. Besides a few knives and forks, that's all they had. It all fit in one load down the hill.

Bridges put them up in an extra house where the Hobe's Hill road met the gravel highway. In addition, Bridges may have been a little smarter about how to get around the system. That summer, rather than give Woods his own acres to work, Bridges gave him day labor hoeing cotton. Now, technically no longer a self-employed contractor, Woods could get a little relief help. At the arrival of 1940, the Woodses were surviving mostly on charity.

Emma was having her own problems over on the bull farm in Mississippi.

BRIDGES

.*i*.

Soon after the Woods family moved to the Bridgeses' land at the bottom of Hobe's Hill, Mr. Bridges had a talk with thirteen-year-old Joe, Jr., about their new neighbors. "Those are a different kind of people," Mr. Bridges warned his son. The son was perplexed. They didn't seem that much different from himself and his own parents.

James Agee noticed this family each time he turned to go up the road to the top of Hobe's Hill. In some unpublished notes for a draft of *Let Us Now Praise Famous Men* that were published in a special commemorative issue of the *Harvard Advocate* dedicated to James Agee, he wrote,

> Just at this first brow or brim of hill, and fully visible to the highway, is a small and most ... pleasing yellow painted house

whose inhabitants fully own it and this land they farm. Excepting their curious and somewhat uneasy watchfulness of us, and the fact of their existence in this place, they have nothing to do with what I write of.

It's unknown whether Agee ever stopped to talk with the Bridgeses. If he did, he would have found a landlord quite different from Margraves.

Though the Bridgeses were landlords, they didn't have the large holdings of other landowners, such as the Margraves brothers, who had title to twenty-six hundred acres in the county, including most of Hobe's Hill. T. Hudson Margraves wore a tie and suit coat. Mr. Bridges, then forty-six, wore overalls. Bridges had no ambition to run a store and manage his holdings from town, as Margraves did, or even to buy more land. He worked hard, just as the tenants did, and didn't seem unhappy with his lot. The entire family accepted that the economics of the Depression forced them to live much as did the six sharecropper families working for them.

Bridges preferred it that way. He didn't like the way Margraves had accumulated his money. Margraves's specialty was making crop-planting loans to landowning blacks; the loans were secured by the farmer's land. If there was a crop failure, he'd immediately foreclose on the family, not granting any extension to the credit, and take title to their land. That's how he had built his empire.

Well as it had worked for Margraves, it just wasn't Bridges's way. "Son," he said to Joe, Jr., more than once, "if you can't help somebody, for God's sake, don't hurt them."

The six families on Bridges's land worked one hundred acres. Bridges and his children worked eighteen. Unless there was a drought or a huge price drop, people who sharecropped for Bridges made money; at the very least, they came out clean at the end of the year. There was an overproduction of cotton during the Depression, so the government instituted the "set-aside" program to reduce the acreage planted in cotton. The amount of the payment not to plant each parcel was based on the value of the crop that land had yielded previously. Many landlords, when land they had title to came up for a set-aside allotment, kicked the tenant off the land and kept the federal money for themselves. The drafters of the law had put in provisions designed to prevent just this substitution of the land-owner for the farmer as the beneficiary of the program, but the pro-visions were rarely enforced. Bridges, on the other hand, turned the money over to the tenant whose earlier harvest had established the amount of the payment. "They made the allotment; I didn't," Bridges said.

Several black families bought their own land after accumulating earnings working Bridges's land. They'd come back and ask permission to hunt. Bridges let them. Some of the white townsmen frowned on all this; they felt Bridges was too permissive with local blacks and spoiled them, causing them to expect too much from their white neighbors.

"The blackest nigger can come piss on your grave, and you can't do anything about it," Bridges said, in explaining his philosophy of neighborliness to one townsman. "Or they can come plant flowers. You can't take nothing with you."

And so they lived a frugal life. Mrs. Bridges carefully saved flour sacks after they were empty, sewing them together to make shirts and underwear for her children. They had oil lamps for light and an outhouse in the back. The couple had nine children, five boys, four girls. Joe, Jr., was right in the middle—he was born June 8, 1924—with four siblings on either side.

It had not seemed at first that Bridges and his wife would find themselves landlords in the tenant-farming system of the South. They met while attending college in Texas, and both became teachers; for a time, in fact, Joe, Sr., was a high school principal. He took full control of the farm in 1937, when his father, then ninety-one, died.

The land meant a lot to the Bridges family. The farm comprised six hundred acres, the same number the family had started off with in the early 1800s. Mrs. Bridges's grandfather was born on a wagon train that came down out of Kentucky, their home in the early 1800s. Four other families journeyed with them to this wilderness in order to homestead and plant cotton. Mrs. Bridges's forebears were not as self-conscious about the mistreatment of blacks as the son-in-law who would later marry into the family; they owned about half a dozen slaves.

Mrs. Bridges's family was lured by the huge new worldwide demand for cotton after the development of the gin and wanted to profit from it. The grant deeding the land to the family was signed by John Quincy Adams when he was secretary of state sometime between 1817 and 1825.

. *ii* .

Those were Indian times and Indian lands.

The main route of travel out of Kentucky for settlers like the Bridgeses' ancestors was the Natchez Trace, purchased by the federal government in 1801 from the Chickasaw and the Choctaw tribes. In 1819, Alabama was granted statehood. By 1820, many whites were entering the state, according to *Alabama: A Guide to the Deep South,* compiled by the workers of the Writers' Program of the Work Projects Administration. It said,

> In the summer months the roads were thronged with settlers, ox-drawn wagons, and herds of livestock. A pioneer newspaper records a fairly typical case of "a man, his wife, his son and his wife, with a cart but no horse. The man had a belt across his shoulders and drew the cart. The old woman was walking, carrying a rifle and driving a cow." . . . Other settlers . . . "rolled them [the wagons] hundreds of miles to the new homestead."

When the whites first arrived in Alabama, they adopted the Indian name for the land, which meant "Here we rest." It was thick with forests, except for the central prairies where the Bridgeses' forefathers were headed. Herds of buffalo and elk grazed on these grasslands, and there were bear and deer.

The first inhabitants of the area arrived two thousand years before the whites. They were crude, Stone Age people and were later replaced on the land by the Mound Builders, pre-Columbian Indians who eventually constructed elaborate cities and earthen monuments as part of a complex society.

By the early sixteenth century, the first white men had come. In 1540, the Spanish explorer Hernando de Soto set the tone for later relations when he greeted the Choctaw Indians with a hail of bullets. Some reports say eleven thousand Indians were slain in his march through Alabama. Another hundred years passed before other white men followed. They were the French from the South and the English from the North.

The French won over the Choctaw, whereas the English gained the allegiance of the Chickasaw. A great fur war was waged in the early 1700s. The English won, and Englishmen began filtering into Alabama, buying land from Indians and marrying into the culture. In 1802, the first cotton gin was constructed in Alabama. In 1805, with the new interest in cotton, the Chickasaw and Choctaw ceded certain lands in Alabama to the whites, but much of Alabama still belonged to Indians of the Creek Federation. In 1813, the Creek War erupted, and Andrew Jackson was sent in to lead the whites to victory at the Battle of Horseshoe Bend. Soon afterward, the influx of whites began.

White settlers hungry for cotton land ignored treaty boundaries. No Indians were exempt, including the Cherokee, who had adopted white ways to such an extent that they owned black slaves. The states' response to the conflict was to start moving the Indians off the land. For instance, in violation of treaties they had entered into with the federal government, the Cherokees were ordered to vacate their land. The Indians took their case all the way to the United States Supreme Court, where their position was upheld, but Andrew Jackson, who by the 1830s was president, refused to enforce the Court's decision, which required protecting the Indians from state and local authorities. The Great Removal began in the summer of 1838. By the end of this mass deportation, most Alabamian Indians had been resettled in the dry plains of Oklahoma. The South was safe for cotton.

. *iii* .

By the middle of the nineteenth century, Alabama was considered the center of the Cotton Belt. Cotton extended itself farther west with each passing decade, until it filled in the entire swath of American real estate in which it could grow, stretching about sixteen hundred miles from the eastern seaboard into Texas, jumping far west into California soon after.

A need to satisfy a growing demand for cotton was not the only reason for this rapid push west. Cotton is not kind to the land that grows it. The crop requires heavy loads of nitrogen, consumes soil nutrients, and quickly leaves marginal land barren. As the soil was burned out and demand continued to increase, it was easier for the crop to move west to new land than for growers to try to reinvigorate the old land.

In 1880, one scientist estimated that an area the size of Belgium had been ruined by this de facto slash-and-burn mentality in the South. In 1920, a majority of cotton production had for the first time shifted west of the Mississippi River.

These new cotton lands were tough competition for Alabama—western farmers on huge open tracts had begun to use tractors to plant and Mexican migrants to pick, and so could produce cheaper cotton.

As world markets drove cotton prices up and down, Alabama remained at the mercy of these markets and of the traders who manipulated them. The region had nothing to replace cotton, and the huge built-in infrastructure created great pressure to continue with the crop—no one seemed to want to challenge it by introducing new crops for farmers and new ways to use the land and people of Alabama. Industry didn't want to move into the area, for fear that the volatility of cotton prices would create an unreliable labor pool, one that would be tempted to move to the land when cotton prices were high, and back toward factory jobs when they fell. Cotton had enjoyed its best time in recent memory during the First World War, when prices had jumped dramatically. But then the Depression lowered prices. Still, clinging to their old beliefs, Alabama farmers were certain that cotton prices would rise again and everything would work out.

In spite of the general westward movement of cotton, and no matter what happened to prices, the Bridgeses weren't about to leave Alabama. In 1936, they had about as much land as they had started with more than a century before—roughly one section. The land that had been in the family so long was expected to be turned over to young Joe and perhaps some of the other children to continue the tradition of raising cotton.

That the Bridgeses had good land helped them stay put. The soil in the immediate vicinity was considered some of the richest in the South outside of the Mississippi Delta. As a consequence, the region was heavily peopled, by rural standards. All the remote forest springs had paths leading to them where children walked to gather water after the field work was done. The forests near the outback houses were scoured clean of deadwood that could be burned in stoves. The county seat of Centerboro, with a population of fifteen hundred, was prosperous by country standards in the 1930s—its business block was lit by electric lamps, and the street was paved. It had a theater, a motel, and several blocks of two-story brick buildings full of shops filled with goods. The seat of the adjoining county, Waynesville, was similar. These were tight, gossip-ridden towns with established orders, leaders exalted by the local press, all others ignored as if they didn't exist, and eyes that scornfully watched the rare strangers who came through. Saturday was the big day, when all the wagons would range in from the surrounding country, as if they had materialized magically on the suddenly people-swollen main street.

When the people left town, they seemed to vanish, swallowed by a land that was vast and terrifyingly silent. It was hard to drive through the countryside and imagine where all those Saturday town-goers spent the rest of the week.

This corner of Alabama, which seemed eternal to young Joe Bridges, was not an endless plain of unbroken fields, as those who have never seen these cotton lands might imagine them to be. Mysterious ravines thick with trees split off open tracts planted in cotton and corn, and eroded hillsides of poor soil worn out from slave times had already been turned over to forests of young pines planted by huge lumber conglomerates that had bought up the ruined land at low prices. These new stands of pines and deciduous brush had grown into tangles so thick that green snakes could slither along through the branches for hundreds of yards, three feet off the ground. The wooded tracts and gullied, snake-infested wasteland broke the earth into segments and subworlds that isolated families one from another. There were no paved roads in the county, outside of the Centerboro main street. The best artery was the highway from Cookstown to Centerboro—the road the Bridgeses lived on—for its twenty miles was graveled and usually passable. The side roads were a web of red dirt that fingered without rhyme between large empty spaces on the map. A lot of real estate separated families from one another and from distant big cities. Twenty miles in those days was not like twenty miles today. A man on a mule or foot was locked in a small world that did not extend much beyond the patch of cotton he raised, especially during the rainy months when the lanes were rendered ribbons of mud. In the best of weather, it was an all-day trip to get into town and back. The pine-board shacks lining the dirt roads seemed inconsequential in the face of this rolling dark land, especially after the dinner hour, when the oil lamps burned in bedroom chambers filled with bodies shrunk against the blackness.

People were drawn to each other and to family. The tenants on places such as the Bridges farm spent a lot of time around the landowners. Even the black families were drawn close to their white landlords. Joe did not like young Pearl, who lived right across the road from the Bridgeses. She could play rough, Joe found, and by the end of the 1930s she stood as tall as a young woman.

GAINES

Far to the south of Hobe's Hill, in a region even more isolated, another group of people were struggling with cotton.

Parson's Cove was different from the counties a hundred miles north. The area was flatter and hotter. It was also near the river, and Spanish moss hung from the trees. Of course, there was cotton, lots of it, but it provided work almost exclusively for blacks. In many other areas of Alabama during the Depression, whites who had lost jobs in the cities of the South were allowed by landowners to replace blacks as tenant farmers. With no one further down the ladder to replace, blacks were left in desperation. But Parson's Cove was a world apart. It never had many whites to begin with, so blacks weren't displaced.

They certainly weren't treated any better than white tenant farmers. In fact, by every measure, blacks fared worse than their white counterparts. Their houses were more run-down and their schools inferior to the whites' already substandard schools (twice as many white tenants as black tenants could read and write); half the white tenants owned cars, whereas virtually no blacks did; blacks were paid far less, and whatever they earned was seldom paid in cash. One 1930s survey of blacks in the Parson's Cove region showed that about 64 percent "broke even," 26 percent owed money at the end of the year, and about 10 percent made some profit. For those who came out ahead, that meant an annual net income of less than ninety dollars per household.

Their plight was mostly ignored. When the *Fortune* magazine editors sent James Agee to do his story on tenantry, they made clear that they didn't want it to include blacks; blacks had always been poor and were expected always to be poor, so their plight was not considered newsworthy. Their poverty was seen as a dog-bites-man story. Besides, poverty is unpleasant. Indeed, few editors wanted to publish stories about white sharecroppers.

That this was so was borne out when Agee returned to *Fortune* in September 1936. While he was gone, publisher Henry Luce ousted Ralph Ingersoll, Agee's liberal editor, and *Fortune* took on a decidedly more conservative tone. Nevertheless, Agee went ahead and wrote his article on the abject poverty of white tenant farmers. It was killed by his new bosses. The magazine wanted more "up-scale" and "upbeat" stories.

It's not hard to imagine, then, that black croppers were not considered proper subjects of study for the northern press. Black family farms in the cotton South, when they were written about at all, were described with more contempt than compassion; a story in *Business Week* magazine referred to them as "nigger and mule" farms.

Parson's Cove was full of such unnoticed farms. The culture of the area harked back to slave times. Residents like Sherman Parson had lived there all their lives, as did their ancestors who were brought over as slaves. Sherman carried the name of the white family that had owned his grandfather, the same family after whom the Cove was named.

Parson's Cove was under little pressure to change. The Cove was surrounded on three sides by water, located within a wide, arcing bend of a river. A visitor had a difficult time getting there, having to negotiate a series of poorly maintained dirt roads, past a store in the town of Magnolia, which was constructed from salvage taken from a ship that had sunk in the river, through a swamp, up a hill, past the community spring bubbling out of mud on the east side of the road and a mile beyond, past the shack of Frank Gaines, a black man who was working the surrounding land for C. B. Gumbay, a white landowner. A little farther, the road dead-ended at the river. That's all there was to the Cove. So outsiders seldom came to pass through Gumbay's land, a wide-open place where cotton was planted everywhere.

In spite of his being a landlord and having a handful of blacks growing cotton on shares, Gumbay found the year 1936 very difficult. People called Gumbay a "little country fella." He had married some years earlier and started out in the relationship with fifty dollars and a desire to work and succeed. He ran a small country store in the town of Destiny, which was no more than a shack with a few tin goods and other staples, just like hundreds of others that dotted rural Alabama counties. It was over the hill from Parson's Cove and didn't provide a living for the Gumbays, just a part of a living. To fill out his income, he delivered the mail and ran a trap line in the winter. His wife minded the store in his absence.

One day in 1935, while out on his mail route, he met a man with whom he'd earlier become friends. The friend told Gumbay about a bankruptcy auction on eleven hundred acres over the hill in Parson's Cove. Gumbay's friend was acquainted with the man who was in bankruptcy and knew that he wanted an honest bidder like Gumbay present, for he feared the local bigwigs would conspire to hold down the bidding and get the land for a song.

Gumbay agreed. He went home and talked the matter over with his wife. The more he thought about it, however, the more he worried, afraid that if he were the successful bidder, he'd be incurring a large debt. He'd never been in debt before. After a sleepless night, he decided he'd better not bid. On Friday morning, Gumbay went to tell his friend that he was withdrawing his promise. The friend was outraged and said he couldn't back out. He was needed. The friend begged. So Gumbay went to the auction, not at all sure he wanted the land he'd be bidding on.

The bidders already gathered didn't expect an outsider.

"You shut up, and I'll pay you five hundred dollars," the man next to Gumbay whispered.

Such attempts to get rid of Gumbay apparently backfired. He kept on bidding. It became very hot in the room. In the end, Gumbay walked away with title to the land for seven thousand dollars.

The year following the purchase was one of hard work and some good fortune. Gumbay lumbered the land, and timber prices were such that he was able to earn back most of his investment.

He inherited the future of Parson's Cove, of Frank and Urline Gaines, of Sherman Parson, and of dozens of others. Some of the land he purchased was already planted in cotton, being worked by some of these families, and Gumbay hired more to farm the newly cleared land, so he soon had three hundred acres in cotton production.

By the late 1930s, tractors were commonly in use on most farms outside the South, but Gumbay would not embrace even that technology. He laughed at the prospect of the new cotton picker. On his land, they raised cotton the old way, with mules and backs.

Frank Gaines had a strong back. He was six foot two, a strong young man of about twenty with a triangular head and strained eyes. He was a powerful sight to watch as he walked behind a mule. It seemed he could pull and manage the stubborn creatures as though they were dogs on leashes.

In spite of his physical power, Gaines was a man quiet in his ways, full of proper manners, especially around Gumbay and other whites. He didn't look them in the eye when he talked with them. That was how blacks got along, especially blacks whose physical size might be threatening to whites. You never said anything but "Yes sir" to the man, and Gaines lived by that well-known rule. Because he was compliant and worked hard, Gaines rose in the respect of Gumbay, who sank all his profits back into buying more land.

Of course, no matter how much Gaines's desire to work and succeed might have matched Gumbay's, he could not have done what Gumbay had done for himself. Had he tried to join the land auction, no one would have offered to buy him off with five hundred dollars. He would have been given another message—that he was out of the bidding.

The Gaines family couldn't have subsisted if it hadn't been for their garden of corn, okra, peas, and sugarcane, which they raised next to their house, built in the 1880s. In 1936, he and Urline began their own family, having the first of their ten children.

1 9 4 0 – 1 9 6 0

GUDGER

It had just rained, a terrible downpour, and the fields were deep with mud. At the woods along the edge, shadows had grown black, but the eighty acres of open field still held the disintegrating light of day. The cotton was knee high to an adult, engulfing the waists of two small children. The children, Debbie and her brother, Sonny, ran down one of the long rows, their young blond heads bobbing along above the cotton. Even in her haste, Debbie noticed how pretty and straight the cotton was. Mud clung to their heels. Sonny sank to his knees from the weight of it all. Debbie pulled him up. At a low spot at the end of the field, a broad puddle separated them from the trees on the other side. They had come far enough that they were just out of sight of their house.

"If we can get across, we'll be free," Debbie told her brother.

Being six—a year older than Sonny—made her the leader in their running away from home.

And so they started wading to freedom.

They didn't know where they were going. They just wanted to get away. They were headed into the unpeopled lands of deep gullies and dark forests.

Debbie could look on the young cotton and find it so handsome. There were other memories. She recalled her mother, Maggie Louise, all torn up over things she couldn't understand, at the time when the cotton was all white and as tall as Debbie's head. They'd all be out there, in that sun, and they'd never stop picking; her mother always stooped, with that vacant face rising over the cotton, those gray, lined eyes, looking, looking—at her, at Parvin, at Sonny, at Mary Ann. These were the eyes that had startled and fascinated James Agee. They had been changed little by twenty more years of planting, chopping, and picking cotton. Those eyes would stalk Debbie the rest of her life, in the night, in that fraction before sleep, the corner of time when it becomes impossible to buttress yourself against the dreams.

This place was so silent. So big. So dark. After the work was done, Debbie and her family would sit on one of their two unlit porches, the damp breath of the night encasing their bodies—dead, thick air tasting of the sweet rot of all things no longer living, the sweat of all things doomed. It caught in their throats, like a sentence never meant to be completed. Debbie was taught to be afraid of the blackness, forbidden to be outside and off the porch after the sun was gone. She would crawl into bed and hear nothing but the whisper of her parents, fading to the click of night bugs and sometimes that distant train working its way up the valley. It was almost possible to hear the cotton growing. Many nights, it was what you saw in those last half moments between the time your eyes closed and when sleep engulfed you. From planting time to picking, it was the only thing you noticed changing. Cell by cell, it climbed, a fraction of an inch each day, until it topped out in that August sun.

Then they'd go out amid the whiteness and "do their thing."

"Do your thing" is what they called it, long before the phrase became part of the slang of the 1960s. Debbie was expected to hoe in the summer and to pick in the fall. She and her siblings would be out there when her mother and father sprayed all those smelly chemicals, and sometimes they'd look up as airplanes swooped down and applied more, enveloping them in misty clouds. Debbie despised the big green worms that crawled over the cotton, which the chemicals were meant to kill but never quite did. She was told to pick what she could. She did, but hated it. Sometimes, she'd pretend to be sick and then sit on the back of the nine-foot cotton sack that trailed behind her mother, riding down the row as Maggie Louise picked along. Parvin was very small, but she picked, too. Parvin would filch bolls from Debbie's sack when she wasn't looking, to fill her own, and it caused more than a few sisterly squabbles.

All the cotton they picked was hauled up to the barn near the big house. As the pile gained in size day by day, Debbie couldn't wait to go there after supper and jump into it from a rafter, losing herself in the softness. She liked the barn. Inside was an old-time junker car that the children could sit in and pretend to drive.

At a very young age, Debbie Franks started to understand that her family was peculiar. She'd been to Cherokee City and saw how other people lived. Her father occasionally took them to see big-screen movies. The children up in town weren't like her. They rode around in cars. They dressed differently and acted differently. After all, it was 1956, modern times.

Down in Madrid, Debbie knew it was old times. They rode around the farm on a mule-drawn wagon. They finally got a television in their shack, and it further pointed up the difference between what they had and what the outside world offered. Even with electricity in the house, they still used oil lamps on occasion. Theirs was a four-room house, built at the edge of a hill and supported by pillars of rocks. Through the cracks in the floor, they could see chickens walking under the house. It was bitter cold in the winter. Their bathroom was an outhouse, and toilet paper was a Sears, Roebuck & Company catalog placed on the ledge near the door.

The children seldom left the immediate area of the farm; only once or so each month they borrowed Mrs. Burgandy's car to go into Cookstown, a dozen miles distant, though they went to a nearby church twice a week, on Wednesday and Sunday.

Debbie and Sonny managed to get across to the other side of their freedom puddle. They looked back and saw the yellow head of their father coming across the cotton. He'd followed their tracks. He shouted in a voice that might have sounded odd to many people but was just their father's familiar voice to them. Floyd was deaf, from a childhood accident in which a swing he'd jumped from struck his head, and his voice was slightly off kilter, not like that of men who hear. He could read lips well, and Debbie and the other kids got used to turning and facing him when they spoke to him. At night, when he lay in bed with Maggie Louise, she talked to him by speaking soundlessly with her mouth against his bare arm—and by the movement of her lips he understood what she was saying. He'd recently traveled a great distance to see a preacher who worked out of a tent. The tent preacher held out the promise of being able to restore Floyd's hearing. But Floyd came back from Oral Roberts just as deaf as when he'd left.

Tonight, his special voice promised the children ice cream if they came back across the puddle. He wasn't about to go into that mud after them if he could tempt them to come out of it. Debbie looked at Sonny—ice cream was a powerful lure—and they waded back across. They got to have ice cream only once a month, when they churned it themselves, so they hurried. Once they were on the other side, Floyd grabbed them and took them home, to a good spanking.

But after that was done, the children got their ice cream. Floyd never broke his word.

He never asked why Debbie had run away with her little brother. If he had any notion why, he never let on.

. *ii* .

Maggie Louise's dream of going on in school, the dream she had shared with James Agee in 1936, survived for a while and then died its quiet death. Her farm chores just took her away from too much of each school year. In 1941, another option presented itself. His name was Abraham Jones, the boy her father never quite liked.

Jones had been eyeing Maggie Louise for a long time, and had intentions. George Gudger, her father, did not want his daughter marrying that boy. She was too young. Annie Mae, her mother, saw the inevitable. Whether she and George agreed to it or not, it was going to happen. Unknown to George, Annie Mae sewed Maggie Louise a yellow dress. It was not as fine as the dress in which she herself had been married, but it would have to do under the circumstances. Jones went to the Centerboro courthouse on December 20, 1941, and took out a license. He told the registrar he was twenty-one and his bride eighteen, thus adding three years to the age of

Maggie Louise. Her occupation was listed as "school girl." That was the last association she would have with schooling.

Jones came from a family of tenant farmers, and he'd left to go on his own, at what was called "public work." That meant he did not have his own acreage on which to plant, grow, and harvest, but was chopping, hoeing, or picking cotton for hire at fifty cents a day. It was a hard way to earn a living. One Saturday, Maggie Louise sneaked away, and they were married by a minister.

George was furious and threatened to kill Jones. The newly wed couple fled to a farm owned by James Black, east of Cookstown. The 1942 season was the first time Jones sharecropped on his own. He and Maggie Louise were halvers. They had twenty-one acres, a mule provided by Black, and a lot of love. They made four bales of cotton and picked every bit of it themselves.

World events caught up with them. Late in 1942, Jones received his draft notice. He was off to boot camp in Virginia, then to service in North Africa. He fought his way across France with the Seventy-eighth Division of the U.S. Army. At first, the letters between him and his wife were frequent and full of passion.

But the letters from home started coming less often. In 1945, right after the end of the war, but before the army brought Jones home, he got a letter that looked different from the others. He knew it was bad news. He could not bear to open it, so he went to his commanding officer and begged him to read it. The officer obliged. Maggie Louise wanted a divorce.

"We lived together until our final seperation in Dec. 1942," Maggie Louise's signed complaint read.

> Several times prior to the date of final seperation I was forced to leave my husband and return to the home of my parents because of my husbands cruel treatment to me. In Dec. 1942 my husband without any provacation on my part struct me with a board on my body particularly on my thigh and leg leaving bad bruises and contusions and lacerations. . . . Since it was reasonable to anticipate further violence on the part of my husband I was forced to leave him and since such seperation we have not lived together.

Even though it appears the document was prepared by an attorney, it contained misspellings. Her father, George, signed an affidavit stating that he saw the bruise and that in fact Jones was cruel.

The court papers left unsaid that Maggie Louise was pregnant by another man. Jones, through his own lawyer, denied he hit her. The divorce was effective in Cherokee City on October 30, 1945. She had been married in one county seat, divorced in another. On November 20, 1945, in a third adjoining county seat, she wed Floyd Franks. Five months later, Maggie Louise gave birth to Mary Ann.

Franks, because he was deaf, had not been drafted and had remained sharecropping in Alabama when most of the young men of that time went off to war. Maggie Louise had struck up a friendship with him, and one thing had led to another. She was nineteen and he twenty-eight when they married. Floyd and Maggie Louise lived with George and Annie Mae for a while, before moving to the Burgandy land.

Jones was wild with jealousy. After the war, he rushed back to Alabama. He came around with a gun several times, but soon realized it was over. He left the county and moved south, where he took a job in a yarn mill and later became a truck driver. Raised to pick cotton, he sharecropped only one season, that summer with Maggie Louise.

. *iii* .

By the 1950s, Maggie Louise, her husband, Floyd, and their four children were on the Burgandy farm, one of the few families left in this corner of the cotton lands. They were the only white family on the tiny branch road about four miles south of Hobe's Hill. Many had already moved out. Not they. They ran this farm for Mrs. Burgandy, a silver-haired woman who seemed very old to young Debbie. Mrs. Burgandy lived in the big white house a quarter mile up from their shack. It was not one of those antebellum homes, with white columns and such, for the Burgandys were not of that high a class, but it was large enough all the same, with five bedrooms and two and a half baths. You couldn't have called the Burgandys truly wealthy. The family, by modern standards, would have been considered barely middle-class. But such things are always relative. Mrs. Burgandy never used a Sears catalog for anything other than mail-order shopping. So Mrs. Burgandy seemed absolutely rich to Debbie.

Maggie Louise and Floyd's four-room shack, with one fireplace and set back a quarter mile in the country, was inferior to the tall, white-sided home of Mrs. Burgandy, but a good deal better than the tiny shacks near them, the quarters for some of the black hands who'd been placed in Floyd's charge.

The Burgandy land had once had as many as ten tenant families farming its acreage. That was before and during the Depression. Mr. Burgandy had inherited this land and, in 1922, married a teacher from Mobile. They built the big white house that year. In 1923, they had their only child, Elizabeth. Elizabeth did try once to pick cotton one afternoon when she was young, to supplement her five-cent weekly allowance, and found she just couldn't do it. Her hands and back hurt so badly that she never tried again.

The Burgandys survived the Depression without losing any land. In 1937, their tenants harvested forty-nine bales—more than twenty-seven thousand pounds, at a market value of $2,354. Soon outside forces they didn't understand would begin to transform everything they knew.

The conclusion of World War II was the start of this new age. When the men first came home, they went back to what they'd known—the land. Many were afraid the prewar economic malaise would resume. But the city lured them with jobs—an outflow that grew as men took their families to the towns, looking for new job opportunities in the postwar consumer society.

Many were like Abraham Jones. They didn't want to cotton farm. Jones had drunk schnapps in Paris and seen the world, and a twenty-acre cotton patch seemed like another kind of death. War had taught him to take chances, that you weren't always safe holding to what you had. Of course, there were others, like Franks, who, because of handicaps or fear of the outside world, or because they knew no better, remained under the old ways.

At this time, the cotton-picking machine proved it could work and started coming into its own. By the early 1950s, it was still a relative novelty in the Old South, but in Texas and the Far West it was taking over. Mules could no longer keep up.

The Burgandy family responded in a manner typical of many cotton lords. They could not afford to buy a cotton-picking machine to combat western growers. They heard that some small farmers were doing that, then charging their neighbors a fee to harvest with it, in a sense creating cooperatives that spread out the investment. It sounded like a good way to stay in the cotton business. But they also heard that it didn't work on the small tracts that dominated in Alabama. By the time the machine worked its way around to farmers far down on the list, heavy winds or rain often came and ruined ripe cotton, or knocked it down a grade. The machine worked best on large, flat arid tracts, harvesting cotton belonging to just one person or a corporation.

The Burgandys, though they did not acquire the picking machine, felt that if they mechanized in part they might be able to compete. They bought a tractor, giving up on the mules. Rather than have half a dozen sharecropper families work the land, Floyd and Maggie Louise were kept on to run the place. In 1952, Mr. Burgandy died. His wife decided to continue.

Floyd became a tractor man. With the tractor, Floyd plowed 134 acres of corn and cotton, five times the amount of land a man could plow with a mule. He'd mount the tractor in the spring, sitting in the shade beneath a big red umbrella given to him by Maggie Louise. At noon, Maggie Louise would bring out his "dinner"— sweet tea in a jug and cornbread—and he'd stop raising dust to eat, then go back to plowing.

Of course, the problem was still raising and picking—although Floyd could plow fives times as much acreage, his family couldn't chop, hoe, and harvest that much cotton.

Because blacks were being forced out of tenantry, there was a pool of hungry people willing to work for any wages. The roads around the Burgandy farm were lined with old tenant houses recently abandoned. They looked ready for the people to return any day. The old store run by Mr. Burgandy, across the street from the big house, was closed just after the war, when it became clear not everyone was coming back to the farm and things would never return to what they'd been.

Mrs. Burgandy left the store just as her husband closed it, a museum to what was. At the age of sixty-six, Mrs. Burgandy was trying to hang on to what she'd known and understood her entire life. She ran things as her husband had, but had Tom Dixon, another landlord, to watch over Floyd and Maggie Louise while she was in Mobile visiting her daughter. Mr. Dixon often came around in his pickup truck to check on things. The big house was also kept the same. Mrs. Burgandy lived alone in it, and Debbie would sometimes peer in and see the piano, the hardwood furniture, the things they didn't have in their house. She seldom entered. Under the old rules Mrs. Burgandy lived by, tenant children were not allowed in the big house. Tenant children could not enter the apple orchard out back, either. Debbie thought that was silly. She'd sneak up through the field and climb the trees to snitch apples when they came ripe. When Maggie Louise caught her, she'd be furious—you didn't get anything off Mrs. Burgandy's land without her knowing—and would punish her. Mrs. Burgandy had many rules, and Maggie Louise forced her children to obey them.

Once a month, when they drove to town for shopping, Debbie watched Maggie Louise approach the big white house with her hands held together in front of her, asking to borrow Mrs. Burgandy's car, a late 1930s Plymouth.

Maggie Louise was terrified of driving. She gripped the wheel tightly for the entire dozen miles into town. Her driving ability was such that if Debbie sat in the backseat, she got sick from swaying, so she always climbed to the front. On the return trip, Maggie Louise would have to negotiate the climb up Wobbly Hill. She hated Wobbly Hill. It seemed so steep. Maggie Louise would gun the car to a full thirty miles an hour, but then lose her nerve with the speed she needed to climb the hill, and she'd stall from slowing. The kids didn't like that, because the car would always stop near the abandoned hotel at the top, a vine-covered house everyone said was haunted, and they'd urge her to restart the engine fast and get away.

Maggie Louise was thirty years old, and seemed much older— she weighed nearly two hundred pounds, filled out by the constant 3-M diet. She'd turned into exactly what she hoped to have escaped, changing in all ways except her eyes. When hoeing or picking cotton, she might have been able to see herself in the children and to imagine them standing as she had before Walker Evans's camera twenty years before, holding her picking sack, looking at him with the same gray, sad eyes that some of her children inherited.

James Agee had encouraged Maggie Louise in 1936, but he never knew what happened to his favorite little Alabama girl much after that. Agee came back to Alabama in 1937, with Alma, who would become his second wife. They'd gone to New Orleans and its jazz clubs and were on their way home to New York. He decided to stop in for one afternoon, to visit the Gudgers and the Rickettses. He told them Alma was his wife, knowing they wouldn't understand his traveling around with a girlfriend while he was still married to another woman, said biographer Laurence Bergreen. The Gudgers offered to put them up, but they declined to stay the night.

That was the last the Gudgers saw him. He did keep in touch

with the Gudger family for several years, writing letters and sending Christmas presents, but as the Second World War began, the letters slowed.

By the time the atomic bombs were dropped on Japan, he'd stopped writing to the family. His career had changed. He had switched to *Time* magazine, writing an eloquent piece on August 20, 1945, about how the globe would never again be the same after the bombing of Hiroshima. "With the controlled splitting of the atom, humanity, already profoundly perplexed and disunified, was brought inescapably into a new age in which all thoughts and things were split—and far from controlled," Agee wrote.

The words could have measured his own life. The man who had seemed so innocent to the people of Hobe's Hill was moving away from those basic values of the Gudgers that had attracted him and, according to Bergreen, toward a steadily more destructive existence. He was drinking more and engaging in bizarre sex, some of it involving him, his wife Alma, and Walker Evans, Bergreen said in his book. In an interview, Evans said he once saw Agee smash a chair over a woman's head because he believed she had faked an orgasm.

Some of his troubles seemed to date to his time on Hobe's Hill. After *Fortune* magazine killed his story, he started writing a book on the Alabama experience and did obtain a contract from a publisher for the work. He felt he could transform his observations into a literary turning point in his life, but encountered great difficulty writing. It consumed Agee. He finished the book in 1939, and the publisher rejected it. He then sold it to another house, which released it in 1941. At first it was called *Three Tenant Families,* but before publication he changed its title to *Let Us Now Praise Famous Men.*

It seemed the book was too late. It was beaten into print by *You Have Seen Their Faces,* a now relatively little-known book on cotton sharecroppers by the photographer Margaret Bourke-White and the writer Erskine Caldwell, famous for his novel *Tobacco Road.* Some critics said Caldwell's writing was strained and contained made-up quotes, that the photographs were almost purposefully brutal. In its behalf, others say it caused Congress to pass laws and awakened the nation to the plight of sharecroppers. It was well known and earned its authors a lot of money. The other bombshell came with John Steinbeck's *The Grapes of Wrath.* Though truth may be stranger than fiction, it is seldom as well crafted dramatically, and this novel soon epitomized for most Americans the Depression suffering of people of the land. Furthermore, the worst effects of the Depression had already ended by 1941, and the country was gearing up for its next national crisis, another world war. By the time Agee reported the story of the poverty of tenant farming in Alabama, poverty was old news and only war was hot.

Agee's book, written in a highly personal, opaque style, was published to mixed reviews. The *New York Times* called it "arrogant, mannered . . . gross," but others gave it raves. The *New Republic* praised its "superior, highly original, accurately poetic writing." However its artistic merits may have been debated, it was not a commercial success. It sold a little more than six hundred copies by the end of the year, going out of print in 1948. It passed quickly into a temporary obscurity.

The families went about their lives in Alabama, unaware of the book's existence. Agee never sent them even one copy of the work that contained countless raw observations of the personal secrets they had shared with him. It appeared for a long while that they might never know of it.

Agee spiraled out of control as the 1940s wore on. He gravitated toward Hollywood, writing screenplays—including the script for *The African Queen*, directed by John Huston and starring Humphrey Bogart and Katharine Hepburn. The lead character, Charley, was written as a boozing loner—mirroring the writer, said Bergreen. Agee's teeth began to rot—he had never had them treated—and he was on a third marriage, womanizing, neglecting his children, the first born in 1940, who were left behind in New York while he was in Hollywood. Increasingly, he lived the Hollywood life—drinking more, sleeping less, declining in health as he approached his fortieth birthday. He suffered his first heart attack before completing the *African Queen* script. The Alabama project still preyed on his mind, but he didn't talk about it much, his friends say. "It was like a dead child," said Mary Newman, a friend of Agee's third wife, Mia. Agee was desperate to complete a novel about his childhood and the accidental death of his father, fearing that his own death was nearing.

So Agee never learned what happened to Maggie Louise. He left her future frozen as it was in the pages of his book, bright, happy, full of promise.

It's clear that he never forgot the families and that he felt a huge sense of guilt over his role in studying them. Perhaps he was glad the book was a flop. He called it and himself a failure, devoured by those thoughts during drunken stupors, sometimes raging and carrying on wildly.

Maggie Louise also became a failure, at least according to the expectations of worldly success Agee's work created for her.

If success is measured solely in terms of dollars, or the kind of house one lives in, yes, it is true that Maggie Louise was a failure. But if Agee had returned to Alabama in 1946, or later, as the children grew, he might have envied her. She was in a love-filled marriage, raising her children and, unlike Agee, doing right by them. But that was not all. It seems Agee projected himself on the little girl he saw in 1936—both were bright, energetic, inquisitive. There was, however, a fundamental difference—namely, that Maggie Louise, at least at that point in her life, had the ability to be satisfied, which, while different from being happy, is essential in finding contentment. In this regard, there may be two kinds of people, or perhaps, more accurately, two extremes, and if so, Agee and Maggie Louise represented them.

Ten years after Agee left Maggie Louise, she and Floyd settled into a routine, simple country life—hard work, few luxuries. Their first child, Mary Ann, was born on May 5, 1946, when Maggie Louise was twenty.

Maggie Louise's first husband had moved away from their county and was having the first of his children. Abraham Jones realized he was blessed to be out of the fields. Floyd and Maggie Louise had no comprehension of the kind of world Jones was living in. But they were, by all accounts, happy.

Big times for the Franks family meant going fishing. They went with their poles to the river and sat on the bank, watching barges go past. They took Mary Ann, spending as much time with her as they could. They went fishing twice in June and twice in July of 1947, months when the cotton crop required less work. The last time they went fishing that summer was in August, on the eighteenth, just before the bolls came ripe. That day, they stopped by the home of Bud Woods, Maggie Louise's grandfather. Mary Ann was his first great-grandchild. On other Sundays, they remained closer to home, always going to Maggie Louise's parents, not far away.

At George and Annie Mae Gudger's home, the ritual was the same each Sunday. The men would take a stick and scratch a line at either end of the yard, in the dust, and then pitch coins. Whoever got a coin exactly on the line won all the money thrown. It was a game for men only. The women cooked, usually chicken, a once-a-week Sunday treat. About once a month, the children would get ice cream. Debbie and the other girls played at jumping rope.

George was always seeking ways to pull pranks. Debbie looked up at her grandfather one day, his teeth already vanishing, the ones remaining stained brown like wood, and he told her he had a treat for her, if she would only close her eyes and hold out her hand. She did. She felt something moist in her palm. When she looked she screamed. He'd placed a wad of his chewed tobacco in her hand.

Maggie Louise hugged Floyd a lot. Their home was one where love was shared and constantly expressed. She loved him in the way she could never love any other man. After the birth of Mary Ann, they waited four years for their next child, Debbie, but after her birth, Sonny and Parvin came in quick succession.

The children were wild in the well-mannered innocent way country children are, running barefoot and half-naked through the fields. Debbie and Sonny would go out to the fencerows, wading into the soft-green vines of sweet honeysuckle, plucking the delicate and diminutive horn-shaped flowers, bringing enough back for Maggie Louise to place in a vase that brightened the shack. She'd keep them until they were wilted and crisp. They became her favorite flower, even more cherished than her cultivated roses.

In the fall, when the honeysuckle was wilting from the frosts and all the cotton was gathered, Debbie started going to school. The schoolhouse was a white frame building in Madrid Junction, and it contained all the early grades, one to four, in a single room. There were thirty boys and only one other girl besides Debbie, and that girl was her aunt, Catherine Annette, the eighth and last child born alive to Annie Mae and George Gudger. One child was stillborn before 1936, another after.

Debbie had to walk about one mile to get to the first and the second grade, down the dirt road that ran due west to the main highway, which by 1956 had been paved from Cookstown to Centerboro. In warm weather, she went barefoot, but had a pair of boots for the many wet months. She was plagued by the same problems that had faced her mother twenty years before—it was difficult to wade through the mud on rainy days. And she had to remain out of school during the cotton harvest. She missed many classes. And the school was not much different from the one her mother had entered back in the Depression—it was understaffed, overcrowded, and used fifty-year-old textbooks. One teacher taught all four grades; even if the woman had been the state's best teacher and had the best materials, neither of which was true, it would have been an impossible job.

Debbie walked down the dirt road many times, across the bridge, going through forest, open clearings, past the "Negro" shacks up near the main highway. She was taught by her mother not to call them "nigger" shacks, a term almost universally used by local whites. She came back in the cold of winter afternoons, and the smell of the woods and fields after a fresh rain was something she thought she'd never forget, like the face of her mother looking at her over the ripe cotton.

. *iv* .

Although Debbie's education was lacking and their standard of living still far below that of city people, their lives were much better, in many ways, from what they had been when Agee had visited. Maggie Louise's parents, the Gudgers, had come a long way in a short period. The end of the Great Depression and the changing nature of tenant farming that came with that end put a little more money into their hands—not much, but enough to pull them up from the hardscrabble bottom. By the mid-1940s, they were actually getting part of the crop they worked to produce, farming for Mr. Dixon. The use of tractors, which allowed larger tracts to be farmed and made the farmer a more productive economic asset, contributed to this new situation.

After the 1930s, as the modern world started to force itself on the Alabama countryside, George and Annie Mae Gudger tried to adjust. George gave up on the mule-drawn wagon and bought a rusted "A-model." In the early 1950s, according to a picture taken by their son, Burt Westly, who'd just come home from the Korean War, when they drove to town they gussied up for the trip. In the photo they resemble a latter-day Bonnie and Clyde, he in a wrinkled topcoat, bell-bottom wool pants, fedora on his head, she in a blazer and store-bought striped skirt.

George never quite caught on to the machine. Invariably, when driving into town, they encountered chickens in the road. Instead of using the horn, George would yell, "Shoo! Shoo!"

When electricity finally came to their farm down by the river, about 1949, George was eager to put it to use and hastily hooked a socket to the ceiling. When darkness fell, the family assembled for the ceremony. George threw the switch. The bulb burned harshly.

"George, cut the light off," said Annie Mae. She was crying.

"Why are you crying?" asked George, bewildered.

"Because now you can see all the dirt," she said, pointing to the walls. The stains upon them had been nearly invisible in the dull glow of oil lamplight.

As soon as they could afford it, George had to have a refrigerator. He and Annie Mae went out and bought the biggest they could find, figuring it was best, but when they got it home, it was just too large—it wouldn't fit through the door of their tiny house. They had to return it and buy a smaller one.

Although they had some amenities, they still worked hard, nearly as hard as they had in 1936. George's skin had withered and cracked beneath the successive seasons of sun, and sometimes, when they went into town, Annie Mae stopped at the store after a hard day of work and bought a cold RC Cola. Often, she'd cry. One of her children asked her why. She told them because it tasted so good.

Annie Mae still washed all their clothes on a wooden rub board, and it was hard to get George's "overhauls" clean (that's how they said overalls), and George was particular about his "uniform"—it had to be starched below the knees, not up in the chest area, and if any starch got up there, he would have a fit. George was still strict with Annie Mae, and he ordered her to keep her hair long, even though she was nearly fifty years old.

Their children were all coming of age, and the shrinking of the cotton world forced some of the boys out of farming. Burt Westly came back from the service and began working in a meat-packing factory in Cherokee City. The wages weren't great, and it was bloody work, but it was far better than laboring under the Alabama sun for an uncertain income.

But some couldn't leave cotton. Gretchen, the girl Annie Mae had been pregnant with when Agee was in Alabama, was having a worse time than her sister Maggie Louise.

In 1956, Gretchen was nineteen and freshly married, to "Boy" Ricketts, a young man unrelated to the Ricketts family on Hobe's

Hill. Gretchen dropped out of school young and could not read, nor could Boy. Boy was afraid to go to the city and look for a job, because he couldn't fill out an application.

Gretchen and Boy started sharecropping, and after their first cotton crop, the landlord gave them a load of corn in payment. They traded that corn for an old car, their first.

They worked their own cotton as well as the fields of others. They got two bucks a day for hoeing, two and a half for picking a hundred pounds. On average, they made about fifteen dollars a week. They had two children and often ran low on money.

One day, Boy came in and sat before Gretchen. He started crying. Gretchen thought he was crying just like a baby. She asked what was wrong. He said they had no money. There was no food in the house. And no prospect in sight for getting either. It was the worst they'd seen. He looked at their young children. He couldn't stand to see them hungry.

Boy was a man who read his Bible, and his belief was strong. He didn't tell Gretchen where he was going when darkness came. He didn't like what he was about to do.

A little while later, Gretchen heard a strange noise outside. It sounded like the squawk of a chicken. She opened the door, and Boy was standing there with a big fat hen. He wouldn't say where it came from. They rushed into the bathroom and killed it, burying the feathers to destroy the evidence. They ate off that bird for one week.

It was very hard. A family couldn't make it any more by farming. But there was little choice for people who were illiterate and had never known anything but cotton, other than to continue trying to make a living at the only thing they knew.

The youngest boy of Annie Mae and George, Walter ("Sonny") Gudger, grew up watching the struggles of Maggie Louise, Gretchen, and his brothers. He knew he couldn't let cotton destroy him the way it was ruining others. (Sonny became a popular nickname in these families, and there soon were half a dozen spread through four generations.)

One day, Sonny went out by the levee and applied soda to the crop. He carried it in a big bucket, tripping and falling down over the clods of dirt, burned by the caustic dust, faint from the sun. When he came home, a heat rash was burning his legs. He was just miserable.

In 1954, Sonny was only in the seventh grade, but he made a decision about cotton. He crossed his arms and refused to do it any longer. He said to hell with picking, to hell with helping his father plow, to hell with hoeing under that sun. He told his father cotton was a dead end.

George became angry. He told his son he had to help work the farm. George had learned only to sign his name. Hard work, that's what got you ahead, George believed. Not education. He ordered Sonny not to start school on time that year, and instead to help with picking, as all seven other children had done or were doing. In George's house, as his sister-in-law Emma had learned so long before, you had to work hard.

"But I have to learn typing," Sonny told him. "If I start late, I'll have to wait until next year."

George scoffed. But Annie Mae intervened. Annie Mae had failed Maggie Louise. It had been impossible to help her little girl escape in 1936. It was the Depression, and she was a girl, and the odds were just too great. The other six children didn't care much about school, but Sonny was like Maggie Louise. If he wanted it for himself, she wanted it for him. She encouraged Sonny to study. It was the 1950s, and maybe he could make something of himself. She talked with George. She convinced him it was important. He gave in.

Sonny went into Cookstown and got a part-time job in the Yellow Front store, bagging groceries. That was the kind of work for a boy who dreamed of going to college. The owner was Mr. Hill. Sonny loved the job and was a good stock boy. He worked after school and on Saturdays.

Word of Sonny's refusal to work the cotton reached back to the Gudgers' landlord, Tom Dixon, a big man around town, as big as the Margraveses. No one set lightly to interfering with the large landlords. They ran Cookstown and this whole county. If you hired their labor away, it was as bad as coveting the landlord's wife, and indeed acting on such thoughts. These men felt that it disrupted the dynamic between landlord and tenant if the tenant was ever paid wages by another or in any other way removed from their control.

Dixon, outraged, went to Mr. Hill to remind him of the way things were supposed to be. Mr. Hill apologized. He said he'd take care of it.

That evening, when Sonny reported to work, Hill told him he

was fired. When George heard about this, he went to see Mr. Hill. George would have been just as happy to get the help of Sonny back, but Annie Mae's influence was strong. Sonny never knew what was said or promised between George and Mr. Hill, but Sonny was hired back in the store the next day. It took a lot of courage for George to fly in the face of the landlord that way. In the old days, George could never have prevailed in this. Much was the same, but a few things at least had changed in rural Alabama.

Sonny studied, all the while hating the work his father did, their way of life. Sonny tried to act as if he were from a higher economic class, and he associated with students he felt were of this upper class. He didn't want to admit he came from a family of sharecroppers. Sonny's brothers resented him for this.

While Sonny was in high school, George and Annie Mae left Mr. Dixon and moved to a new landlord. The tenant house on this land was back in the swamp, raised about eight feet off the ground to avoid the spring floodwaters. When Sonny first saw it, he commented that it was ready to fall down. The walls of his room were made of bare pine boards, and the floor was bowed. A big family fight ensued. Sonny said he wouldn't move into such a dump. He said he'd take an apartment in Cookstown.

George shrugged. He went and purchased wallpaper, pasting over the pine boards, trying to make the room look like one fit for a city boy. Sonny moved in.

When the day that Sonny was to get his diploma approached, he was ready to grab it and escape Cookstown, moving on to college and whatever big time the city, and the greater world outside cotton, held in store for him.

Sonny desired to graduate in style and wanted a class ring, but couldn't afford one on the wages of his store job. Annie Mae did some outside work that fall of 1958, above and beyond what she had to do on their own farm. She picked thirty-seven dollars' worth of cotton to buy the ring for him. "I don't want you giving this to no girl," she told him as she handed over the money.

She picked some more, to pay the rent for his gown, and for the invitations. She was extremely proud. If only Maggie Louise could have worn a gown and flashed a high school ring.

If Sonny's sister Maggie Louise was jealous, she never showed it. She and Sonny were close. She encouraged her youngest brother. They were known for their "cutting up" when they were together.

They were always joking and couldn't go anywhere together without breaking out in laughter. In all ways, they were the two most alike of all their siblings.

While Sonny was poised to escape, the cotton world appeared as though it would never change for George and Annie Mae, and for their daughter Maggie Louise and her husband Floyd. George was only in his early fifties as the 1950s neared an end, and Floyd was even younger. They were still able to make a living, no matter how bare, from cotton, in spite of all the problems associated with growing the crop. They were making it without those picking machines that were talked about so much. But machines weren't their real worry.

. *v* .

It was 1958, the third week of June. The crop was in the ground and growing. Floyd didn't have to hear the thunder—he could see a gray mass of clouds stalking the western horizon. He eyed the clouds in the way all farmers do. Too much rain would make the cotton grow all green and thick, but throw no bolls. Too little would parch and stunt it. This rain was a strong one, and Maggie Louise and the children ran to the storm pit, a cavern carved in the red bank of earth about a hundred feet to the east of their home on the Burgandy land.

Ever since she could remember, Debbie had been rushed by Maggie Louise into that pit to wait out storms that came frequently to these tablelands. It was cut in the bank, about waist high to an adult, and ten feet deep, a dark and cold place that Debbie imagined to be full of snakes lurking beneath the benches on which they sat. She felt that the danger of getting bitten outweighed the chance of being struck by lightning or buried under their house by a tornado that might level it, but the fear of storms instilled in Maggie Louise by her parents remained strong. As the door closed behind and they sat in the pit, Maggie Louise's face was probably similar to what it had been that day twenty-two years earlier when Agee sat in the bedroom with them during the storm.

The rain came, pounding the metal roof covered by a skin of concrete, and the baby, Parvin, was crying. Floyd decided to make a run across the road and ditch to the house, to get her bottle, which they'd forgotten in haste.

Big round drops were falling. When he returned, climbing up through the entrance, between the dark forms of his family on either side of him, they were amazed that he was absolutely dry. They worried that it might have been some kind of omen. That seemed silly. But they kept talking about it.

One week later, on June 29, about four in the afternoon, Floyd was out by the barn, working with a hand they had hired from the county home for the retarded to help out during cotton-hoeing time. It seems he suffered an aneurysm, a weakened blood vessel that ruptured, probably a congenital defect. They said it appeared his head exploded, with blood coming from everywhere. The death certificate said he died from an intraventricular hemorrhage of an "unknown cause." No autopsy was performed.

Floyd died at one in the morning on June 30, 1958. He was forty-one. Cotton sharecropping was over for Maggie Louise. She could not continue with four young children, the oldest twelve. She gathered the children and closed the door on the shack, forever leaving cotton behind.

Life as a cotton landowner also changed for Mrs. Burgandy. Since the death of her husband, in 1952, she'd been spending some time in the winter down in Mobile, at the house of her daughter, Elizabeth. For a few summers beyond the death of Floyd Franks, she'd go back and live for several months at a time in the big, silent house, trying to cling to memories and to a life that once had been. Over the years, she came to spend less and less time there.

Maggie Louise went north, to Cherokee City, into a public housing project on the rough south side, occupied by many others who, like her, were refugees from the land.

Later, they moved a little way out and lived in a duplex. The other half of the duplex was rented to Maggie Louise's brother Squinchy, the baby whom Agee saw in 1936 and whom Maggie Louise had held in her arms the day they sat in the bedroom during the storm. They still had no inside toilet, only an outhouse and a metal tub to wash in. There was little she could get in the way of public help, and she didn't want anything for nothing, anyway. She told Sonny, her son, that you never get anything free, that the only way you get ahead is to get off your ass and go work for it. She was to repeat that piece of philosophy many times.

She got a job as a waitress at Gas Island, a crossroads joint on the road south of Cherokee City. She worked eleven hours a day, six days a week. The wages were low, and tips were her mainstay. By that time, her brother Sonny had just graduated from high school and was working in a shoe store as a salesman. Maggie Louise went to visit him one day. He gasped when she entered, walking in on her tiptoes, because she couldn't use the balls of her heels, so blistered were they from constant standing. She had lost all her excess 3-M weight, turning almost gaunt. She didn't complain to Sonny, or to anyone else. Work was what she was supposed to do.

Meanwhile, the sun still burned down on Cookstown and its environs, and George Gudger labored harder, minus many of his sons who no longer were around to help him. He seemed old as he neared his fifty-fifth birthday. In the off season, he and Annie Mae were borrowing forty bucks a month from their landlord to survive. George seemed to become crazed with work, worse than anything Annie Mae had ever seen. One afternoon after a day in the fields, he came home and started rubbing the liniment he always applied to his skin to sooth his aching muscles. Annie Mae saw that he'd begun to drink it and was now out of his head and wild. She fought to restrain him, and he didn't recognize her or anyone else. They forced him down with pillows until he stopped thrashing. It was the beginning of a series of nervous breakdowns.

Not much later, George fell ill, unable to recover from exhaustion, and Annie Mae was worried. Her son Sonny drove her and George to the doctor in Cookstown. George had been there before, and the doctor said he was fine. But Annie Mae knew deep down something terrible was wrong. During that last visit, she dropped to her knees and begged the doctor to do something or to send George to a specialist. The doctor looked down at her and told her to get up off her knees, to go back home. George was just tired, he said.

George dismissed her concerns, but finally, when he continued to decline, they talked him into seeing another doctor. That doctor found cancer in his throat. But it was too far along now for anything to be done. George's sickness worsened just before the cotton was ready for harvest. Sonny went to the landlord and told him he could keep the crop. That more than settled the debt George had incurred at the start of the season—they didn't want to pick or have any share of the cotton George had planted. They were done with cotton. The last cotton George Gudger ever picked was after his son-in-law had died the year before, when he helped Maggie Louise gather their crop.

George Gudger died on December 27, 1959, in the time of year when the withered, brown, and beaten stalks born of the seeds he had put into the earth the preceding spring were plowed deep beneath the frost-covered ground, and the land he last farmed waited for a fresh season, a tractor driven by another man, the green lines of new cotton, new life, a new decade, the return of another August sun and another field of white to be gathered.

Annie Mae moved north, toward Cherokee City, nearer her sister Emma and her daughter Maggie Louise, who had also been driven out of cotton by the loss of her man. Emma helped her get work at a nursing home. Sonny helped support his mother when he had to on the thirty dollars a week he made in the shoe store.

RICKETTS

. i .

The two decades before 1960 were critical to cotton, marking a quiet revolution in the old cotton South. Finally coming to pass were all those predictions made when the inventors John and Mack Rust demonstrated their cotton-picking machine in the Mississippi Delta that hot August day in 1936.

In 1936, the total U.S. production of about fourteen million bales of cotton was almost entirely raised by hand and mule on forty-three million acres.

By 1960, the same amount of cotton was being sent to market each year. But because of machines and improved cultivation, it was grown on just seventeen and a half million acres. Fewer people were needed. One million farms had vanished since 1940, representing a loss of a majority of the nine million cotton tenants.

Machines were on the march.

Most cotton in 1960 was planted with tractor power. Even more significant, for the first time in history, better than 50 percent of the U.S. crop was harvested by mechanical pickers. In 1955 just 25 percent was machine-harvested, according to James H. Street in his book *The New Revolution in the Cotton Economy* (1957). It was a trend that would accelerate even more in the few years after 1960.

Even though many farms were phasing in machines, some hand labor was still used. This was so, said Street, because a

> factor in the preference of planters for hand labor over machines is the genuine concern some of them feel for loyal employees of long standing who remained on the farm during the difficult war years and who are now too aged or untrained to find adequate employment elsewhere. Some of the larger operators, of whom a few have as many as one hundred cropper families, are introducing fuller mechanization only on that land from which the tenants have departed. They reorganize the plantation by stages, pulling the empty houses down where necessary, and begin a new system of farming.

Most of the old-time cotton farmers left on the land were black. Whites had vacated the farm first, after the war, taking the relatively good jobs in new factories that had moved south—three whites quit cotton in the first years after the war for each black who did. By 1960, only the hard-core poor—and that most often meant blacks—were left on the land living under the old ways. But a few whites remained.

Fred Ricketts was one of these few.

. *ii* .

Fred Ricketts was eighty-eight. His wife, Sadie, was seventy-three, still sickly. They lived with their daughter Margaret and her fourteen-year-old son, Garvrin Arlo. Margaret had never left home. She lived her life within that clannish family that refused to change its ways.

They were still planting by mule, still using the same old equipment, including the animal-drawn seeder used on Hobe's Hill twenty-four years before, and, of course, picking by hand.

But there was a critical difference—Fred Ricketts now owned the land he cultivated. He kept all the crop he grew. There were no more thirds and fourths to share with any landlord. He alone, among all the relatives who had farmed near him back on Hobe's Hill, could boast of having achieved the dream of all cotton tenants—title to his own farm.

Back about 1940, Fred bought 149 acres under a New Deal loan program designed to turn cotton tenants into landowners. He apparently got the land through the Bankhead-Jones Tenant Farm Act, administered by the Farm Security Administration, though records in Atlanta were incomplete and exact details are skimpy. The government loan at 3 percent interest enabled him to buy the property, about three miles due west of Hobe's Hill, near the river. After he signed the lease, a storm came and knocked down many trees on the property. He sold the lumber, which had been felled at no cost to him, and with the proceeds was able to pay off the loan and keep $1,300 for himself.

It should have been a time to rejoice. But his family had fallen into bitter factionalism and hate, something many of them would never get over.

Most of Fred and Sadie's seven children wanted to escape. Fast. John Garvrin was only fourteen when he struck out. He was the first. The rest left as soon as possible. After the youngest, Clair Bell, who had been just four years old when the writer James Agee visited, took off about 1950, only two remained—Margaret and her brother Richard.

Margaret and Richard were different from the others, trapped in their father's world. They could not escape the old man. The others were upset with all the things Agee hadn't seen, things that were just beginning about the time of his visit. Fred was crafty and concealed them well from the outsider. Oddly, Agee observed that Fred always stared at him in a funny way, as if hiding his fear. There is no suggestion that Agee knew anything about the special secrets Fred Ricketts kept from him.

Ricketts took delight in the use of a horsewhip on the kids, and this would have saddened and maybe shocked Agee. But it was those other things, whispered by townsmen, that would have intrigued Agee. It was all seen by Bea, the wife of John Ricketts, the first of Fred's sons to leave. She was astonished at the family she had married into.

There was the time Fred held Margaret out on the porch, just as the Foster men were passing. The Fosters were black landowners on Hobe's Hill. Fred unfastened her flour sack dress, so as to expose her naked front. "How would you niggers like some of this?" he asked, according to Bea, and then he laughed crazily.

Fred once came after Paralee. She wouldn't put up with what he did to Margaret. To escape her father's wrath, she jumped through a window, shattering the glass. Paralee soon married and left.

Margaret did try to get away. She married once, to a man named Jones, but Fred broke that up. He made her come back home, to plow behind a double team of mules. He let no one date his Margaret after that.

On June 6, 1946, Margaret gave birth. Margaret said Mr. Jones was the father. The child was named Garvrin Arlo, taken from Fred's middle name. His last name was Ricketts. Fred and Sadie and Margaret raised him, and Margaret would call him both brother and son. Seven years later, she had another child, but she could not put that off on Mr. Jones. That boy died from disease within a year of his birth. Margaret would walk to the cemetery behind the tall white pine-board church to visit the grave, marked with a plain rock the size of a basketball.

Their house wasn't much different from their previous place. It was just as nasty as the house on Hobe's Hill, and inhabited by rattlesnakes to boot. They once killed one in the bedroom that had seventeen rings on its rattle. That was a lot of snake. The home threatened to collapse from rot beneath its own weight. Neighbors who stepped inside could not believe the foulness they witnessed.

John Ricketts, repulsed as he was by what was going on, felt sorry for his mother. He entered the service and went to Korea. According to Bea, he sent money to his mother, so she could finally buy some nice things. Bea, who, like many in the family, hated Margaret, said Fred and Margaret never gave Sadie the money her son sent her, but used it instead to buy things for themselves.

One of the many people shocked by the unsanitary living conditions of the Rickettses was Annie Mae Gudger. Fred Ricketts was related to her only by marriage, Fred having married her father's half sister. Fred had a brother, Tommy, who was a favorite of Annie Mae's. He was ill and quite old, eighty-nine in 1950. Though the kinship was far removed, Annie Mae could not let Tommy live in that house. She took him in, letting him stay with her family for one year.

Annie Mae's daughter Gretchen said Tommy was in sad shape. He had a huge and ugly sore on his leg and was emaciated.

"They was just that kind of people," said Gretchen. "Mama felt sorry for him 'cuz they just dragged him around. She babied him. We kept him about one year. Then Daddy, he just didn't want to keep him no more. It really hurt Mama. She cried and cried. Daddy wouldn't back down. He was in good shape when he went back."

Tommy had put on weight and looked healthy under the care of Annie Mae. But once back in that soiled home, he quickly degenerated into a pale and ghastly shadow. Gretchen visited him. "I squatted down in front of him," she recalled, "and he didn't know me." Tommy died right after that, in 1952.

The next to fall ill in that house was Fred and Sadie's son Richard. For years, a violent cough had been his trademark. One day, he coughed up blood. They were reluctant to take him to see a doctor. He had a fever for two days, then died in their home at 10:50 the night of April 27, 1956. Richard was thirty-three years old. He was in awful shape—the death certificate listed the cause as pneumonia, "probably tuberculous with pulmonary abscess."

James Agee never met Tommy—so of all those he wrote about and knew on Hobe's Hill, Richard was the first to die. In his book, Agee hazarded a guess as to when some of those in the families would perish, that "in two years, in five, in forty, it will all be over" for most of them, that one by one they'd all "be drawn into the planet." He predicted a few of them would be dead within months after his departure.

But in a strange twist reality put on the story, Agee was the very first to die, a year before Richard. Agee collapsed in a New York taxi on May 16, 1955, from a heart attack, brought on by a hard-lived life. He was forty-five. He'd just barely finished a novel that would posthumously win a Pulitzer Prize.

The Rickettses didn't know anything about Agee's death. They were concerned with the loss of Richard's labor. Richard was a strong cotton hand. Without him, it was much harder for Fred to farm. But they went on. After the death of Richard, Fred and Margaret put aside the pretense that may have served to protect a shred or so of Sadie's dignity and took to living in the same half of the house. Sadie was made to live in the other half, according to Bea.

By that time, Garvrin Arlo had permanently dropped out of school. Although his mother never made it past the fifth grade, he didn't even get that far. He left in the fourth grade.

It happened one afternoon, when the teacher told him to write down an answer to some school problems. He refused. The teacher, frustrated with the child, sent him to the office. The principal told him to bend over his knee. He was going to spank him.

"Over my damn daid body," said Garvrin Arlo. "You maht run a-this school. But you ain' wuppin' me! I ain' stayin' and you can't do anything!"

Garvrin Arlo went to his homeroom to pick up his book. He started to walk out the door. The principal and two teachers blocked him. "You can't walk out," said the principal.

"I ain' walkin' out. Ahm knockin' my way out wit my haid. The one I hit with my haid is the one that's gonna hit the ground."

They parted. The boy ran home. Margaret was enraged—not at Garvrin Arlo but at the principal. No one whipped a Ricketts. She pocketed a .32 semiautomatic and went off to the school. Margaret told the principal he'd never threaten to hit her son again, because her son was done with school. Garvrin Arlo stayed home after that, working the cotton, withdrawing further into the world of Fred Ricketts. She bragged about her deed, constantly retelling the story of how she showed those know-nothing teachers.

While Fred Ricketts captured the loyalties of his daughter and her son, he inspired fear in some of his grandchildren. Nancy Ann, one of his granddaughters, recalled a visit as a child. One of her cousins was playing behind the rocker in which Fred sat. Fred rocked back, unknowingly crushing the cousin's finger beneath the wood stave. Her cousin was too terrified to yelp, for fear the old man would go into one of his rages. Finally, an adult noticed the cousin turning purple. But the cousin never cried.

Four years after the death of Richard, Sadie's health began to degenerate. Sadie needed medical help, as had her child, but it wasn't made available to her, either. The family believed that the doctor who had come to visit Richard when he was spitting up blood killed him with the shot he administered. Bea felt that something could have been done for Sadie, but little was. She died at 2:30 the afternoon of February 7, 1960.

"Sadie used to come to me and just cry her heart out," said Bea.

"I held her hand when she died. I was glad she died. It was better that way."

Meanwhile, not all the Ricketts children were living like Margaret. John had moved north to Cherokee City, working as a mechanic for the city, and led a normal life in a clean house with a bathroom. Clair Bell was the only one to finish high school, and she had good grades. She moved to Illinois with her husband, living in a suburban-style home. To distance herself from the memories, she shortened her name to just Bell. She never liked Clair Bell—she was given that name by Fred, after his favorite mule.

. *iii* .

Fred Ricketts could ignore what was going on in the outside world by controlling his own world so tightly. But many cotton tenants could not.

The impetus for change came from several fronts. World War II, of course, altered American expectations and the economy of the world. Here was what is called a "pull" factor, inducing cotton sharecroppers to leave the land. The enticement was better jobs than had ever been available to them.

Then there were the machines, a "push" factor to force them off the land. The machines came, and the tenants had little choice in the matter. Some had nothing to go to.

John Rust retained his vision of helping them. He and his brother, Mack, worked frantically in the early 1940s to perfect their mechanical cotton harvester, but continued to have problems. Their successful demonstration in 1936 must have sent fear through the huge companies that manufactured agricultural equipment. International Harvester had spent $3 million since the turn of the century to do what the Rusts seemed to be perfecting.

No matter what its merits, nobody was buying the Rust brothers' contraption, with all those rules they had imposed to help the sharecroppers. So they sought their own financing. They managed to convince a group of liberal New Yorkers that the machine could liberate the tenant farmer and be the salvation of the South. The New Yorkers invested $43,000.

Their new company sold two machines to the Soviet Union. John Rust went to the USSR to set them up, believing they'd be used "to lighten man's burden rather than to make a profit at the expense of the workers." They also sold models in Argentina and Australia.

Still, no Americans were buying. The Rusts decided to change course. They would not impose any rules on the use of their machines, selling them on the open market for $4,800. To hold faith in his earlier dream, John Rust said the company would set up a trust fund from which the profits would be drawn to assist farmers forced off the land and to encourage cooperative farming. The brothers also announced they would not earn more than ten times their lowest-paid employee.

Financing was a problem during the early years of the war—the New Yorkers' money was not enough. And the machine continued to break down. Also, the small new company had trouble distributing the device. All the Rusts had was a development shop and no plant to manufacture their picker commercially, no marketing people, no sales force. By 1942, they had sold the shop tools to pay debts. The moribund company was then dissolved.

Mack Rust was finished with the dream. He took a few of the machines and moved to California, setting up a custom cotton-harvesting business for Central Valley farmers.

John Rust was left alone, heavily in debt. Forty-nine years old, with no property except a company with no net worth and a house heavily mortgaged, he had nothing to show for fifteen years of work. He remained undaunted. He decided the machine was just not good enough for the market. He went back to the shop, to redesign it and eliminate the problems.

Meanwhile, his largest rival, International Harvester, was putting more money and manpower into perfecting its own version.

All this activity had been spurred by the news in 1944 of the first cotton crop ever to be produced totally by machine, in the Mississippi Delta, which proved that the mechanical picker was not only possible but even inevitable.

International Harvester finally broke through when its engineers decided to put the cotton intake at the front of the machine rather than the rear, as Rust had. That eliminated the destruction of cotton plants by being run over and made the machine easy to operate by one man. International Harvester turned out twelve machines in 1941 and 1942 and, by 1947, was producing seventy-five a year.

In 1948, that company announced it was going into commercial production. The firm completed a plant in Memphis, producing more than one thousand machines that year, each costing $7,600.

John Rust saw only disaster ahead if he continued to try to go his own way. He decided he had to turn to another large corporation, and in 1944 he signed with the Allis-Chalmers Manufacturing Company. But the firm was plagued with problems and was producing only forty-nine machines by 1950. Allis-Chalmers lost its exclusive rights when it failed to live up to its contract, so Rust also sold the rights to Ben Pearson, Inc., a small company in Pine Bluff, Arkansas. Ben Pearson agreed to give Rust 10 percent of the gross sales on each of the first thousand machines sold and 5 percent on each after the first thousand.

In the fall of 1952, the International Harvester Company said it had produced more than eight thousand cotton harvesters, four times the number produced by Allis-Chalmers and Ben Pearson combined.

Even so, in 1952, Rust reached a milestone—paying back more than $250,000 in debts to 125 investors who had given him money since his quest began in 1927.

He had an additional $200,000 in earnings that he put into the foundation he had formed a decade earlier. Fifty percent of all royalties were to go to that foundation. Furthermore, he assigned all patent rights to the foundation, taking a salary of just $25,000 a year.

Rust dreamed the trust would grow and help former tenant farmers. He continued to try to make a cotton-picking machine even more affordable to a small farmer. He also set up an experimental farm near his home in Pine Bluff.

Just as this next stage of his dream was under way, John Rust suffered a heart attack. He died on January 20, 1954.

Rust's was one of the few voices calling for help for the sharecroppers through the 1930s, 1940s, and 1950s. The media and politicians of the 1950s almost totally ignored the millions of cotton exiles who were being driven into the cities, some to poor jobs, with no retraining. Few wrote about them or spoke in their behalf. America was preoccupied by the wealth of the postwar years; not until the 1960s would it see the start of the War on Poverty. A significant part of that poverty, particularly in the urban areas of large northern cities, was a result of cotton tenants' fleeing the land.

When Rust died, his dream was a failure. The trust fund didn't amount to enough to help many sharecroppers, said G. E. Powell, president of Ben Pearson.

Most of the market was eventually taken by International Harvester. What royalties that did come into the Rust estate were never seen by tenants. After his death, Rust's second wife took much of the money to invest in a chain of hotels, according to Powell. She had never shared his vision, Powell said, and before he died, Rust would often vanish for days at a time to escape her. Rust's daughter said she and her uncle Mack sued to keep the wife from getting the estate. Eventually, the fund was depleted. The hotel chain never caught on, and all that remains today is one hotel in Pine Bluff.

Even if Rust had lived and earned many millions of dollars in royalties for his fund, it probably wouldn't have been enough to extend any kind of real help to all the families hurt by the introduction of technology to cotton farming. It was a job so huge only the government could handle it—and the government did very little. The Ricketts children and millions like them who were trying to assimilate into society were ill equipped. They had to contend on their own.

. *iv* .

Fred Ricketts didn't want to meet the modern world, but he could not forever insulate himself and his family against the realities of the cotton market and the national politics that controlled it. His shrunken family was about to be forced to face reality. By the 1960s, Fred, Margaret, and her son were already living on borrowed time.

A *Reader's Digest* article summed up the predicament through the lens of economic Darwinism:

> The trouble in cotton began in the 1930s. At that time, the United States supplied nearly half of the world's requirements, selling an average of 6,300,000 five-hundred pound bales of cotton overseas annually, at a profit. Then, to help the small, depression-ridden farmer survive, the U.S. government started propping up the prices of cotton with public money. . . . This kept poor marginal farmers in business. But it also raised U.S. cotton prices so high that our cotton began to lose buyers in the world market.

By 1956, the government subsidy of about one thousand dollars to each cotton farm cost U.S. consumers more than one billion dollars.

Just when this subsidy program was being established at this level, cotton's share of the fabric market was shrinking. In 1960, cotton provided the material for only 66 percent of all clothes sold. In 1930, the comparable figure was 85 percent. Rayon became cheaper than cotton in 1944 and soon established a place for itself with the clothes-buying public.

The export market for cotton was virtually lost by 1956—only a little more than two million bales were shipped overseas. The government kept buying up the extra cotton that American farmers were producing. Finally, in the late 1950s the United States started "dumping" cotton overseas. U.S. textile mills had to pay $167 a bale for the same cotton the government was selling to its overseas competitors at $129. This gave foreign textile manufacturers an insurmountable advantage over domestic manufacturers and helped ruin the domestic textile industry.

All this was done mostly to save some small southern farmers like the Rickettses. If that one billion dollars had been used to educate and train them to enter more useful professions, it would have been money better spent. But that would have smacked of social engineering and been politically unacceptable.

A spokesman for the world's largest private cotton dealer told *Time* magazine that the expensive price-support system tended to keep cotton production in the old, uneconomical mule-power farms of the Southeast, retarding a shift to the more economical big farms of the West. A loss of subsidies would make the large western growers better able to compete in world markets.

It was inevitable as the 1960s began that those subsidies would soon have to end, radically lowering the price, making it impossible for anyone to earn a living on thirty acres of cotton. The last of the Rickettses would then be forced to give up on cotton, no matter how hard they worked or how much they feared the modern world.

WOODS

. i .

Much had happened since that summer day in 1936 when Emma
left Cookstown in a pickup truck, looking back over her shoulder at
the shrinking figures of her sister Annie Mae Gudger, her brother,
Gallatin, the writer James Agee, and the piercing eyes of her niece
Maggie Louise. The truck crawled and rumbled along, carrying her
and that iron bed—all there was to her marital property—to the
place where she would lie upon it with her lawful husband. She
really didn't understand why they had to travel so far to make their
home, but Lonnie had been told that Mississippi bull farming
looked promising, and so they were on their way to Mississippi.

By the time they arrived in Mississippi it was too late in the year
to plant a crop, but Emma and Lonnie found work here and there

to earn money until the spring season, when they'd be able to put in cotton as tenant farmers.

Emma was used to seeing in front of a plow. But even in this small way of going to the bull farm, Emma was not to see anything new in cotton farming. "They called it bull farming," she wrote in her diary. "But he got a mule instead of a bull."

Emma learned that the Mississippi sun was no kinder than the Alabama sun had been. The cotton wilted beneath the numbing advance of late summer, just as it had in Alabama; the fields, their house, lay yellow in the heat. And then soon after the last cotton was gathered, the winds of winter came, shaking to its primitive foundation that mausoleum for the living to which her husband had brought her. But it was not all the same. Missing were those sights and smells and sounds of family that had sustained her back home—her father, Gallatin, Annie Mae and George, little Maggie Louise—now all miles removed. In their place were signs of married life new for her, the soft cries of her own babies, the early jealous stares of Lonnie, later becoming bored glances—ever reminding her of the deathly loneliness that was growing between them. Some nights he was in bed next to her, often not.

It was easy for Emma to believe that the wrath of God had been visited upon that house. Her burdens were harsh, but in more ways than those of the tenant farming that she had known all her life. When she had left Cookstown, Alabama, she had not known—or if she had, she hadn't told Agee—that she was already pregnant. After her first daughter, Judith, the others came fast. She remembers that Ruby, who was the third, born in 1941, was from the beginning small and sickly. Ruby's poor health was to be a special trial in Emma's life.

What made it more difficult was that over time her worst fears about Lonnie were realized, though she would have trouble admitting this even to herself. Her diary tries to put the best face on things:

> Now dont misunderstand me. I growed very close to Lonnie and we had a lot of good times together. With his toung he was real good to me. . . . I know he loved me and the children with all his heart. I wont try to write about how and the way we lived but we was happy. I followed him arond like a child would there dady and he treated me like I was a child.

But other entries, those dealing more with the facts of the relationship, clearly reveal he was not as committed to the survival of the family as Emma was, and amid all the rosy memories that fill her journal she does concede this. "If he couldnt find a job like he wanted," she writes, "he just wouldnt have one. If he couldnt make good money he just wouldnt work. Now that is the truth." Her husband also thought it his right to come and go as he pleased. If he wanted to go off somewhere, the fact that he was a married man with a family did not stop him.

> Bless his heart. In his way he was good to us and I cared a lot for him but when he wanted to go some where he went. If he wanted to stay a month or 2 or 3 he did, then come home when he got ready.

When Lonnie was home, he spent much of his time trying to perfect a waterwheel from which he hoped to make electricity. But the stream was flat and shallow, unable to drive a turbine, and it was a doomed dream from the start. In a pattern very different from what she had known in the homes of both her father and her brother-in-law, where everyone had to work in the fields, and the father of the family the hardest, it was Emma who wound up working the cotton crop most of the time, contributing not only that greater half of the marriage bargain that was the woman's part but also the burden of what she had always known to be the man's part.

> When Judith was borned I tryed hard to be a grown woman but I didnt know how. I still wanted Lonnie to pet me just as mutch as he did Judith. Then in 17 months Missy was borned. I worked in the field right up till she was borned. I put out soda with Judith in my arms. . . . I picked cotton all the fall. Oh it was hard but I done it.

In fact, she not only did most of the field work, she made the contract with the landlord and pledged her own credit.

> I dont meen to be braging for it is nothing to brag about, but we farmed on the halves and I had to be the one that had to get a place and I had to give my word and they looked to me for them crops to be made.

In addition to working their own crop, Emma hired herself out to hoe other farmers' cotton. The pay for this work was poor—

either four pounds of lard or fifty cents for a full day's work. Lonnie would never reduce himself to work for fifty cents a day.

In the middle of this period of toil, the event that would be both the joy and the tragedy of her life—the birth of Ruby—was not far off. She was alone when it happened.

> The day before she was borned I washed for the children my self and 3 men on a rub bord. I can rember I was so tird the next morning. About 8 oclock Ruby was borned befor the Dr. got to me so me and Ruby done that.

Ruby grew, but before the end of the decade, she fell seriously ill with rheumatic fever. Emma felt terribly guilty forever afterward about Ruby's illness because, having been on the farm without transportation, she had not been able to get Ruby to a doctor at the first fever. By the time she was able to do so, Ruby's heart had already been permanently damaged by the infection. This was 1950, just about the time that rheumatic fever in children was starting to be treated with penicillin, with a dramatic change in the long-term course of the disease, but we have no way of knowing for sure that even if Emma had been able to get Ruby to a doctor promptly, she would have been given this treatment. As it was, Ruby was condemned to the life of a near invalid.

> Ruby she tuck sick when she was jut a little girl of 9 year old. She had just went into the third grade. . . . I rember when they told us she would have to stay in bed for 6 months to a year. She was so happy for she wouldnt have to go to school. But what we didnt know was that she would never be well again. Of corse the Dr. told us after the first year that she couldnt last long. He told us her life was like a candle. We could just look for it to go out any time.

When with all Emma's work they still found it hard simply to survive, Lonnie responded not with greater commitment but by falling back on his mother. They went back to Alabama, and Emma, who had once been unable to remain in her father's house because of the presence of his new wife, was forced to go back to Alabama and move in with her mother-in-law. It is not clear whether Lonnie's father was still alive or, if alive, whether he continued to have any contact with his wife and son.

Emma had three children at the time, but was treated like a child in her mother-in-law's house. "It was dont do that dont do this," she recalls. She also says her mother-in-law didn't want her singing in the house, and after all those years of marriage, Lonnie, too, suddenly found it objectionable. It wasn't the musical quality of her voice that bothered them, but the messages in those songs of love and hope. They especially objected to the love songs. She was discouraged but not defeated:

> Oh my nerves. . . . I sung love songs and all kind of stuff and they would say that was what my mind was on. Well I stoped singing my songs out loud but I sung in my heart.

With the volatility of the cotton economy in the years right after the war, it was sometimes possible for a tenant family to survive even with only one reliable, full-time contributing member. Emma and Lonnie managed to get themselves a mule and a cow, some pigs and chickens. But better times, as short-lived as they were, meant that she and Lonnie got close again, and that led to where it had often led before:

> I was the happiest woman arond. And then I got pregent with Sonny. And that year I planted the cotton seed with my hands. Lonnie covered them. Sonny was borned the 20th of April and believe it or not I choped cotton. I could see the house and I would call to Judith and tell her what to do. When Sonny got to crying hard I would tell her how to pick him up and bring him on to the porch and rock him. Then every once in a while I would run to the house and feed him and then go back to work. It was hard but I done it and we got by.

More forgiving times or not, Emma and Lonnie managed to lose it all—mule, cows, hogs, chickens. Lonnie left for a job at a shipyard in Mobile, and Emma's worst fears for herself came true: "Then back to his mother we went, me and the children." As Emma remembers it, in all the time that she and the children were at his mother's, he sent her money only once—thirty dollars. "The rest of the time," she reports, "he always got robed."

Emma tried not to be a freeloader. She worked in the field and did all she could to help. Apparently some kind of truce was worked out with her mother-in-law because her diary entries for this period reflect not much more than usual and familiar family tensions. Judith, Emma's oldest, was her grandmother's favorite. "Ruby and Sonny was mine," Emma writes, "with the help of God we made it.

Well I had 4 of the sweetest children I thought in this whole wide world—so I just built my world around them."

Lonnie got a job as a guard at North Hospital near Cookstown and moved Emma and the kids to an old Civilian Conservation Corps camp close by. Soon afterward, Emma's last was born, a ten-pound baby girl they called Sister. The next year, they were back in cotton, farming as tenants for a man named Ed Jones.

How could they have been tempted to return to a life that on the whole had treated them so poorly, and that at its best required a level of work and commitment Lonnie seemed incapable of providing? Emma does not let us know.

Unlike some other tenant farmers who were leaving the farms for postwar jobs in town, Lonnie could not make the transition to paid work. He was simply too unreliable to be hired. Emma, too, was trapped. While today, women in her situation would go out to work themselves, in the early 1950s few women considered such an option. And Emma and Lonnie were acclimated, to put it kindly (brainwashed, to put it bluntly), to a cotton lifestyle; if not overtly, subconsciously, at least for Emma. With that crop, she could provide for the family and herself and not rely on Lonnie to dole out whatever portion of his paycheck he chose to share with her. Whatever their true reasons, they were back in cotton.

It was in 1950 that Ruby fell ill. In those early months of her sickness, little Ruby lay in bed each day. At night, Emma would peek in at the girl's empty eyes fixed on the ceiling. Then Emma would go to her own room and take the Bible into the bed. Every night she whispered the same question: *God, did you bring this upon me, because I married a man who had a living wife?* In her heart, she was sure she knew the answer, and that God was not through with her yet, that other, even worse fates would befall her for her sin. But why make Ruby pay the price for her transgression? Many diary entries confirm her anguish over this.

Poor thing.

She just had to suffer so mutch.

God do have mercy on her.

Of corse there was a lot of praying going on. I have shed enough tears to do a washing and God seen me and I bet he felt sorry for me for I prayed as I worked so many times. I cant help but believe that he heard my prayers and saw my tears.

What hurt me so bad and know one realy knew but God but I would have to go to the field and leve her and some time she cryed for me just to stay home with her. But believe it or not I couldnt. We all had to eat. I have left Ruby a lot of times with my heart braking and the tears runing down my face.

While she was a child she never complained. I know she wanted to go and play with others but she wouldnt say a thing. She just tuck things as they was. And Ruby was such a good child she learned to read the Bible and she belived in praying but she thought she had to go in the closet to pray so she would slide of the bed and crawl, for the Dr had told her not to stand on her feet. She was good to mind her Dr. but she had to go to that closet to pray.

. *ii* .

Emma's best year as a sharecropper was 1953. Lonnie had run off to Florida the first day of cotton picking. He stayed away until Emma and the children picked the last of it. Emma cleared nearly one thousand dollars. Lonnie came back just as she was paid and remained until he'd spent all of it.

He continued to come and go as he pleased, and she wound up, as usual, shouldering much of the work. On the bright side, she was at least close to home, drawn here at first by Lonnie's job at the North Hospital, which in the end, like all the others, didn't last. She was at least again near her sister, Annie Mae, and her father, Bud Woods.

It was now the mid-1950s. She tried to continue to tenant farm, but fell into worsening health, debilitated by asthma. We don't know what would have happened to Emma and her children at this point had an agency of the state of Alabama not intervened. We hear many horror stories about governmental programs gone wrong, about their achieving ends opposite to what they were enacted to achieve: millions of people still below the poverty line years after the War on Poverty was launched. It should provide some relief to know that there are people helped by state programs, and in just the way the programs were designed to help people. Emma was one.

One of the tasks of the state rehabilitation office in Alabama was to help a few tenant farmers, especially women who were ill, such as Emma. An official of that agency came to Emma's house and told her that she wouldn't have to suffer under the sun any longer, doing that heavy labor that aggravated her asthma. Not only would he help her get medical care; he'd find her work she could do. And he did—a job in a nursing home. She was one of the few tenant farmers to get any kind of assistance in freeing herself from the bondage of cotton. It brought her into the twentieth century.

> I was working at oke knoll nurcing home making $35 a week. It was the first time that I got a pay day. The first job I ever had only in the cotton field. Rehab bought my glasses my teeth my uniforms my shoes and what I made went to keeping a home. I was taking care of all the expence. I even paid the rent. I never got to buy me anything new.

This last line tells us something about how Emma was pro-grammed to feel guilty about any good fortune she didn't work hard enough to earn. It is almost as if she thought buying any small article for herself would be unfairly milking the system.

She worked for a couple named Clayton at the home and appears to have gotten on quite well with them, especially considering she'd had no experience working directly under a supervisor. They both liked her; she was particularly proud that they trusted her, reporting in her diary, "Mr. Clayton belived any thing that I told him for he found out I wouldnt tell him a lie."

To complete her indoctrination into the American work-for-wages scene, all she had left to learn was the art of engaging in a little on-the-job goofing off.

> All them old men just loved me. After lunch I would go in a room and go to bed and one of the old men would set out side the door and watch to see if any body was coming over there and if he seen some one he would call me. I had it so easy. . . . Oh I had a good time. I was almost happy.

Lonnie hated her going to that job, and she says he was jealous. He wanted her on the farm. He saw she was making easier money than he had ever made. But rather than be happy for her, he came up with a scheme to continue to collect some of the state's money without even having to lose his wife for the workday. If it had been so easy to get Emma certified as unable to work the cotton fields, why not get her certified as unable to work at all? Now that she had been on salary for a while, she would qualify for state disability benefits.

But Emma would have none of it. Lonnie did not lightly take being frustrated in his scheme.

> The dr. wouldnt have said I was disable to work for I was in better health than I have ben in for a long time and I was happy with my job and the people I was with, but he got mad and left me and went to Polly + Bill and he wrote me the meanest letter. He called me every thing but a lady and I wasent doing any thing but working. I got a nasty letter from him every day. Missy and ruby got to where they would tear them up befor I got home.

Emma's children started marrying and having children of their own near the end of the 1950s. Sickly Ruby remained home, living with her mother, but had her eye on Warren, a boy she'd known as the son of a tenant farmer in Cookstown. When he came home from the Korean War and started driving a truck, they became sweethearts.

After Annie Mae's husband, George, died of cancer in 1959, Emma got her a job in the nursing home where she herself worked. The sisters helped each other through the trauma of leaving the land and starting new lives in the city. Emma believed the nursing-home jobs were the best things that ever happened to them. The jobs gave them confidence and independence, showing them they could survive on their own.

. *iii* .

While all this was happening to Emma, the years after Agee's visit to Hobe's Hill brought some improvement into the life of Bud Woods and his new family.

The Woodses stayed on the Bridges farm until the middle of World War II. As during World War I, the wartime demand for cotton increased dramatically, making it attractive to farm and putting the tenant in a better negotiating position, even with the less-than-scrupulous landlords. Woods left the Bridges land to once again tenant farm for T. Hudson Margraves, but this time on better land, at Indian Lock, where ships plying the river had to pass. He was farming with two mules. His oldest boy still at home, Thomas, who had earlier been called Buddy, was old enough now to help him, as were his daughters Pearl and Ellen—Ellen was the one who had been photographed by Walker Evans as an infant on the lap of Ivy Woods. Even Marion, born in 1937, could pitch in.

Prosperity of sorts reached down to cotton tenants, and Bud Woods changed from the hardened, Spartan figure caught by Walker Evans's camera, standing alone with his picking sack in the cotton field. A family picture taken after the war shows him relaxed, wearing a red-and-yellow Hawaiian shirt and tennis shoes, his hair slicked and tall on his head. It was hard to imagine he still stood behind mules and picked cotton by hand. Gone also were the floursack dresses worn by Pearl. She changed to store-bought clothes and stylish hats that raked over her forehead. Pearl, always precocious and large for her age even at eight, had grown to over six feet tall, with strong bones and sensual eyes that commanded the attention of boys.

Pearl had large hopes. She was exploring many possibilities in 1946 and into 1947, even writing a column for the Cookstown weekly paper. It featured small-town gossip and included many folksy items about her own family, her getting a job at the local hospital, the coming of harsh spring storms. The columns reveal something about their life down by the river.

LOCK ROAD NEWS
By Pearl Woods.

January 10, 1947:
Mr. Clint Jefferson and Thomas Woods, son of Mr. Bud Woods, and Mr. Bud's dog, Jack, ran a wild cat up a gum tree Monday afternoon and Mr. Jefferson shot it with a 22 rifle. The cat weighed about 25 pounds.
Mr. Thomas Woods and sister Ellen, visited their half sister, Mrs. Annie Mae Gudger, and family Thursday night.
Mr. Bud Woods and family killed hogs Friday.

February 7, 1947:
We sure were glad to see the river go back in its banks, for we were so nervous we could not stand our own self. There were only 13 of us in one 3 room house and only had 4 beds, but we made it okeh, no one got drowned.
Mr. Bud Woods is ill at his home and we hope him a speedy recovery.

The wind is blowing so hard it seems like a March wind.
We noticed some plum trees budding out on Indian Lock road and some in bloom, but we are afraid they will get killed.

June 5, 1947:

Little Ellen Woods is suffering from a fish bone which she stepped on Thursday night and just got it out Friday morning.

July 17, 1947:

Miss Pearl Woods celebrated her 20th birthday Monday, July 4 and received many nice presents.
Mr. and Mrs. Clayton Woods spent Saturday with his brother, Mr. and Mrs. Gallatin Woods and family of Route 1.

July 24, 1947:

The people have had so much rain until they can't get through hoeing their cotton and will be a week or more before they can plow their corn in the swamp.

August 7, 1947:

Mr. and Mrs. Bud Woods and family had an ice cream supper at their home Monday night.
We are sorry to hear of Mrs. Floyd Franks being ill at the City Hospital. Our wish is for her a speedy recovery.
Mr. Bud Woods grieving over the loss of his mule, which died Thursday night.
Miss Pearl Woods was ill at her home Monday and Tuesday.

September 26, 1947:

Miss Pearl Woods stepped on a black racer snake Thursday afternoon, but the snake did not bite her, only hit her ankle three or four times with his tail.
Little Marion Woods celebrated his tenth birthday Sunday. A fine dinner of chicken, cake, potato salad, peaches and banana pudding was served to the family.

November 20, 1947:

Miss Ellen Woods celebrated her 13th birthday Tuesday, November 11. As she was in school at dinner, she was served for her supper, chocolate cake, potato salad, pineapple sandwich, hot chocolate, banana pudding, vanilla wafers, and fried chicken. She received several presents and the present she was the proudest of was a $5 bill, which her father and mother, Mr. and Mrs. Bud Woods, gave her. She received lots of spanking, but she reports a grand time. After supper, home-made peanut candy was served.

November 27, 1947:
Mr. and Mrs. Bud Woods and family were on their way home from Cookstown Saturday when the wagon wheel broke down between Mr. Dimes and Mr. Earps, but no one got hurt. Mr. Woods got Willie's wagon to carry his groceries and new stove home.
Mr. Bud Woods is 72 years old, having lived long enough to see two great-grandchildren, a great grandson of Mr. and Mrs. Junior Gudger, the little boy came in Sept. and has been given the name of R. W. Gudger. The great-granddaughter is around two years old and belongs to Mr. and Mrs. Floyd Franks of Madrid. The little girl was named Mary Ann.

December 5, 1947:
Miss Pearl Woods, daughter of Mr. and Mrs. Bud Woods, is work-ing at the Health Department in Cookstown now and is going to work in the Centerboro Hospital as soon as there is an opening.
Mr. Bud Woods and daughter are planning a business trip to Cen-terboro Friday.

December 11, 1947:
Mr. Bud Woods lost his other mule Monday. She died sometime Sunday night, so he will have to buy him another pair before he can start another crop.
Many thanks to grandmother Miss Molly, for the pecans, candy and raisins which she sent to us Saturday.

It was the last quiet year the Woods family would have. The loss of the two mules would become the least of their concerns.

. *iv* .

Pearl didn't mention the biggest piece of gossip around Indian Lock and Cookstown in her column—that she was pregnant. On Decem-ber 31, 1947, she gave birth.

It was a boy, and they named him Bobby. There was a question about who the father was. The birth certificate filed with the county listed a blank for the father's name. In later years, she talked bitterly

of men to *New York Times* reporter Howell Raines, who came calling at her house. "I always said when I got grown, no man would
lay a hand on me without getting something back. And they haven't.
I don't believe woman was put on earth to be abused by man." Her
dislike covered many men. Of her stepfather, she said to the reporter, "That man would kill you in the blink of an eye."

About the time she had Bobby, her world fell apart in other
ways.

The trouble started in a nearby swamp and ended near the de-
pot station in Cherokee City. It was a fight, and several men were
involved. One man crawled from a car bleeding profusely, and when
he was taken to the hospital, health workers found he was castrated.
The story has become part of the folklore in this rural Alabama
county, retold again and again over the years. Some say the man lost
only one testicle. An assistant district attorney from that time said
there was no prosecution.

One day, Ellen says, she watched as the castrated man visited
their house, looking for Pearl. In one hand he had a knife and in the
other a salami, says Ellen. She heard the man say, "I want to fuck
her with the salami, and then I want to kill her."

Bud Woods turned the man away. Pearl boarded a bus, headed
south. She would never again be seen in Cookstown. She left Bobby
behind, to be raised by his grandmother, Ivy. She wound up in
southern Alabama, in the town of Jefferson, not far from Parson's
Cove and the Gaines family and others who lived there. She changed
her name to Ruth Ann and met a man whom she married in 1951.

Bud and Ivy Woods farmed on. In the middle of the cotton-
picking season of 1957, Bud stopped picking. A few days later, he
died.

Ivy felt compelled to move the rest of her family to Jefferson, to
be near her outcast daughter. Ellen had been going through her marriages. She followed her mother with her young children. Ellen was
reunited with her sister, but Pearl would fly into a rage whenever
Ellen called her Pearl. She was Ruth Ann. So Ellen took to calling
her Pearl, just to rile her.

Still, Pearl was the favorite of Ivy, and no one, not even Ellen,
could speak against her. "I'd remind my mother of it when Pearl
would be fussin'. Yes sir, my mother would get real mad at me whenever I would say somethin' to her about it."

Pearl was trying to get on with life. She would tell tales about her past, to gloss over the bad years. When Bud Woods died, Ellen says, Pearl told all her friends that her stepfather was a cotton and timber baron up in northern Alabama and that, now that he was gone, she would be coming into great wealth.

BRIDGES

In 1940, the Bridges family gave up using mules and bought a tractor. The family was still using tenant farmers, producing about one hundred bales of cotton a year.

Joe Bridges, Jr., was going through school. He made it to the eleventh grade, but had to drop out to take care of the farm as his brothers went off to fight in the Second World War. His brother Barney had terrible luck—he had three ships blown out from beneath him in the Pacific. His luck wasn't the very worst it could have been, however, for he lived through each one. He came home early, and they said he would never be the same again, though in those days they didn't have the term "posttraumatic stress syndrome."

In late 1944, Joe, Jr., was drafted, but the war ended before he was sent overseas. Life on the farm went on as normal, and the county paved the main highway in front of their farm, leading from Cherokee City to Centerboro.

In 1948, Joe, Jr., landed a job in a newly opened tire factory in Cherokee City. He worked the farm in the morning, laboring nights in the factory. He was making good money, and he fell in love. In December of 1951, he married Kate. Joe, Sr., sold his son ten acres of land on the highway, and Joe built a house for his new wife. They had four children, and it seemed early on that Huey, born in 1955, would be the one to take the farm over from Joe, Jr.

Things were good on the farm—overhead was low, and prices, while not as high as they had been during the war, were such that they provided a farmer a fair profit. Joe, Sr., kept some of their older tenants on his place through the 1950s, but phased them out as they died or quit, renting their excess land on a straight cash-for-rent basis, growing cotton on other of their land holdings, hiring labor to pick and chop on an hourly or price-per-pound-picked basis.

GAINES

After the Depression years, in the 1940s, and, to an even greater extent, in the 1950s, whites left the land to take jobs in the many factories that were appearing in the South. Wages were up more than threefold over prewar levels, creating an almost irresistible lure for those who had not had great success farming, or were simply no longer interested in putting in the endless hours and back-breaking work farming required.

Many of these new jobs were closed to blacks. One study found that 27 percent of the whites left the farm after the close of the war, compared with 9 percent of the blacks. As a consequence, cotton tenantry became a mostly black occupation. But with the perfecting of cotton-picking machines, local blacks, who had not been lured out of cotton, were soon being thrown out of it. Cotton-picking machines were entering the state, or other growers simply stopped planting cotton.

Few studies exist documenting the change, but one conducted in seventeen Arkansas counties found 482 mechanical pickers in 1952, but by the early 1960s, there were nearly 5,000. In the same period, the number of black tenant farmers dropped from almost twenty-two thousand to under seven thousand. Small farmers in Alabama seemed more reluctant to buy machines—only 2 percent of the Alabama cotton crop was harvested mechanically in 1954.

Blacks had nowhere to go but north. They flocked to Chicago, Detroit, Cleveland, and the industrial Northeast, a pattern of migration among tenant farmers very much restricted to blacks. For example, among the three white families Agee lived with, none had to leave the region to find work, and census figures show that this was not atypical among white tenant farmers in the area. There was little migration of Deep South whites to the North during the 1940s and 1950s.

There were some few pockets of resistance, however. The growers of Parson's Cove did not buy cotton machines; it seems the dirt roads, the remote hills, and the protective river that served as a natural border for the region kept the outside world at bay. As a result, amid all the social dislocation beyond the river, an uneventful two decades passed at Parson's Cove.

This time marked the peak of Mr. and Mrs. Gumbay's plantation—they employed thirty sharecropping families. Frank and Urline Gaines raised their ten children under conditions similar to the 1930s.

In 1953, Sherman Parson became one of the few blacks of Parson's Cove to leave the area and go north. He went because he lost his job on the railroad and had never worked cotton. Parson was amazed at what he saw in Washington, D.C.—many hundreds of southern black men, roaming the streets like refugees. Some told Parson that they'd been up north more than five years, but that no one would hire them. They warned him never to say he was from the South; it would be the kiss of death, and he'd never get a job. Parson was luckier then most—he landed a job after "only" two years of searching. Many of the other men he came to know ended up in hopeless despair, drained of all drive by constant rejection; they eventually made up a large part of the mass of unemployed blacks occupying northern ghettos.

As for Frank Gaines, he continued raising cotton. Because of a special ability, and a willingness, to play the white man's game,

Gaines succeeded as well as any black man could. But he couldn't do it just by farming cotton. He got a job driving a log truck between farm chores. He took hundred-foot logs down to Mobile, where they were putting in long docks. He drove the truck out on narrow, shaking piers, sometimes a mile out on the water, unloading the timbers, which would be driven as pilings for the docks, coming back through the big city to his little shack. He got home at ten at night, ate dinner, went to bed, and woke up before the sun, ready to strap himself behind a mule and do his farm work. When his farm work was finished, he'd do his truck run all over again. It was a brutally hard life, but it allowed his family to survive.

1 9 6 0 – 1 9 8 6

GUDGER

. i .

The Cookstown cemetery is south of the crossroads at the town's only traffic light, on the crest of a hill just off the main highway that leads to Joe Bridges's farm and beyond to Centerboro. Most residents, at least the white ones, have some kin buried in this ground.

Blacks of the area, even in death, remain mostly segregated, excluded if not by racial restrictions then by financial considerations. Most cannot afford reserved, parklike sites for their final resting places, and the after-care these places provide. Their tombstones will more likely be found clustered in small groups, in small forest clearings, discovered by surprise when one is looking for something else, back in the old home places. Hearses still travel muddy roads to these family plots, such as the one at the terminus of the Hobe's Hill road, several miles from the white graveyard in town, where kudzu vines and tree roots are chopped away to make space for new graves. Some of these grave sites have formal headstones—small, yes, but at least cast of concrete and properly engraved. The greater number, however, are more simply marked—with rocks, plastic signboards, names painted in black on the surface.

In contrast, there are some grand markers to be found in the Cookstown graveyard. The oldest monuments, nearest the highway and under the canopy of three large white oaks, are of eroded sandstone, honoring early settlers of the area and Civil War veterans. Far to the rear, where the sun is strong, is the new section for those who have died in the 1980s.

At a point between the oldest and newest arrivals is a granite marker in a treeless part of the cemetery. Between the chiseled image of hands brought together in prayer is this inscription:

George Gudger	Annie Mae Gudger
Sept. 11, 1904	Oct. 19, 1907
Dec. 27, 1959	Jan. 26, 1979

Sometime in the early 1970s, Annie Mae came to visit and kneel at George's grave. A plot was already reserved for her to the right of where George lay, and now she noticed they'd recently buried Mr. Dixon, their former landlord, in the site adjoining hers.

"Oh my," she said to her son, Sonny. "Look who I'm gonna be buried by. He give me hell when I was livin'." She paused, thinking of all the things that landlord had done to hurt them. "I'm gonna rest when I'm gone," she announced, taking satisfaction from the fact that she would lie down right next to him, that he could no longer decide how hard she'd have to work and what she'd get paid for it, that she and the landlord would finally be equals.

. *ii* .

To the northwest of George and Annie Mae Gudger's stone, at the corner of the graveyard nearest to town, you find a steep and thickly wooded ravine. The heads of the gums and water oaks jump with the promise of a summer storm still far away, somewhere over in the piney woods country of Mississippi. The advancing thunderheads deliver a cold wind into the face of the summer day, the sudden force of it liberating a scatter of leaves yet green, dead before their time, falling slowly to the bare earth at the foot of a granite marker bearing this inscription:

FRANKS

Floyd	Maggie Louise
Jan. 19, 1916	Feb. 2, 1926
June 30, 1958	Feb. 21, 1971

The stone is near the edge of the hill, close to a wire fence climbed over with wild honeysuckle, star-speckled with flowers. Beyond, the wooded slope is littered with discarded domestic flowers that had once been brought into the cemetery to grace other stones. At various levels down the hill—depending on the strength of the person who had pitched them—are dead roses amid the blackness of the trunks, petals still red and white and yellow, and it all makes a path of color down to the thin line of the creek that flows into the big river and on to the ocean.

The storm works its way north, over Cherokee City, leaving the trees heavy, numb, the dry land cheated of its promised water.

To the right of the headstone, next to the side with Maggie Louise's name, are several fragments of a broken red brick. They abut the marker, acting as a weight concealing some dusty object. It is a piece of paper, yellowed from several months or more of weather. The brittle pages unfold to reveal a street map of Orlando, Florida. Two roads are underlined. One is Alabama Avenue.

. *iii* .

In 1986, the public housing projects on the south side of Cherokee City resemble military barracks. The forty-seven red brick buildings, now occupied mostly by blacks, are lined up in precise rows, sterile and worn, making that statement of defeat that taints so many attempts by the government to house the poor.

In 1960, when these projects were much younger and had not yet trampled the many souls they would in time crush, they looked grand to white cotton refugees who had never lived in anything more substantial than sharecropper shacks. There must have been quite an army of these sharecroppers passing through these projects: by 1964, so many tenant farmers would have left the land that the

Census Bureau would decide that it was no longer worth counting them.

Maggie Louise and her children, fresh from the pain of Floyd's death, would live in this project for five years, until moving to the duplex with Squinchy. It was the first time any of them had lived in a city, crowded in tightly with other people. No longer could the children run through the fields and collect flowers for their mother, lose themselves among the cotton rows, the apple orchards, the secrets of the barn. There was nowhere to be alone. It was not silent at night. There were new sounds, new people, new things to do, new ideas about what one ought to do and what not. The children could not really measure the many ways they were changing, or understand why. Many years later, they'd look back and realize that this world was vastly different from the world that had made them what they were, that they were quite unlike the city children whose style they tried hard to imitate. They did not know the term "culture shock" back then. Even if they had, they wouldn't have known precisely what it had to do with them.

Parvin, the youngest, was seven in 1960. The eldest, Mary Ann, was nearly fifteen.

It's hard to say how long it took before Maggie Louise felt she was losing control of the children. Those things happen on a scale that defies measure. She was gone many hours at work in a roadside café. She tried hard to earn the money they needed to survive, to be a good mother, to be there for them. Maggie Louise could not afford baby-sitters on her thirty-five dollars a week. When she dated, one of her brothers who lived nearby called her a whore. She went on in solitude. She received no welfare cash benefits, sometimes getting charity food, often not. As her family came apart, she became bitter but full of self-determination.

> Debbie: *It is 1965. I am in love. He is a special man. My baby will soon be born. Mother married when she was fifteen. I am fifteen. I am a woman. I quit school in eighth grade. When I was thirteen, mother told me I should not shave my legs, wear makeup, but I did. She got angry. I got so I put lipstick on after I left the house. She made Parvin go with me on my dates. Why is mother so old-fashioned?*

> Parvin: *It is 1968. There is a whole world out there. I want it. I want to make my own money. We never have any money. We never had anything. Why were my parents living that way back on the*

*farm? I want to get away from this place. I hate Alabama. I have
been robbed. My parents were robbed. I want to go to Florida. I
am fifteen. I look older. I feel older. Look at my eyes. They are of
an older woman. Everyone believes I am older.*

Sonny: *It is 1969. I am in a work-study program. This summer, I
will graduate from high school. I will be the first in my family. I
have a wife and child. I met her in tenth grade. Before then, I catted
around, ever since the urge came to me. I learned blond hair, blue
eyes, an innocent look works with women. I had many girls. I
stayed out to all hours. Mother never cared. I could not get pregnant. Mother worried about my sisters. I was the boy, the man of
the house. I will be a house painter.*

Maggie Louise's brothers and sisters: *The kids, they are so wild.
They are turning on their mother. She works so hard. They don't
seem to care. They go places and vanish. Why do they do this?*

Mary Ann was the first to leave. She married on March 28,
1962.

Debbie gave birth to Andy in 1965 and ran off with the father
to live in St. Louis. Maggie Louise raised Andy for several years.

Parvin married and went to Miami. She lied about her age and
at fifteen became a waitress. Later, she moved to Orlando, where
she worked at a K-Mart store.

Sonny stayed around with his new wife and son, working as an
apprentice painter, eager to become a full tradesman.

. *iv* .

Maggie Louise felt alone. It was 1969. She was forty-three. She had
never forgotten her Floyd. Floyd Franks was on her mind every day.
Could it have been eleven years since he died?

> *What could I have done different? How could it be that I failed my
> children? My mother comes to visit me. I sit and refuse to talk with
> her. She talks with me. I don't look at her. When she rises to leave,
> I cry and make her stay longer.*

The late 1960s found Maggie Louise drinking; the bottle now
filled the hours of her life. Neighbors reported seeing her coming
home covered in mud after binges. She started hanging around with
a man named Geeson and told people they were married. Her sister

Gretchen doubts they ever formalized the relationship, and no local marriage records exist, though they could have wed elsewhere. It was a long way from a real marriage. What a far cry he must have been from the dedicated, loving Floyd.

Maggie Louise alternated between living in the Cherokee City duplex and living with her sister Gretchen and their mother, Annie Mae. She often would not talk. Gretchen recalls that she pulled knives on her and struck her mother. The first time she tried to kill herself, she cut her wrists, says Sonny, her brother. The second time, she tried to swallow dry rat poison. They got to her before she drank the water to activate it. She survived again.

They tried to get help for her, but Maggie Louise could not, or would not, be healed. Not by any means any of them knew or understood. Nor apparently by any means known to the doctors who examined her. The family put her in an institution, and when she was discharged she seemed better.

After she came out of the institution, Maggie Louise was as "innocent as a puppy," says Gretchen. They felt better about her. Maybe the worst was over.

"I remember the last Christmas with her," says Gretchen.

> We was decorating the Christmas tree. And there was a little round ball, inside the ball was an angel, and she picked that ball up and said, "Well, this is me." And she hung it on my tree. She stood there so bright. And for years, I kept that ball and at Christmas I hung it in front. But one of the kids broke the ball and the angel in it.

Then came that February day in 1971.
"We was milkin' the dairy cows," says Gretchen.

> Mamma called me from my house. She called me, she says, "Come quickly." So I run and when I got to the door, Mamma was just standin' there screamin' and telling me, "Gretch—do somethin'." Well, I looked into the bedroom, and she was standin' in the middle of the floor and she had the bottle—rat poison. I run to her, and I knocked it out of her hand. And she shoved me backwards, and she had the rage in her that hurt me. Well, I kind of manhandled her and got her on the couch. And we tried to put saltwater in her mouth to make it vomit back up. I told Mamma, "Get me a spoon." I tried to get that spoon between her teeth. I

couldn't budge her teeth. She died that night about twelve o'clock.
She just tore apart.

When their attempts to get her to vomit up the rat poison
failed, they rushed her to a hospital, but the doctors could not save
her. These are the notes Gretchen found in her purse after they got
her to the hospital:

> Maggie Louise Franks
> at my Death I want Mary Ann to
> have my lot at Canton, Ala.
> at my Death my dis-ality lup
> —sum I want each child of mine
> to have $100.00 dollars each
> the other part of it in a
> hospitle insurance on Andy Jr. and
> All the other thats left put
> presants for nurces aid maids
> just ——— like roped just alike
> > (over)
> 2. Doctor cards just alike fix
> just alik the one that gave me
> my x ray a card. a card
> something real funny
> Maggie Louise Franks Geeson
> at my Death the car of mine goes to
> Debbie
> The support from Andy Jr.
>
> ——— ——— ———
>
> In case of Death Andy Jr. goes to Burt
> Westly Gudger, works at ——— ——— Southern
> Mills Cherokee City, Ala.
>
> But until my death Debbie get the support
> for Andy
>
> *(A page of squiggles.)*

How had that special, vibrant ten-year-old child of James
Agee's pages and Walker Evans's photographs come to such an end?
Maggie Louise's life seems to recite clearly the old lesson that a life
not lived to its full potential, or close to it, will be destroyed by
bitterness. Why didn't Annie Mae and George make sure that she

went to school? If it couldn't be done by a family farming cotton on shares, why didn't they just leave?

It's easy to look back half a century later and see all the things that could have been done.

Not long after the suicide, Annie Mae told Scott Osborne, a writer for the *Tennessean* magazine,

> Every year, them Margraves'd strip us out of everything. Now, we wasn't treated as dirty as the colored people, but it was somewhere in the neighborhood of that. They didn't sell us. But they would've tried to sell us if they thought they could've got away with it. How can I begin to tell you what we was athinkin? We just didn't know no better. All we knowed was, we was barely livin. You know, I don't see where I could've helped out to make things any better. I think I done the best I knowed how.

Cotton killed Maggie Louise, Gretchen believes. It started with the institutionalized cruelty with which the tenants were treated. It was drilled into her, and by the end "she didn't care which way she went," says Gretchen.

Maggie Louise always wanted more, says her son, Sonny. If she had only gotten one break along the way, instead of always being cheated, always being denied, always put down. Everything always seemed to go against her.

James Agee, the urbane writer, poet, man-about-town, and Hollywood celebrity, and Maggie Louise Gudger, Alabama cotton picker, lived strangely similar lives. They were both dreamers and, deep down, tragic people who yearned for something they could not define even as they came to know finally that it had irretrievably escaped them. They died, though far apart in years and miles, at the same age—at forty-five—as if defining a limit for the number of years of failed dreams a dreamer can be asked to endure. Neither could journey any further, and so they ended their lives, though Agee chose an indirect route to self-destruction, defying doctors who repeatedly told him to stop his drinking and smoking, and Maggie Louise took a direct path to where she chose to be.

Of course, the conflicts that defined the lives of each, the events that chronicled the lives of each, were very different. Maggie Louise's antagonists were real and exogenous; Agee's were for the most part within his head, conjured up by his troubled and fertile mind.

Agee commented, after raving about Maggie Louise's abilities, that bright as she was, serious and dutiful as she was, she already showed signs of a "special sort of complacency" that would eventually "destroy all in her nature that is magical, indefinable and matchless." He hoped it would not. But he knew the cotton system and the things such relentless oppression did to the human spirit.

Before her death, say her relatives, Maggie Louise saw the Agee and Evans book, the copy owned by her mother. It is unclear how she reacted to reading Agee's prophecy of success for her in adulthood. It is certainly reasonable that it may have provided for her a cruel reminder of the dreams she had once dreamed, at the very time when she realized that they would never come to be. But she never gave up her affection for Agee, say her aunt and son. She didn't seem outwardly upset over the book.

In a passage Agee seems to have written to apologize in advance to her, he said, "Good God, if I have caused you any harm in this, if I have started within you any harmful change, if I have so much as reached out to touch you in any way you should not be touched, forgive me if you can, despise me if you must. . . ." But she didn't seem to blame him, or anyone else.

There were the landlords, but, though they took much from people like the Gudgers and gave little in return, there are many who will remind you that they themselves were trapped in the system. Indeed, as the world turned against them, the landlords ascribed many of their problems to their tenants. "Both are teamed together under a yoke of debt," observed a writer for the federal Work Projects Administration in 1941. "Each lays the blame on the other, whereas the fault probably lies more with the system than with either."

An uneducated person who is simultaneously kept poorly nourished and physically exhausted, forever at the brink of personal and financial disaster, does not think in any logical manner. If people are repeatedly told they deserve their fate, they'll begin to believe it. And why not? They have no frame of reference, no knowledge of the commonality of their lot with many of those around them, and even their place among many of the oppressed people throughout history, no understanding that the mind games played on them create and nourish their feeling of guilt, turning it into an agent of the oppressor.

Gretchen believes that it was the cotton system that killed Maggie Louise, but that it would be difficult to point to specific culprits, that there is no one country teacher who failed her, no one landlord, one boss to hold responsible. And it may be so. The course her life ran was in the end the vector created by a balancing out of all the forces having acted upon her. If so, when Maggie Louise saw that she would never be able to control the direction of her life, she chose to escape from a world that had long and successfully conspired against her. Agee's personal guilt was very likely no more than a conceit. Much as there surely were demons he had tempted to life in her, or at least nourished, and fond as her memories of him remained to the end, he was no more than a moment in the long continuum of her life.

If we look for the perpetrator of the crime among those who stood to benefit most from it, we will find that it was bankers and merchants who really made the money. One-fourth of the expenses of a typical planter went to pay the interest. Even then, the WPA writer said, it was obvious the tenant system was doomed. Both landlord and tenant were simply playing their assigned roles, as had their fathers before them. Mrs. Burgandy, Maggie Louise and Floyd's landlady, surely did not see herself as an evil person. She would have told you she treated her people kindly. And relatively speaking, within what she knew, she did.

What would have happened if Maggie Louise could have attended a decent school, become the teacher or nurse she had once dreamed of becoming, if there had been real child-labor laws so that cotton could not have robbed her of her childhood and kept her from the classroom all those days?

Of course, fate is never an equal-opportunity oppressor, and some do find a small measure of success in situations where others can find only failure. All those factors having to do with cotton aside, Gretchen believes that if Maggie Louise had simply remained married to Jones, rather than dumping him while he was off to war, she would still be alive and probably happy. Jones is married with seven children and has a wife with whom he attends week-long religious camps. He escaped cotton. It isn't that he became rich—he has a modest home in a modest town—but that he probably would have pulled Maggie Louise away from cotton with him. What does Jones think about this? He shrugs his shoulders and says, "She had a lot of ideas. None that turned out." It is said in Cookstown that he is still madly in love with her, but he would not exhibit any emotion at all when asked about her. He barely acknowledged that he remembered her when first shown a picture of her in *Let Us Now Praise Famous Men*, though he can remember the brand of schnapps he drank in just-liberated Paris. It apparently remains a painful subject for him.

It must be remembered Maggie Louise was not from a family like the Rickettses. It can be said—maybe at the risk of cutting things too fine—that Gudger poverty is different from Ricketts poverty. Ricketts poverty is sometimes tragic, though more often simply pathetic. Gudger poverty is often tragic because of the element of crushed potential so often present.

From the weeks Agee was there to the time she divorced Abraham Jones and went to the arms and bed of Floyd Franks and to her later years when she despaired over the course her children's lives had taken, there was one thing, Gretchen says, that was always certain, one thing that always drove Maggie Louise: "She was just looking for love. Searching for love."

. *v* .

Defeat.

It is written across the face of the once great land, in all the brittle shells of towns that once were, in all those little-town eyes that wait (but for what?), and in the cemeteries, the abandoned sharecropper fields, the vine-covered shack on the Burgandy land where Maggie Louise and her children last grew cotton. That home still stands, valiant and silver against thirty empty seasons of frost and sun, containing fragments—the last straw sun hat she ever wore out in the cotton, a pair of high heels—all rotting, rat-chewed, faded. It is going the way of the gin down the road, abandoned in 1977, finally, to rust, pigeons, vandals.

It is no surprise some of these people react negatively to the outside world, that Junior Gudger sat on his porch in 1969, even before his sister committed her ultimate act of rebellion, and vented his fury. He was holding a copy of *Let Us Now Praise Famous Men*, the first he had ever seen, it is said. He fumed that it made them look like slaves.

The Gudger family had at last learned about the book. It was a long process to that discovery. They might never have known about it had Agee not posthumously won a Pulitzer Prize for his novel, *A*

Death in the Family, published in 1957, two years after his fatal heart attack. The award created an interest in his earlier, "lost" works. First to emerge was a collection of his film reviews. They were well received, and in 1960 *Let Us Now Praise Famous Men* was reissued. It caught on and was instantly popular. It became required reading in many college courses, and sold tens of thousands of copies.

Word slowly drifted back to Alabama that some of their own had made up the cast of characters in a famous book. It was with some shock that many of them first viewed its pages. Mostly, they were upset with the photographs, which had a startling impact. But the text was brutal in its portrayal of some of them.

Junior was described as "jealous and lazy, malingering" by Agee, and so has special reason for anger. His anger has only heightened with the passage of years.

In the late summer of 1985, we made a telephone call to his home. He was not in. His wife said it would be okay to come talk about the book. At that time—those were still naive days—we did not know how he felt, for he was going to be only the second person we interviewed for this project.

Later that afternoon, Junior was out on the road, waiting. He had a cracked and whiskered face, sun-formed triangular eyes, hardened after fifty-eight Alabama summers. He is the only one in the Gudger family left farming, working for pay for a man who raises soybeans. He so resembles his father that when a copy of *Let Us Now Praise Famous Men* was shown to townsmen, they would swear the Evans picture of George, Sr., taken in 1936 was a recent one of Junior.

As our car rolled to a stop, he spit out his lack of interest in being exploited again, as he thought had happened in the Agee episode, for the profit of others. He started the conversation, and seemed prepared to end it, by saying, "Everyone gits rich offn us. I ain't talking."

He stood there, fists clenched. He mumbled some words about how they wanted to be left alone, unless they were paid some real big money. He could not understand, even when told, that when people do a newspaper story, they work for a salary, just as he does, or that when they do a book such as Agee's, or for that matter such as this one, they most likely will not earn back what they spent to do it. He may not have known that Agee died before he had earned a nickel from the book, apart from the small advance he received prior to its first publication. His bank account had $450 in it when he suffered his heart attack; Evans had to borrow money in one of the last years of his life to throw a birthday party for himself. In Junior's view, any words he might utter had to be worth many thousands of dollars, or else how could people afford to fly across the country and rent a car on credit just to talk to him? He seemed to believe that there were fortunes to be made.

That, too, was something newspaper people understand but would have been virtually impossible to explain to Junior. It would have been absurd, really, even to try. Agee could not have paid these people, even if he'd wanted to and even if he'd had the money to do so, which he didn't. It would have corrupted the process. People who are paid to stand before a camera, or to speak, are called actors. It is not journalism when people perform for pay, because actors, like others who get paid for their activities, will inevitably try— with their posture and with their words, their inflection, the meaning they put into things—to please those who pay them. Agee did give the Gudgers some money for room and board, which was fair, for he did stay with them and eat their food, and he did send them small presents for four years after he had left them, including a check with which they could buy other things. But he did not pay them for what they told him, and Evans did not pay them to pose. Such distinctions, real as they are to newspaper people, would have sounded too convenient, no matter how carefully put. And naturally so.

Years later, Annie Mae Gudger, who did not harbor the bitterness her son did, told Ross Spears, a filmmaker who documented Agee's life,

> I don't care what they done with their books and things; if they got rich off it, it was all right with me. It was the truth. But now, my oldest boy, he just don't go for it. They even talked about suing them when that book first came out, some of the kids did. And that's when I told them . . . I wouldn't want to hurt 'em if I could, because they was so good to me.

Junior had obviously not changed his mind in the seven years since his mother spoke those words. His wife was there, a kind-voiced woman, sitting by a roadside stand where she tried to sell some used dresses to supplement their income. She tried not to look at her husband and the men he was talking with.

Some fifty years earlier, journalists came and paraded his family's poverty for all the world to see. It's now in a famous book. The Gudgers got nothing out of it in real terms. Even if Agee never saw any real money out of the project, he did receive other rewards— professional, for sure, in terms of prestige and respect for having written the book. The Gudgers were put down by the book, this theory would go, but received nothing of substance in exchange for the use of their private lives. Why didn't anything ever come Junior's way? If it was up to the Gudgers themselves to demand a bigger share of the pie, rather than wait appreciatively for whatever was thrown to them, then they'd start right now.

On the other hand, he could have used our appearance, if he had wanted to, to correct some bad impressions created by the original book, to make the point that some of the Gudgers, at least his family, were certainly doing better than they had in the Depression. It was hard to say what Junior's income was from working for the soybean farmer, but in 1978 he had told a writer for *Southern Exposure* that he was earning $125 for a fifty-hour week working five hundred acres of ground. He had finally come to own some land, a patch far too small, however, to farm. It's a reasonable guess that his income had gone up in the interval in proportion to the changes in incomes of others through the same period, which would still place his family in a very low income bracket, by national standards. Yes, it is true he is out of abject poverty, and that is a great improvement. But in this materialistic age, it is all relative. It was not that Junior and his wife were dressed in rags; their clothes were old, yes, but nice and certainly still serviceable. The family also had cars to drive, owned a five-room house on half a dozen or so acres. The house was adequate in size, and Junior's family certainly had a television set and probably the normal American complement of gadgets.

Yet many of the Gudgers are poor by modern standards, and, worse, they know it.

Tolstoy wrote that he often envied peasants for their illiteracy and lack of education. The closer he came to peasants in his later life, the more he said he came to know truth. In many ways, Agee derived the same benefit from his Alabama experience—he found a vision of religion and life through examining the simple lives of the three families. Of course, it should be said that both Agee and Tolstoy would have had far different attitudes had they been prisoners of poverty rather than simply visitors to it. At any rate, the poverty seen in Czarist Russia by Tolstoy and in Alabama by Agee was different from the poverty under which many contemporary Alabamians now find themselves.

The kind of poverty Agee reported in 1936 exists in America today only among the urban homeless, who make up their own category. It does exist outside our national boundaries—nearby in certain places of Latin America and, commonly, in many other places farther away.

There is a village we once visited that comes to mind, located in the heart of guerrilla territory on the island of Mindanao, in the Philippines. It is a day's walk from the nearest road, across a whitewater river and through a thick and roadless jungle. The people there live in thatch huts, eat meager rations almost exclusively of rice, and use oil lamps for lighting. They have nothing. But they are a wonderful and seemingly happy people.

While they do not have color television sets, as do some of their low-income American counterparts, they are not in all ways more deprived. All they know is poverty. Everyone they know is poor. Millions of others are in the same predicament. They have nothing else to compare themselves with. There is no ever-present standard of acquisition against which to measure their status. It is a natural state and therefore one to which no stigma is attached. It can easily be argued that Third World poverty has a harder edge to it than anything found in the United States, and this is surely true. Yet it is also true that in America the word "poverty" labels losers, that to be poor and to accept your poverty is to exhibit not stoicism but a sense of defeat.

The poor of 1980s Alabama know that they have failed in the American game of life. They're reminded of it every time they watch television. Junior Gudger, as he lives today, would have been rich in 1936. The material things he has provided for his family by his own work would have been impressive in 1936. Today, they are nothing to brag about. He climbed heights his parents could never have dreamed for him, but the rest of the country around him moved up at about the same rate, leaving him still near the bottom. Later, in 1988, he could go to the store and pick up a copy of *Life* magazine, a special historical retrospective on photography, and see a picture of his mother, with the title "Best Buy" over her head. Annie Mae Gudger's tight, worn face was backed up against their sharecropper shack, frozen in the microsecond it took the shutter of Evans's camera to click that sweaty afternoon fifty-some years ago. Now she was sandwiched between a smiling picture of the actress Farrah Fawcett, showing plenty of breast and leg, and a nude Edward Steichen entitled *La Cigale* that sold for $82,500.

What *could* he say? If everyone wanted to know about his family, what's the harm if a little money were to stick to him?

Junior's eyes remained on the rented car as it drove away, not quite fast enough, and his face, framed in the rear-window mirror, became smaller. It remained tense, his fists at his sides, on his hips, little balls of white against the tired blue of his overalls.

. vi .

The children of Maggie Louise had the greatest cause to be bitter. If anyone among the Gudgers had a chance to make it, it was Maggie Louise. Now that she had failed, what could be expected of them?

We had reservations—in going after them to hear what they had to say, we might be doing something dangerous: perhaps merely to find them would be a violation. They were living anonymous lives. To uncover people who had run from their identities could not easily be defended as an act of innocence. It could be seen as a callous reopening of a very painful sore. It might not be without consequence.

Could it be that Maggie Louise's children, like many of the young in rural Alabama, were still living within the mind-set of defeat impressed upon them by the cult of the cotton system? Men like the old landlord Margraves aren't around any longer, but might the curse live on in the attitudes men like him helped establish?

But Debbie, her brother, and one sister were quite unlike their sour Uncle Junior. In fact, they were introspective, and used our many visits to seek answers to fill in their own blank spaces, as well as to provide answers for the questions we had. It was as if they had been expecting someone to come knock on their doors.

. vii .

Cherokee City is thirty miles and a lifetime north of the Burgandy plantation in Madrid Junction. This community has grown considerably from those 1936 days; it is now a real city, with all the attractions that would draw one to live in a city.

This is where Debbie lives.

She left, for a while, but came back from St. Louis after divorcing her husband. She has since remarried, and this has been her home.

Occasionally, she will drive south out of Cherokee City. And so it is today. She heads down a modern four-lane freeway, leading to Cookstown. South of the town crossroads, the highway is two-lane, mostly unchanged from the time of her youth.

Debbie arrives in Cookstown and has a green light through the intersection. She turns into the cemetery to walk among the stones.

Parvin has her mother's eyes, as does her brother, Sonny, and her sister Mary Ann. Debbie's four boys also have the eyes of Maggie Louise, but Debbie does not. Hers are round, bright, swimming beneath a blond curl of hair.

She is familiar with the cemetery path. A winter has passed since the discovery last year of the map of Orlando, and it has crumbled, leaving only the broken brick paperweights. Debbie cannot understand why Parvin placed the road map and other icons on Maggie Louise's grave. She does understand, in an obscure way, but the meaning troubles her. A chickadee sounds a call. The hum of working bees comes from the honeysuckle.

Debbie stands at the foot of the stone of her parents, the whiteness of her lace blouse reflecting the sun. This cemetery is as far south as she has come on this road in many years. She has never before gone back to the old place down in Madrid Junction where she and her mother and father and brothers and sisters farmed cotton together. The cemetery has been an imaginary line past which she has forbidden herself to travel.

The line is crossed. She is back in the car, air-conditioning set on high, going a clean sixty-five, and she passes the Bridgeses' farmhouse and the dirt turnoff to the top of Hobe's Hill, into the territory of her past. Her hands are tight on the wheel, and she is quiet. She comes to Wobbly Hill, the slope that gave her mother so much trouble in that old Plymouth of Mrs. Burgandy's. Her car never slows, and the grade now seems not at all steep.

After the top of the hill, her eyes scan the woods and fields on either side of the road. She sees not what there is before her at the moment but a land as it was frozen in the mind of an eight-year-old girl.

There is the turnoff for the worn dirt road leading to the Burgandy mansion—a slow mile bounces past, dust filling the road behind the car. Now everything is lost to her recollection. The Burgandy house burned a few years ago. The land has been overgrown with kudzu. Only a few gnarled remnants remain of Mrs. Burgandy's apple trees, the orchard from which she once used to sneak fruit. Little is left to tell her this was where she was born. It all seemed so big and powerful in those days.

"I can remember the fun times," she says. "A lot of it I have blocked out of my mind, because some of it was so terrible."

One field is left, the one her father used to plow in cotton, the one she ran through when she and her brother, Sonny, were attempting their escape. Dust rises from the middle. It is now being plowed for soybeans by the farmer Joe Bridges, who has taken over the land.

It is not hard to imagine Debbie as a little girl standing out in that field two and a half decades ago, amid the cotton. Maggie Louise would be standing nearby.

Maggie Louise would be proud now, looking at Debbie parked at the edge of the field, in a new air-conditioned car, dressed in white lace. She certainly hadn't wanted Debbie and Debbie's children to pick cotton. Some poverty can be beaten. Could she have imagined how far her daughter would come in the twenty-seven years after leaving this place?

There was a bleakness after her mother committed suicide, and Debbie compensated by concentrating on her children. They came in succession, four of them, the last born in 1975, four years after her mother's death. She divorced the U.S. marine, later marrying Ron, who is a painting contractor. Two of her children are young enough to remain home. They live in a modern apartment complex in Cherokee City. Debbie recently quit a job she had held for a long time. She started in a fast-food restaurant, at the bottom, flipping hamburgers, working her way up to being a manager and then to training other managers.

By any definition, Debbie attained a middle-class life, and nothing would differentiate her from others who make up what has been called Middle America.

The past remained, however, lurking. She decided early on to deal with it by covering it up with fun times. She has adopted a philosophy of enjoying life, going about it with purpose, aggressively seeking good times. She enjoys water-skiing and going to country-music bars. When she feels depressed, she tries to find things to laugh about.

Debbie lives life intent on not missing any part of it. She goes about living as if tomorrow might be her last day, not with reckless abandon but aware that every action and word counts, that no moment should be wasted, for she craves to feel, touch, and experience it all.

Now that most of her children are older, she has come to face herself again, and for the first time she wants to deal with the past. Looking for something to laugh about is no longer enough. Maybe this process started two years ago, when she became a grandmother, after Andy Lee, her eldest, and his wife had their first child.

Debbie has journeyed far enough away from those days when there seemed to be no answers and no hope. As recently as a few years ago, she was still dealing with survival. Now, she can wonder, *Where did I come from? Who am I? What should I do with my life?*

Debbie was robbed of her education by circumstances, just as her mother had been.

> Don't you think the people up North get a better chance at education than people in the South? I always say I wish I'd been born someplace other than Alabama. That may be it. I don't know. Schools here are terrible. We're so far behind. I wish we had chances like a lot of people. Because considering the way we were brought up, we've done fairly good for ourselves. I would like to have gone to school. I feel too old now to do anything. I don't want to spend the rest of my life in a fast-food joint, slinging chicken, even if I am the manager.

She asks, "Do you think I could go back to school?" She explores the idea. It sounds ridiculous to her, a grandmother, trying to go back. I tell her it is never too late. Nothing is stopping her. Opportunity is there.

True, she says, but it seems so improbable.

She blushes.

Debbie is different from many of her cousins. She has drive, a yearning to understand more, to be more. Many are content to live a little behind. Debbie inherited her ambitions from her mother.

"Mama always made sure we kept up," she says. "But some of them didn't. Some haven't changed in fifty years. Did you run into people down here who still live like that, have no teeth?"

Among these people, there are two classes: those with rotten teeth, with no sign of ever having had any professional dental care, and those whose teeth are perfect.

Debbie is a member of the latter class. She believes that the rotten-teeth people use their mouths as a badge to prove they have not joined the outside world. They tend to stick together, she says. She works hard to tone down any hint of backwoods drawl, while some of the rotten-teeth people have accents that set them apart even from other southerners. When Debbie once talked about her father's wearing overalls, she said the word as it is written. Her cousins still say *overhauls,* a common pronunciation Agee noted among the rural cotton farmers. The old-time rural Alabama voice has a cadence exact and reassuring in tone. People still speak that way in the rural places, but among the young ones like Debbie it is muted. They have more generic southern speech patterns, like those of Atlanta people.

> There's still some of them dirty. All of them could be attractive looking, if they took better care of themselves. But they don't. They're just stuck back in country living.
>
> You can tell they're self-conscious. They won't associate with us, with me, Parvin, and Sonny. It's because we look a little different, we act a little different. We don't still talk country like they do. Some think we think we're better than them. But we're not. I still feel the same way inside. I just tried to better my appearance. I'll go down to Judith's, like the wedding when I stopped off at her house, and I was in heels and a dress. I went in and her kids just walked around looking at me strange, checking me out. They thought I was rich. I'm not rich. Just different. I don't want to sound like I don't like them. We got out and explored the world, and they never left Cookstown. They seem defensive. If they moved this way, they'd be better off. They're set in their ways. They don't want to change.

Two days after she went to the cemetery and the Burgandy land and said these things, Debbie decided to obtain her high school equivalency degree. Then she enrolled in a two-year business school, the first among the forty-seven grandchildren and great-grandchildren of George and Annie Mae Gudger to attend any school of higher learning. Of all her grown relatives on her mother's side, only one uncle attended any college. She made her decision on the basis of the conversation that day and after reading a copy of *Let Us Now Praise Famous Men* that she was given. She said Agee's words, coupled with talking to someone about them, had inspired her. She was getting B's and C's, with most of her trouble in English. But the letters she wrote were grammatically fine.

She eventually graduated and for a time became the office manager for a group of doctors. It took fifty years and a delay of a generation, but the dreams a ten-year-old shared with a poet from the North are coming to something.

As for Debbie's children, Roland, the youngest, is uncertain of his course after high school. Westly, in high school, is also not sure of college, but is leaning that way. Debbie's other two boys have good jobs but, for a variety of reasons, never went beyond high school. It was hard on them. For much of the time that the two older ones were growing up, Debbie was struggling simply to exist, and this may have limited their chances. But they will do well. All of Debbie's children have native intelligence and a gift for dealing with people, though the most hope lies with Roland, for he is watching his mother go back to school and is learning from what she has done. Also, her life is now more stable than it has ever been. Debbie wants Roland to have opportunities. He says college now, but he is yet young. She fears he'll change his mind a dozen times. There are still many distractions. But it seems he's listening to her. Someone will be able to look back at these boys and report they and their children have done things.

. *viii* .

And so there is a chance for greater accomplishment among some of the children.

Among other third-generation children of the three families, there is a great mix of abilities. Most have the rudiments of education. None seem illiterate. If they are, they have hidden it well. Many write with pain, misspell, and butcher grammar. To more than a few, school was a chore to be escaped as soon as possible.

In the cotton years, for the tenants, literacy was not wide-spread. Among the adults in the families in 1936, according to Agee, Sadie Ricketts could not read or write; Fred Ricketts could, some, and was smug about it; George Gudger never made it past the second grade, could write his name, and no more; Annie Mae was adept at language and perhaps the best among them. Bud and Ivy Woods could both read and write, though it's unclear how well. The landlords did not want their workers educated, for they might lose them to better jobs in the city.

Emma Woods wanted desperately to learn. When her mother died, she had to quit school at thirteen. In other cases, education was rejected, as with Margaret Ricketts. That most in the third generation are functionally literate is a vast improvement.

Or is it really so vast an improvement? One who thinks it is not is a young teacher from Cherokee City who instructs a first-year college course for many of the youths who come from the high schools of Cookstown, Centerboro, and other nearby rural towns. She says she can tell where her students are from simply by looking at the first papers they turn in. She has never failed in her assumption, she says, for the ones from these former cotton towns invariably do poorly. Many drop out or fail. She says the kids can't help it—many of their parents can't read, or don't care, and there is thus little home support for education. The schools they came out of are inferior, a holdover from the cotton days. So the kids grow up deprived—of knowledge, of motivation, of a culture that places education in a prominent place. The parents are happy if the children can write a little, do some arithmetic. They enter college at the level of seventh-graders, if they're lucky, she says. Ignorance seems to be honored. Kids of this area look to go into the coal mines or other basic labor jobs. The goal, she says, seems to be to latch on to any kind of job so that they will not have to leave the region. The teacher, from Florida, is terribly frustrated. She clenches her fists when talking about this.

The larger issue here is that the cotton society and the culture it bred have left a legacy of an inferior educational system. At this time, Alabama has the lowest property taxes of any state in the nation. There was a recent increase that raised howls from large landowners, but the rates are still low. Property taxes could be elevated by one-third, and Alabama would remain at the bottom in the nation. Low property taxes translate into meager allocations for schools. The state is just beginning to recognize what this means. An editorial in the Montgomery newspaper told about a man from the state economic-development department who went to Cleveland to talk with a large industrial firm about relocating in Alabama. The official trotted out the glories of cheap labor and low taxes, lures that worked well in the not-so-distant past. The industrialists told the Alabamian that what they now looked at most in areas they might move to was the educational system. In today's world, they need educated workers, not muscles. The old days are gone. If they just want low-cost labor, they can go to places overseas that even Alabama can't compete with. Company officials expressed disbelief at Alabama's taxes—they even snickered. They asked how the schools could be funded with such ridiculous rates.

Even if taxes were doubled, there would still be the problem of a system in the rural areas that is set in its ways. How can there be an escape when ignorance is so institutionalized? The third-, fourth-, and fifth-generation children of tenant farmers have little chance of changing their fate as long as they remain in those rotting onetime cotton towns. Only those whose parents have escaped, such as Roland, have a chance.

. *ix* .

It would be wrong to stop and say Debbie has reached success through a good job, for that measure would ignore the deepest part of her life, her children. Her richness is her family and the love its members have for each other.

One warm spring night, in the middle of her schooling, Debbie decides to have a cookout. The barbecue is scheduled for the eve of Mother's Day, and her four boys are going to be there in her apartment, which is typical of the 1980s, with a microwave, a video recorder, tasteful furniture. It is neatly arranged and freshly cleaned for this occasion.

First to arrive is Andy Lee, Debbie's eldest and the one raised for a few years by Annie Mae and Maggie Louise. He is twenty-three. His wife is quietly beautiful, and their son, just barely able to walk, is inquisitive. Wayne, twenty-one, is single and loudly proclaims he will never marry. He is curious about all the places you can travel in this world and asks a lot about them. Westly, the one in high school, is here with his wife-to-be. He is very bright and gets straight A's in school, but is not sure about college. It may be the military instead for him. Roland, twelve, is talking of baseball. He is perhaps the brightest, but his report card shows B's and C's, not reflective of his ability. He could get A's if he put in more effort—he knows his material—but does not want to. He is outgoing, taking the offensive with visitors, sitting in on adult conversations and holding his own. He seems much older than his dozen years. This is not unusual in the three families. The young even today grow up fast. Many of the twenty-year-olds appear to be in their thirties. A ten-year-old here is not like a ten-year-old in an average American family. This could be related to the fact that in days of cotton, the young were treated like adults early, beginning at about eight on the farm. Much was expected of them—picking, chores, and so on. The adults today, because this is how they were raised, seem to expect such maturity in their youngsters.

For Roland, at an age when girls are normally attracted to older boys, this maturity, and a skill with words, means that he can seduce older girls into liking him. It's not that he's some junior womanizer; this is his natural way. He has the problem of too many girls chasing him. Debbie says he dates just one, a girl of fifteen. He has those Maggie Louise eyes, sandy hair, and this, too, is part of the attraction.

Roland is afflicted with the disease of youth—a sense of indestructibility. He jumps bikes and skateboards over all sorts of obstacles. Showing off his bicycle tricks, he falls several times, but picks himself right up, seemingly unhurt, to do them again. He won't let failure stop him, nor does he get flustered. He repeats them until he gets them right.

Everyone drinks beer, except for Roland and Andy Lee, who declines because he says that he still has trouble drinking in sight of his mother, that it makes him feel disrespectful. It is a habit he cannot break. Debbie does not understand this deference.

Ron, her husband, arrives from work. He is a traditional man of the house in many ways and takes over the duty of preparing the steaks. He is a good businessman and has more work than he can handle. He is a strong disciplinarian with the children and spends much time with them. They seem genuinely to like and honor him. The marriage between Ron and Debbie is one of mutual respect. Debbie went through her troubles with Ron. They separated once, but found they couldn't live apart.

Debbie is alone on the porch. It is an apartment balcony, looking down on a parking lot where children play. Across the asphalt are six other buildings just like this one and, behind, a thick band of woods where the bobwhite gossip from a convention of quail can be heard. In the fading light, she discusses life. It is intimate talk, with all the others in the kitchen. Debbie's voice is low. She covets the outside world and the travel a single man or woman can accomplish. She wanted adventures and instead had children at an early age, and so feels she missed out.

But she looks too much at the good side of that kind of life, and not enough at the down side. What about the world then missed, the love of children? Someone her age who is still single has lost something she takes for granted. She should cherish it. It is not too late for her to have adventures, and she is doing well to start with her schooling. She can do almost anything she wants to do, and her children will support her in it.

The solitude is broken by the entrance of Ron and of a few other visitors. The grill is ready. The steaks cook. In the living room are her sons and their women. They whisper, conspiring.

The boys and women march through the kitchen, crowding onto this narrow band of cement. There is a look of a well-kept secret. Andy Lee, being the oldest and therefore charged with such duties, walks forward. Debbie is standing with her back against the railing. She turns red, awkward at being the focus of everyone's attention. From his pocket he produces a tiny box wrapped in gift paper. She has forgotten that tomorrow is Mother's Day. The sons' eyes are expectant. Go on, open it, Andy Lee says. She picks at the paper, seeming to want to make the moment last. Beneath the lid is a silver ring, exquisitely carved, of deep luster, set on a snowy puff of cotton, and she holds the box in hand, staring. She plucks it from the cotton and slides it on her finger.

Debbie has no words for all this and cannot control her tears. She hugs each of her sons. Andy Lee says she will get the bill for it tomorrow, and everyone laughs.

. *x* .

That same Mother's Day, Debbie's brother, Sonny, was also crying.

It is always that way on Mother's Day, his wife says. He tells his wife that if his mother were still alive, he could do a great deal for her.

Sonny is the only one of Maggie Louise's four children to complete high school when still a youth. He was in that work-study program, which taught him a trade—house painting, hanging Sheetrock. After he graduated, in 1969, he remained in Cherokee City with his wife and child, looking for work. He rushed over on the day when his mother drank the rat poison, driving her to the hospital with Annie Mae and Gretchen.

Sonny does not talk about it. He cannot even remember the date his mother died. Everything before and after is sharp. It is as if he had been in a coma that day and the days that immediately followed.

After the funeral, he fled Cherokee City with his family, moving to the Gulf Coast of Mississippi. He could no longer live in Cherokee City again. He took a job in the paint department of a shipyard. He remained there for six years. He and his wife have four children. They are grandparents. In 1980, he opened his own business, as a painting, drywall, and wallpaper contractor. Sonny is thirty-five years old.

The Gulf Coast of Mississippi lies at the end of roads traveling the empty piney woods country of that state. The sharpness of an afternoon bleeds into night at the dank edge where a line of neon meets the blackness of the sea.

It is a hot night. The home of Sonny and Susan Franks is set back from the old mansions along the shore, in a new suburban tract. It is one of those homes that resembles all others around it. In the 1960s, when it was popular to trash American culture and look-alike suburbia, it was said that if you came home to your development house drunk in the night, the only way to tell which home was yours would be to go out back and smell the garbage. If it contained the remains of your dinner, you had the right house. There is something wonderfully comfortable about that idea, at least in the context of Sonny and the shack he once lived in, which did not have even running water.

The door opens, and Sonny is standing there. His is an instantly recognizable face. He has the eyes of Maggie Louise, mysterious, gray, kind.

Everything about this home is solidly in the middle, the furniture, the microwave, the Sesame Street swing set in the backyard, the parrot named Cowboy, two teenage children who peer at strange visitors with curiosity and timidness.

It is nine o'clock, and he has just arrived home from a job. He works seven days a week. He is too modest to say he is an accomplished musician—Debbie is proud of her brother for that. He learned to play instruments by ear, with no formal training. He started playing at fifteen, driven around to bars by an uncle. He once made a gospel album in Nashville, right after the death of Maggie Louise. Sonny talks for hours over the chatter of the parrot, late into the night, drinking through several pots of coffee.

As far as Maggie Louise's children, we're doing great. We've come a hell of a long ways. You know where we changed? When we came off of the farm and into the city. I'll take the city any day. After that, all the farming we did was a garden, you know.

You know I remember a lot of stuff from when I was seven, eight, ten years old. It makes me want to work hard. Back then it was plain physical manual labor. If you're a kid and you see these people get up and go to work, it sticks with you. That's the way I saw a man made a dollar. My mother worked hard. She was a survivor. We always made it. She never went for charity. Basically, the way we made it, the way my mother raised us, was working our ass off. You do make a living, you do survive . . . if you keep doing it long enough and don't give up.

We've been in this house for seven years. This is the second one we've had. It's middle-class. The rich are more on the south end. The houses there run from eighty to a hundred and fifty thousand. These run from thirty to fifty-five thousand.

I work from about seven until nine at night, twelve to fourteen hours a day. I don't sleep much. I'll work crazy hours for three or four weeks, then I'll take a weekend off, and I have slept from Saturday morning until Sunday morning. Right now, we're surviving. Your bare necessities will tear you apart. If you're in the middle, you're dog-paddling, you're surviving, you're staying on top. In the middle, you're paying both ways. You're paying for the poor people, which we need to take care of, but you're also paying for the rich man's Cadillacs.

Unless you're turning five hundred, six hundred dollars a week, you're not making any money. My minimum is four-fifty. And I've got to make that every week, just to stay on even keel. I can do it, but I can't do it in a forty-hour week. I've got to stay out there. A forty-hour week to me is gone, if a man's going to survive. Now it takes sixty.

I work for people who can afford it, an upper bracket. But

me, the people I associate with, are scrapping, are barely making it.

The way I do it now? If I can make one week at a time, I'm doing good. People don't have—what you call it?—any kind of security. Job security is gone. There's no more of that. . . . The big companies have got the upper hand right now on the average working man. Like this job I'm on at this hospital out here. I'd say twenty-five workers are temporary part-time. You don't get any benefits out there, you don't get the vacation, paid holidays, all of that. But if you want a job, you'll stay there. Supply and demand. There's not enough jobs out here.

They're going to have to give the common man a break for a change. If a man is already rich, that's good. I'm not saying take all the money from the rich people and kill them because they're rich. But you're going to have to go back to giving the poor person a break because they'll appreciate it, they'll go on with it. If I made a million dollars, I would reach back and help somebody somewhere. There needs to be a limit. If a person gets rich, makes a million dollars, there should be a limit. The big bugs shouldn't have all these breaks.

People making forty or fifty, they're set. They got what they need. They don't think about the people out there. If we don't do something here in the United States, if we don't correct this problem one way or another, get it on an upward trend, we're gonna find things a lot more difficult. People's gonna start taking what they want. . . . My son? I don't know if he'll do the same thing I do. But he's talented with going out and picking up money. He's been through grass cutting, then he went through this aluminum-can thing. He's just got it in him. I don't worry about him at all. I know he'll make a dollar somewhere. He'll go out there and get it if it's available. The availability of it is what I worry about.

His youngest boy enters the room. Sonny is looking at a picture of his mother in *Let Us Now Praise Famous Men.* It is the first time Sonny has ever seen the book.

The son asks, "Is this for real?"

Sonny's eyes never leave his mother's.

"This was the Depression, Son. It's for real. Yeah."

Several years later, Sonny was tracked down again. Things had not gone well. He and Susan had lost the house—work turned down, and they had to sell it. And as bad as that was, it got worse. Since that first visit, his real wage fell another two dollars an hour, and he had to drive to Mobile to get any work.

"What can I do now?" he said. "From where I am, the Depression is here. I make the same as I did ten years ago." He'd like to get out of his field, go to school for three years to become a nurse. But he still has mouths to feed, and so that plan seems impractical for now. Like Debbie, he is not complacent and is always thinking of ways to better himself. If only he can. Moreover, his oldest son—also named Sonny—dropped out of high school for a while. The good news was that the son started working with his father and realized he had to do something else. He went back to school and now plans on going to college to become an engineer.

Sonny and Susan were renting an apartment. Still middle-class. Clinging.

. *xi* .

The other two children of Maggie Louise are harder to understand.

Several years ago, when this project began, Mary Ann was working in Texas, managing an apartment complex with her husband and their five children. Like the other children, she had fled Alabama. In 1986, she returned home, just as Debbie and Parvin had before her.

She came to take a job in the Cookstown Junior Mart, that convenience-store chain with a goofy-face logo of a kid, where they sell overpriced toilet paper and milk, reasonable gasoline, greasy chicken, badly brewed coffee. The eldest of Maggie Louise's offspring, Mary Ann is five years older than Debbie. She saw a lot more and had important family history to contribute. The first time we approached her, she was withdrawn, though not nearly as hostile as her uncle Junior, and so we did not interview her.

I attempted a second approach. It came one evening, and Mary Ann was at work inside the Junior Mart. She was easy to watch from a car parked by the ice machine. She could not see who was spying on her, for the brightness of the store interior made vision into the dark night world outside impossible. She looked just like Annie Mae Gudger in 1936, or a picture of her mother just before death. Her hair was pulled back tightly. She had the thin lips and gentle smile. And those eyes, lines sinking into the center of their reflective whiteness, a look that runs in most all of the Maggie Louise line. She was working behind the chicken counter, dipping a batch of breaded parts into smoking grease. Then she was lost from sight, behind a window sign that advertised two chicken pieces and a roll for ninety-nine cents. A customer entered and everyone laughed. The customer was some good-old-boy type, and they were probably talking about some town gossip incomprehensible to an outsider. The good old boy left. The store was empty of customers.

At that point, it seemed unnecessary to talk with her. It would have been such an intrusion, it seemed, but weren't our approaches to the others also intrusions? Who knows how such decisions are made? She was left alone.

Perhaps Parvin should also have been left alone. How sweet, special, and fragile she is. She is much quieter than Debbie. Debbie has dealt with the past by opening up; Parvin, by withdrawing. Parvin does not embrace new experiences the way her sister does. Parvin, the youngest child of Maggie Louise, is childless and, at thirty-three, on her third marriage.

How could she be asked about the map on the grave? It is impossible for me to ask some things. The map was discovered by us a few months after she came back from Orlando. Could it have been placed there to tell her mother that she had come home? Parvin seems to want to atone for a past she cannot reclaim. She and Hubbard, her husband, had driven their thirty-two-foot mobile home from Orlando to Cherokee City. Before she came back, she had a cancerous breast removed. She also had a hysterectomy and an operation to remove the other breast.

Like many of her kin, Parvin is not in good health. Marion, the son of Ivy and Bud Woods, succumbed to cancer when still young, as did his brother, Thomas (Buddy); Thomas Woods and Ethel had a retarded son; Mary Lee was born premature to Ellen and is still thin and small; Emma suffered her whole life from asthma and general weakness; Emma's daughter Ruby had rheumatic heart disease; George Gudger died young from cancer; Squinchy Gudger's heart is weak, as is that of his sister Gretchen, and both face shortened lives; the Rickettses' boy died of tuberculosis. The list is much longer and equally sad.

It's impossible to ascertain how much of the disease is related to genetics and how much caused by diet and other environmental factors. Debbie cannot help believing that some of this disease was caused by exposure to chemicals: "The crop dusters would come and spray, and it would go all over us. Before that, you had to go out there on this machine and spray around, before the planes came." Parvin can only suspect the cause of her cancers.

In that first meeting, Parvin talked about her earlier move to Florida, how she worked her way up to become a bookkeeper:

> I left home and didn't know what an inside toilet was. I was going on sixteen when I got married. Back then, that was the thing to do. Hurry up and get out. I did grow up fast. Quick, hard. I learned everything by just doing. I have learned nobody will give you anything. Waitress work, that's all we could start at. I learned typing by common sense. I feel like I was cheated all my life. Behind the times.

With a bit of wistfulness, she adds, "We're just different."

Some relatives believe that the children of Maggie Louise, out of malice, turned against their mother and that this led to her despair. That does not seem to be true. They were confused teenagers fleeing from the brutal cotton days into life. Parvin later wrote a letter and addressed the issue:

> I sure hope you know that my mother was a very beautiful lady. When my father died, she had four kids to take care of and at that time it was very hard on her. My father is the only man mother ever loved. I have already talked to Gretchen about this. Don't take me wrong but I was her baby girl. I didn't understand myself until I got older. I realize it was very hard on her.

Many months later, after coming home, Parvin landed a job as a bookkeeper in Cherokee City.

Her husband, Hubbard, was not working. He had a bad back and said he could not work at his trade of repairing mobile homes. They were still living in the motor home, parked at the back of a lot where house trailers were offered for sale.

He is a jealous man, says Debbie. After the first meeting, he told Parvin that any men who come to Alabama talking about the old days are up to no good, if they are talking to men's wives. Debbie does not like Hubbard. She feels he rules Parvin's life and manipulates her desires.

About a year after that first meeting, Hubbard was lured to a healing church. He went to a service and was convinced that the church would be their salvation, that it could physically restore his wife to being the woman he had married.

"I went back to that church twice and watched what went on," said Hubbard.

> You see demons come out of people. There's a woman who got a brand-new kidney. I've seen legs grow. It'd be hard to pull the wool over my eyes. I'm not from Alabama. I said, "I think you should come with me and go to church." I'd been praying for the Lord to give her back to me just the way she was when I met her.

Now they both belong to the Double Helping Tabernacle Church, run by Sister Wanda and Mr. Hainey. Sister Wanda is the one who heals people. Hubbard has told Parvin that God must rule their lives. All their radios are tuned to the Jesus station. Fifteen faces of Jesus decorate their trailer. They go to the church five times during the week and twice on Sunday. They once went sixteen nights in a row.

Parvin has stopped taking any medication for her health problems. She believes she is cured.

> I was of this world, but when I came here, my maker, Jesus Christ, he just stopped me and showed me he is still alive. I've totally turned my mortal body over to him because he is now my doctor, he's my everything. I haven't gone to a doctor since. I totally refuse. People talk about us, laugh, but I could care less. I'll receive all my treasures in heaven. I can't wait for the glorious day when I'll see Maggie Louise Franks and Floyd Franks.

Many years before, Floyd Franks had once gone to see Oral Roberts to get his hearing back, and Annie Mae had gone to a healer when she found she had cancer, but Parvin's brand of religion is far different from anything the Gudgers have ever practiced.

The night comes for one of their church services. The building gleams in a neighborhood of lower-class homes on the south side of Cherokee City. The raised voice of Mr. Hainey is heard a full block from the church, the name of Jesus traveling through the night air.

Inside, Mr. Hainey is found to be a short and obese man, working hard, running around behind the pulpit. He's not as good as some—they say Sister Wanda has it down better—but he tries. Sister Wanda sits on the side of the altar, quiet this night, a stern parrot-nose redhead. She sways, eyes closed, to the words of Mr. Hainey.

The congregation is a mix of black, white, old, young, thin, grossly fat, well-dressed, threadbare. The common tie is desperate hope—a retarded woman, a bulb-nose alcoholic, and legless people are all trying to reclaim something. Mr. Hainey talks about how God will take the last and make him first. Do you want a car? Pray for it! He will see that you get material wealth. This assurance raises the level of interest. People sing, and Parvin is the first to walk forward on the altar call, eyes closed, arms raised. She falls forward, gripping the carpet. She repeats loudly the name of Jesus, her voice rising above the rest. A dozen others follow. A one-legged black man hobbles and falls next to her. Parvin shakes violently, as in a seizure, repeating, "Jesus! Jesus! Jesus!"

The service ends. Hubbard and Parvin decide to visit a waffle house for coffee. He drives the car, and she follows in his pickup truck. He is enthusiastic. Wasn't Mr. Hainey great tonight?

Hubbard arrives first, and Parvin enters the waffle house behind. He asks where she parked the truck. She says in a space. Was it near any other car? He becomes frantic. Women don't know how to park trucks, he says. He insists on going to move it and park it "properly."

While he is gone, Parvin taps her hand to a rock tune on the jukebox. She says Hubbard forbids her to listen to rock music. When he returns, she stops tapping. He speaks twenty words for each of hers.

The coffee gone, good-byes are exchanged. They walk off, the thin, still-sensual body of Parvin next to that man.

A year later, they separated. He sold everything she owned. She went back to Florida. Mary Ann also went back to Texas. After that, Parvin had another operation, discovered she had ulcers. Two years later, she was back living with Hubbard, in that trailer in Cherokee City.

. *xii* .

The journey of the Gudger family is one of many paths and mixed successes. Annie Mae took a job in a nursing home with her sister Emma, and, Gretchen says, "she just blossomed like a rose."

Her hair, always long and tied back on the orders of George, was cut. She started wearing makeup and even had an occasional drink, something George would never have tolerated. Her children say she grew more youthful as she got away from cotton and that work-crazed life, and the pictures bear this out. A family photograph of her in the early 1960s shows her actually looking younger than when Walker Evans took his famous photograph in 1936.

The family revolved around and revered this woman, after a life so hard-lived. We found many who speak against some of the Rickettses and Woodses, even against George Gudger and some of his children, but we found no one who will speak against Annie Mae.

Annie Mae met a man who visited the nursing home where she worked, and later married him. She was with that man for six years until he died. She later said they were the best six years of her life. She finally found some joy in life. One day, she noticed her stomach bloating, and she didn't feel well. She told Gretchen she didn't have to go to the doctor—she knew what it was. She believed it was the same liver cancer that had killed her mother, Lulla, in 1929. Annie Mae held on long enough for her son, Sonny, to make the drive from Georgia. When he arrived, she said, "I love my boy." Then she closed her eyes and was gone.

Many Gudgers today live on a few acres in a tiny group of trailers south of Cookstown, forming a circle like some pioneer wagon camp. The place is about three miles from Hobe's Hill. Annie Mae's children Catherine Annette, Gretchen, and Squinchy live here, and they are surrounded by children and grandchildren. Squinchy was the baby in 1936 who Agee said would not grow. He did grow—into a shy man with a bad heart. He has undergone surgery several times and was recently laid off by a bankrupt meat-packing plant in Cherokee City.

Of her other children, Elizabeth Anne is married to a man who threatens to kill people, especially reporters who come to Alabama asking questions. Burt Westly, her brother, is shy and does not want to talk. He learned his welding skills on the GI Bill after the Korean War. In 1978, *Southern Exposure* magazine said, "He is bitter about the past and would not live in his home county." According to the magazine, he abandoned welding after fifteen years because the fumes gave him serious sinus trouble, and he became a supervisor. He told *Southern Exposure,*

> I helped organize the place that I'm working now. . . . This guy that
> owned the place came from up north. He came down here looking

for cheap labor. He was paying us two dollars and a quarter to weld. Now, they're paying a welder about six or seven dollars, and some good fringe benefits.

Junior, already mentioned, lives in a small house surrounded by a few trailers belonging to his children, in yet another compound, withdrawn into their own world. Gretchen says she has tried to get him out of that world, but he refuses. He just doesn't want to change.

Sonny, the son who lives in Georgia (the uncle of Maggie Louise's Sonny), is the most financially successful of all those descended from the three tenant families. This is the son who rebelled, who absolutely refused to go on picking cotton, who chose instead to bag groceries for a living, the son in whose name George Gudger challenged Mr. Hill at the Yellow Front Store when Mr. Hill had been told by the Gudger landlord that it wasn't a good idea to be giving jobs to boys who belonged on the farm picking cotton. He lives now in Valley Town, Georgia, managing a jewelry store for the man he shares a home with. Twenty years ago, he and the man started working together, and they now own two jewelry stores.

The two men reside in a tall and spindly dwelling, its exterior peeling, interior ceilings water-stained, plates of plaster ready to fall in pie-size hunks. The seediness of the house stands in contrast to the care lavished on its contents. The home is filled with untold thousands of dollars' worth of dark antiques—Victorian, Art Deco, Greek Revival, Chinese—splashed in red velvet, corners occupied by silver urns and candelabra, fifteen-foot mirrors, a baby grand piano, statuary, oil paintings, a book turned to a favorite poem by Ezra Pound. This is the only child of George and Annie Mae to have attended any college. The town in which he lives has three country-music bars and not much else for entertainment. The community lacks the culture Sonny craved when growing up. But he is, apparently, here for good.

Sonny is a fine jeweler, proud and fair in his dealings, with a nice way with his customers. He spends much of his leisure time in the silence of his home, playing the piano for two tiny poodles. He has not gotten over the death of his mother, one of the few people who understood him, and it seems he never will. He draws tears when talking about her. Since her death, he has spoken little to his brothers, Burt Westly and Junior, for whom he reserves contempt, an emotion he feels they return.

Debbie says her uncles hate their brother. For a man who dreamed of the big city as a boy, it's hard to imagine how he manages in that small redneck town, a place of unenlightened isolation.

Although many of the Gudgers are backward, some at least have progressed, and it is with this group that the greatest hope for the future of the families lies.

RICKETTS

. i .

Our very first evening in Alabama, every sensation was new and striking.

There were the insects. It is still unclear what species comprised their ranks—but it can be said in less-than-scientific terms that there were two distinct types, day bugs and night bugs. Both made the same racket. To imagine the quality and cadence of this sound, tune a radio until there is nothing but static, then turn the volume as high as possible, quickly lower it, and repeat the process in a rhythmic pattern that oscillates between extremes. At a roadside stand, we inquired what insect makes such noise. "What noise?" asked the woman, who was selling ice cream. Attempts were made to call her attention to the chorus rising and receding from the kudzu across the road, but she had grown up with the bug talk and simply did not hear it.

There was heat. It is another presence, unseen, alive, encompassing, ever there, impossible to commit to words. It does not lessen much with the night. Again, only outsiders seem to notice or complain about it.

There was solitude. It would become very familiar: the measureless land lying out, sleeping, between infrequent houses, the feeling of being lost even when in a known place, a succession of kudzu and pines stretching across all those endless miles.

There were things very "southern"—blood-colored earth, gleaming churches at almost every crossroad, Coca-Cola signs. As for the latter, it is in the nature of things that the poorer an area, the larger and more ubiquitous these signs, and this holds true on these Alabama back roads. The soda company promotes itself by providing signs to store owners in exchange for the use of the store-owner's premises as a permanent free billboard. In fact, the company often makes it part of the deal—if the retailer wants to have the product to sell, the store has to display the sign. Back when Walker Evans took his pictures, the signs were made of steel; the ones supplied later are larger and made of plastic. In places such as the outback islands of the Philippines, the Coke signs are as large as barns, and a Coke costs a dime. In rural Alabama, sodas can be had for thirty cents from machines in front of little country stores, half the price charged in large American cities. It appears that consumption must be encouraged at whatever price local markets will bear.

It seemed necessary for us to feed one of these machines three dimes and drive on, past the Forks, on the road to Centerboro, caught by full darkness in Waynesville, a mostly black town, unlike mostly white Centerboro, a dozen miles west. Many homes within this black town are not much better than the country gray-board shacks. There are some nice homes, to be sure, but they seem a minority. All houses, regardless of soundness, have porches. They aren't decorative, but are a functional part of the architecture, for the interiors of these small homes—whose owners are unable to afford air-conditioning—are uninhabitably hot most summer evenings. Summer life is lived on porches. The town pastime is to sit on rockers in the early shadows of night, all house lights extinguished, and the best porches have banks of chairs lined six, seven strong, all rocking with deliberation, to conversation or the silence amid conversation.

A hot wind entering through an open car window conspired with the whirling voices of insects. In a nameless town in the county where many members of the three families live, everyone stared, and we deemed it proper to drive slowly and stare back dumbly. Rural Alabama may have the most suspicious small-town eyes in America, though we later found there was nothing overtly violent or threatening behind them. The look is one of amazement at what business would bring anyone so far off the main path to their town. Nevertheless, the eyes are disquieting, and one never gets used to them. The road led out of town, the eyes soon far behind, and the comfort of night returned. The course was uncertain and the road narrow. The beams struck a mailbox that contained a road number.

And there was the name: Margaret Ricketts.

The chance discovery came one day earlier than Margaret was expecting our visit. She had been the most easily traced and therefore the first to be contacted. We knew nothing about any of the families that initial night, and we thought it important to try and learn as much as possible, as fast as possible, as quietly and secretly as possible.

We closed the car doors with great care, so that only a click was heard. In the distance two tiny squares of window light burned. All houses look the same in the night, and we couldn't tell whether it was a rich or a poor house. It looked rich. Our light steps failed to silence the gravel of the driveway, alerting a counterspy, some canine that put a halt to our reconnoitering with dog shouts of alarm.

. ii .

Daylight revealed a simple dwelling. As our car pulled up, the front door opened. Margaret emerged, flashing gums studded with stumps of bituminous teeth. Her feet were naked, apparently a normal state, as her toenails were split and ragged. A right finger was thrust up her nose, pulling a hunk of whatever had dried up there, and she started hugging these visiting journalists, snot still stuck to the finger, lips sinking tight around memories of molars in smile.

From behind Margaret came her son Garvrin Arlo, who also

hugged his guests. But his off-center eyes, distorted behind thick glasses, looked fearful. We later learned that the townsfolk talk about him, as they have for the forty years he's been alive. How he wanted to show them wrong, show just how smart and skilled he was. He ran inside.

"Watch me! Watch me!" He clasped his hands behind his back, slamming his belly down on the floor with such force that the walls of the shack shook.

"Think I can get up? Huh? Huh? Think I can get up?"

And he squirmed to his feet, hands still together, throwing back his head, false teeth clicking out a stutter of words.

"I'm gonna call you Cous'n. You, Hoss. Hey Hoss, I butt heads with goats! See this head? C'mon. Butt it!

"Cous', can you spell incomprehensibility? Betcha can't. Lissen! I-N-C-O-M-P-Ree-E-H-E-N-Sss-I-B-I-L-I-T-Y. Hippopotamus? H-I-Pee-Pee-O-Pee-O-Tee-A-M-U-Ssssss.

"Ssss. Ssss. Huh? Huh?

"I'm a writer. I'm a photographer, too," he said. He produced a cheap Polaroid and snapped pictures. He began adding whole strings of numbers. "Yesssir, Cous'n, bet you never met anyone like me."

And Garvrin Arlo took his fists and slapped his head with a force that knocked him backward, and he laughed and laughed and laughed.

While Garvrin Arlo was involved in all this, a car came up the drive. In it was Katy Ricketts, Margaret's sister. Margaret mentioned that Katy does not like talking about the past.

Katy entered, hair thrown like gray straw, and sat down.

"Tell how you're in that book," Garvrin Arlo said. "Tell them! Tell them!"

"I ain't in that book!" she announced.

"Sure you are. That's your picture in there!" Garvrin Arlo said, laughing some more.

"No it's not," she said, as if denying all the decades of her sorry life. "Nothing in that book concerns me! I hate that book! I hate them! I hate you people!"

She announced she had to go to church. She rushed out. Her car threw gravel as it pulled away.

"She always gets that way about it," said Margaret.

. *iii* .

Their house comprised four small rooms.

In Garvrin Arlo's room, the bed was perched on crates. Next to it was a large zinc basin full of liquid. Urine! It had not been emptied in a week. There is no plumbing. They defecate in the weeds out back and dump the piss buckets out there, too, when they get around to it.

In Margaret's room, bed sheets, once white, had matured to slate from lack of laundering. The living room contained a wood-burning stove, the sole source of heat. Next to it was a color television set. ("Didja know Garvrin figgers out them dee-tective shows?" Margaret said. "He could be one of them dee-tectives.") There were plastic flowers beneath a coat of dust, bottles of prescription drugs—Margaret's health is not good. On the walls, seven pictures of Jesus, the fourteen eyes, some looking left, some right, knowing all corners of this room. There was also a picture of Margaret's mother, Sadie, taken by Walker Evans, given to Margaret by film-maker Mort Jordan. Sadie is wearing a flour-sack dress, barefoot, sad-eyed, emotionally barren. This is the woman who was sent to live in the other side of the house when she got older, so she wouldn't get in the way of Margaret and Fred.

The kitchen was the worst of it. From there emanated a scaly black crust of grease that found its way through the whole house, painting walls, floors, ceilings, the cup in which Margaret offered coffee.

The smell was a mixture. Unwashed flesh. (They bathe every few months by rubbing their bodies with a damp washcloth.) Stale urine. A blend of milk, vinegar, cheap sardines, stewed every few days on the stove, a recipe created by Garvrin Arlo ("I'm a chef, too!") Wood smoke. Chain-saw fuel. Toxic chemicals bled from the factory clothes worn by Garvrin Arlo. It combines, rushing the nose. Unlike some odors that grow less sharp with familiarity, until easily ignored, this one stays conspicuous. Each component takes its turn welling to the forefront, depending on the part of the house in which a person stands, but each smell is present every minute you're there.

In town, they like to talk about Margaret and Garvrin Arlo. One man said that going to see them is better than watching television and that he's been meaning to take his new wife up there just to get a look. Townsmen guffaw at every chance, a hideous small-town cruelty. The Rickettses were the butt of jokes all over the county in 1936, and some still are today.

But how were the Rickettses supposed to turn out?

The reality is that Margaret and her son are the "worst" of the Rickettses, in the sense of having never attained the "good life." Those terms are relative, of course, and will be dealt with later. For now, it will suffice to say they are what people in the county think of when you say Ricketts. They do not think of those of Margaret's siblings who did not wind up living under such weird conditions. Margaret and her son have also been popular with occasional journalists and filmmakers who have come this way the past fifteen or so years to do stories on these families. Why? They are easy to find. They cooperate, because they are ignorant of why any human would want to cause them any harm, to hold them up to ridicule, to be gawked at like zoo creatures. And they are convenient for confirming an image of a South living in shacks, backward and uneducated. They make good copy. They make good pictures, good stories—that is, they are easy journalism.

It's much harder to examine and treat on film or in a few inches of newspaper column how her four sisters dealt with their sick father, how the surviving brother, John Garvrin, retreated into his own head after fleeing to Cherokee City. It's not easy, perhaps it's even confusing, to describe how he reacted to the pain of his boy's being struck by a car and killed, how he became lost in his job as a mechanic for the city, or how he lived his last year of loneliness, when the cancer was eating at him, still bitter at some in his family who came around those last days for the sole purpose of trying to get a hold of what few possessions he acquired in the four decades after he left Hobe's Hill. There is much more to the Rickettses, but most of it is too complex to be useful for understanding; it's much easier to focus on the surface truth as confirmation of a convenient stereotype; gawking at Margaret and Garvrin Arlo exposes an ugly and voyeuristic side in the townsmen, in journalists, in readers, in this book, in society; these are human beings whose every action, whose occasional offense, came out of their limited understanding of the world.

How do you capture the rage of Robert Allen, the son of Margaret's sister Paralee? There were his years of combating alcoholism, his tour of duty in Vietnam, and now his struggle to make a living in that furniture factory in Tulip City, Mississippi.

And there are the quiet struggles. There's Paralee, who reads her Bible every day and listens to the "Gospel Hour" on the radio, secluded from the world. Or Nancy Ann, daughter of Flora Merry Lee, whose husband left her. She raises a daughter afflicted with cerebral palsy, living in that cheap apartment outside Birmingham, working fifteen-hour days as a secretary to support the two of them.

Each of Fred's children, grandchildren, and great-grandchildren has dealt with those Hobe's Hill events in his or her own way. It is a family divided by bitter factionalism dating to those days, so they seldom get together, except for funerals, and there is much hatred.

Many exist in limbo, neither middle-class nor poor, carrying this great weight of the past. Most are not as hard-pressed as Margaret and Garvrin Arlo, though many do the work that replaced the cultivation of cotton in the South—basic jobs in textile factories, mills, lumber operations. They had more to surmount than the children of the Woodses and Gudgers did, and such normality as is found within their ranks should be viewed as success in itself.

Two of the five surviving children of Fred and Margaret Ricketts would not talk for this book; a third was not approached for comment. The motives of the two are different from those of Junior Gudger. They care less about someone's getting "rich" writing about them than they do about the wounds. They know everyone goes to Margaret, if not first then eventually, and the "worst" about the Ricketts family will be learned. They know how townspeople talk and journalists act, and they know they have nothing to gain by making themselves part of confirming gossip. They have spent lives trying to forget the stories and the snickers.

. *v* .

Clair Bell is the youngest of the Ricketts children. She is fifty-four. She was four when James Agee and Walker Evans visited.

If a line were drawn on the map due east of Margaret's home, it would cross the highway and head up Hobe's Hill, where they lived in 1936. Continuing past where the dirt road comes to an end near the black cemetery, you find a tangled mile of forest, beyond which lies another dirt road, unconnected to the first, and a frowning green trailer. Clair Bell lives here.

This is a serious collection of dozens of ancient and unworking cars, trucks, tractors, nameless wheeled and stationary objects. Kudzu has tried to cover this two-acre whorl of iron, steel, and wood, but not even that relentless vine can hide it. The trailer, with its cracked door, is lost in the center.

All this suggests that Clair Bell is another Margaret. It is true she's a recluse who dislikes the outside world, but unlike Margaret, who has never left this county, Clair Bell has ventured out into modern America. She was always a good student, the only Ricketts to finish high school. For a while, she moved to Illinois with her husband and led a suburban existence.

After ten years, she and her husband decided to come home to the South, as all in the three families have eventually done, pulled back to these barren tablelands. None seems able to make a permanent break. This is unlike the pattern evident among many back-country southern blacks, who seem to stay away once they leave. Only one of the 128 members of the three families and their offspring was living outside the South, and that one, a Ricketts, was planning to return home soon.

Many are afraid of the outside. They call it Alabama pride. But Alabama pride is not like Texas pride, based on boosterism. Alabama pride has an inferiority complex at its root. Even other Alabamians, with college degrees, say that they feel put down, marked by their accents when living in the North or the West, that the instant association with Alabama is "stupid." It follows that poor Alabamians will suffer even more from this same complex. They fear that everyone is onto them, that they will be discovered and exposed as one-time cotton pickers. Even some South Carolina and Georgia people laugh at Alabamians as being "backward." Whether real or imagined, this sense of the world's scorn drives them to the haven of sweet home Alabama, where they can live their lives unjudged and comfortable in what they are.

Not long after Clair Bell and her husband returned, they were divorced. Clair Bell came here to the forest after marrying Albert Margraves—not one of the monied Margraveses but one who works the "logwoods," lumbering trees. This Margraves has no teeth. He is conscious of his badge and whom he shows it to. When talking with outsiders, he speaks through lips narrowed to a slit to conceal those blackened chops.

It is a strange couple. Clair Bell resembles a schoolteacher in appearance and manner, with wire-rim glasses, a face as round and soft as the cotton balls she refused to pick as a child, hair the color of seed. She has all her teeth, and they are in fine shape. She looks like any average American. She fared better than some of her older siblings. The younger children were more advanced not only because they came of age in better economic times but also because they learned early, by the painful example of their elders, that they had to reject absolute loyalty to their father to have any hope. Clair Bell wanted to be a stenographer and would have become one, except that she married first. Now she is here.

Clair Bell was one of two children Agee said would not live much longer after he left at the end of summer in 1936. She was the one who was hurt in that playtime accident, the one Agee made an oblique reference to in his book, about her "six-month image" lying sleeping, referring to her being in a coma. She would die, he predicted, going on to envision even the form her parents' grief would take: the Ricketts family would place atop the grave of the four-year-old child the tea set Agee had given her as a present. His small gift to the dying child, who had had so little in her short life, would be a logical choice as a symbol of love of the family for their lost member. It would be a poignant, beautiful act. Why else could he have imagined that the family would choose to place this gift from a stranger on her grave?

Then we learned the secrets.

As it turned out, Clair Bell was not in a coma for long—she was laid up for six weeks, not six months, and obviously did not die.

And it was revealed that it was either Agee or Evans who had accidentally caused her injury.

This information is not offered in Agee's text; indeed, it is also not stated in the text that Agee found Clair Bell alive and well when he revisited the families in 1937, after his material had been rejected as a *Fortune* article but long before he completed his manuscript and had it published as a book in 1941. It's unclear exactly why Agee ignored the facts regarding Clair Bell. It could be argued that the way he chose to describe her imminent death and the family's grief had too nice a sound to it to be altered just for the sake of historical accuracy. Or it could be said he was dealing not with journalism, not simply with a setting down of facts, but with a creative enterprise.

We cannot now hear Agee's side of this. But there is Clair Bell's recollection of the incident.

> We were in front of the porch, playing "poison oak." They wanted to learn to play the games southern people play. It's one where you hold your hands and run through people. Being a kid, I wanted to play. One of them—I forget which one—ran between my hands and sister Paralee. I fell down and hit my head on a porch rock. I was hurt real bad. I almost died. I had to lay flat on my back for six weeks. I'm the one who was supposed to die. Well, here I am. That's what makes me the most mad. I wonder if this arthritis of the spine was caused by that. I had a big knot on my head. A doctor took X rays of me, and told me I was in a bad wreck. I was never in a bad wreck. That's all that ever happened to me.
>
> They went to Birmingham, came back, and brought the tea set before they left. I never played with that tea set. Southern families will let you in if you're in need. That's the way we are. They took advantage of that. If I saw them again, I'd tell them they were stupid, that's what I'd say. They was nosing, sneakin' around in bedrooms. They went under the house, crawling around. I wish he'd got snake-bit under there. Somebody's crazy to crawl under a house when folks is gone. The crazy idiots wouldn't sleep on beds. My father offered them a bed, but they slept on the cotton pile.
>
> I don't want to be splashed all over the newspapers. We tried to sue when some stories came out. The judge said we're historical figures and have no right to sue. I don't have no rights, because I'm famous. If I'm famous, why ain't I rich? We never got anything out of it. They never gave us any money, never sent us anything. You can take my picture the day when that tea set sets over my grave.

. *vi* .

It's not surprising that Clair Bell didn't want her picture taken. Evans's original, signed photographs came to be worth many thousands of dollars after his death. Clair Bell once went to a show of his pictures in Birmingham. There was her face, bigger than life, the tight shot of her as a wide-eyed, beautiful child. She told no one she was the child in that photograph. She just wanted to see what it was all about. She left after she believed that the head of the gallery began staring at her, that he recognized her from the picture on the wall. She went home to a job in a textile factory that does not pay in one month what the picture of her would sell for in that Birmingham gallery.

Later, she was laid off and had no work.

The story of Agee and the Rickettses is one that deals heavily with the practice of journalism, how one human views another and puts that impression into words.

There is no room in this volume to properly explore the role of journalism—indeed, there could be an entire book written on the subject in relation to these families. Journalism practiced one day can have an impact fifty years later.

Perhaps Mort Jordan said it best when he stated, "Walker Evans later wrote that the families understood and applauded what Agee was down there to do. It isn't true. And now I wonder if Agee understood the families any better than they understood him."

Emma Woods later said, "He must have been drunk when he wrote it and got things mixed up. He shouldn't have done that, no matter how cute I thought he was. There's a whole lot in there that's true, and a whole lot that isn't true. He was a mess. My goodness, I could turn around and write a book on him."

. *vii* .

In those last days before he died at age ninety on November 6, 1962, Fred Ricketts was given *Let Us Now Praise Famous Men.* He was nearly blind, but kept looking at Evans's pictures. He was so happy that he was a famous man, Margaret recalls.

After he died, Margaret inherited all the land Fred bought using that federal government loan. That enraged her siblings. She was later cheated out of it by a swindler. He told Margaret he would build her a new house, if she gave him most of the 120 acres. He built them a shack without plumbing, the one she lives in with Garvrin Arlo, and built himself a fine brick home next door. Margaret remains happy with the deal.

To most members of the family, Margaret and her son are a hub of hate. The hate is explained on the basis of her gaining the land and not sharing it, and then giving it away, but the land is not the only issue. The hate is by now institutionalized, sadly for Margaret and her son. The relatives cannot be entirely blamed. The memories are just too bitter. The way she continues to live reminds them all of what they themselves were once forced to endure.

Margaret and Garvrin Arlo are starved for familial warmth and outside friendship. In their isolation, they have been drawn to each other. It is a curious existence. She talks, and he does not hear. He hoots, and she smiles. Margaret dotes over her boy, treating him like a schoolchild. He returns the love with his form of care. A year after they were first interviewed, he was proud to have bought her a kerosene heater to replace the wood stove, moving them one more notch out of the 1930s. He talked about its technology for an hour. He says he is providing for his mama. He loves his mama and is not too shy to say so. He runs right home to her at night after work in the chemicals factory, and she often waits up for him.

It's true Margaret and Garvrin Arlo live in a shack without plumbing, but he drives a nearly new truck. He makes about $250 a week at his job. It's enough for them to spruce up the house, at least put in a toilet, if they so chose. Garvrin Arlo's net income of about $13,000 qualifies them as poor, or nearly so. But theirs is a queer kind of self-imposed poverty. It is the way they know best.

Margaret has dealt with the early madness by simply blotting it out. She has created her own reality of the days under Fred Ricketts. She worships her father and calls him a great man. Indeed, it is strange that many of the descendants of Fred Ricketts revere the old man. In one breath, they condemn and whisper about his excesses, and, in the next, pledge undying love. It is probably related to how highly southerners value loyalty, especially to superiors, to one's father, to one's cotton boss.

In the hearts of many, there is no room for the same forgiveness toward Margaret. She is very near death and has seen little kindness. She and Garvrin Arlo are utterly alone. Nancy Ann, Margaret's granddaughter, is one of the rare ones who come to visit. Long after the day we first met them for this project, I made a return trip. Garvrin Arlo had just celebrated a birthday, and I had forgotten that we made a loose promise the preceding year to visit on the day of the party. "We must get together again soon" and "Let's have lunch" are little more than social pleasantries in the urban and urbane world. But in their world, such words really mean something. They were truly hurt, for no one else came—the birthday party was just the two of them. They offered me some of their sardines, milk, and vinegar stewing on the stove. They dished out seconds and quickly forgave the failure to show up for the party as promised. When it was time to leave, Margaret hugged me tightly, not wanting to let go, insisting on a promise to return and see them soon. She stood in the door after she released her hold, her breath keen against the cold night air.

It seemed Garvrin Arlo was doomed to a life of solitude. What would he do after Margaret died? Be alone in that primitive house? He never came to find out. He was at a picnic some time later and saw a man slap a big woman. He walked up and told the man never to do that again. The man responded by slugging the woman straight in the face. Bystanders had to haul Garvrin Arlo off to the side.

While Garvrin Arlo was held back, the man said, "He can protect you all he wants, but you fat bitch, no one will take you! This is it, bitch! You're out. You'll have nothing. No one will take you in."

Three weeks later, Garvrin Arlo and the woman were wed.

Jeannie Kay weighs well over two hundred pounds. She thought all men beat their wives. She had known nothing else her whole life. Garvrin Arlo would never hit her. They are happy. She moved in with Garvrin Arlo and Margaret, insisting on fixing up the little house, painting it, and having a modicum of sanitation. They live there with Margaret, who is now bedridden most of the time, with that Bible at her side.

Margaret was once asked how she felt about her life over the past fifty years. The look in her eyes revealed that she understood the true question: How is it that you have continued over fifty years to be as poor as you were at the beginning? Some people start poor and work their way up. Others make money along the way but are wasteful and end up in poverty. But you have been consistently poor, through depression, three wars, the end of the cotton South, economic expansion and dislocation, through the War on Poverty and the surrender to it, through the Reagan years and their let-the-devil-take-the-hindmost attitude.

"I'm rich-poor," she said. "You see, I got my son. I got my Bible. That's all I need. I don't treasure nothin' on earth."

Outside the Ricketts home, rotting and rusting, is the horse-drawn cotton seeder they used on Hobe's Hill and, later, on their farm down by the river. The Ricketts family last planted cotton in 1963. Garvrin Arlo tried to continue the farm one season after his father died, but the world had finally caught up to small farmers like them.

The cotton-price-support program that propped up small farmers was at its nadir in 1963, a great scandal of a failure in what it had done to the American cotton industry. In 1965, the government abandoned artificial price setting and started direct payments to farmers, letting the market dictate the price of cotton. The new market conditions encouraged growers to get larger and larger—the day of the small cotton farmer was closing. That made inevitable the fact that mechanized western growers on large open tracts would come to dominate cotton growing. By the 1970s, the U.S. cotton market had stabilized, and most production was in Texas and California. This nation's share of the world market settled at a steady 18 percent, says the Cotton Council. The crop was grown totally by machine.

In 1930, it took 270 hours of labor to produce a bale of cotton. Today, thanks to the cotton-picking machine and other improvements, it takes 23. Alabama was left behind in the technological rush.

It was hard on Garvrin Arlo those first years after cotton. He recalls,

> For a while I was travelin', pickin' up work here'n yonder and e'where else—North Carolina, South Carolina, Virginia, then farm work down here. Shoot, I worked that about four year straight.

In 1977, he landed what he feels is the best job he's ever had, in a nearby chemicals factory. He is essentially an expendable human mule, lifting two fifty-pound sacks of toxic chemical onto a conveyor belt each minute, sometimes fifteen hours a day.

> I'm baggin'. Resin. I'm the fastest bagger they got there. Most'm can't keep up with it. Everybody's tryin' to get a job makin' what I'm makin'. I'm makin' six-forty an hour. It's fair, but not fair for the danger to your health. There's a fella, he retired up there. He had 'bout nineteen year. Shoot. No, twenny year. He done got

twenny year and retired. He lived 'bout six months. Cancer. It's nothin' they can really prove. I'm not gonna stay there no twenny year. I might stay fifteen.

This is the world the introduction of the cotton picker opened up to the Rickettses.

Slowly the benefits of a changing economy did reach former cotton tenants, even if it meant jobs like that of bagging resin. After World War II, jobs in rural areas such as the one-time cotton lands were on the upswing. The poverty rate in these areas dropped dramatically from 1945 to 1973.

But then it reversed and started climbing, until it far surpassed the rate for urban areas. At last count, eighteen million people in rural areas across the nation were considered below the poverty line—that is, one out of every five rural families—according to the Population Reference Bureau. Many in this book have been affected by a meat-packing plant closing in Cherokee City and by textile factories' cutting back their work force.

The trend is worsening, especially for blacks: in 1979, some 46 percent of young black families in the rural South were poor. Seven years later, the figure grew to 68 percent. There seem to be few corporate managers willing to go into the rural areas to create jobs, for either blacks or whites.

Those few jobs that pay more than the minimum are often hazardous for the former cotton farmers. As Rust feared, the new rural South has not been kind to many former tenant farmers, some of whom find themselves inadequate to the task of dealing with the new dangers it presents. Within the three families, it seems that a disproportionate number have died or been maimed in car wrecks, industrial accidents, and freak occurrences, as if they had an inherited inability to deal with modern machines and the modern world. This is admittedly just an impression, and it is not offered as statistically compelling. A proper analysis of the pattern to see whether it indeed differs from the frequency of these occurrences in the population at large to a statistically significant degree is beyond this author's mandate and ability. Still, for whatever it's worth, here's a quick rundown of some: in the Woods family, one boy was blown up when an engine exploded on the barge he worked on, one boy was killed in a car wreck, and a girl was maimed in a car wreck, as were a man and another woman; among the Rickettses, one man cut himself open by accident with a chain saw and died, and one boy was killed by a car; in the Gudger family, a brother was killed by a car, one boy was maimed in a wreck, one husband drowned, another husband was killed in a truck wreck, and so on.

Most of the cotton landlords would be happy if people were still picking cotton by hand today, living under the old rules. Much bitterness is expressed by former cotton landlords in rural Alabama. More than several of those interviewed felt theirs would still be a King Cotton region if it weren't for "them civil rights that caused us to lose our labor." They blame civil rights because blacks were the last to be freed from tenantry. Not one landlord interviewed ever pointed to machines that put the region, with its small farms, at a competitive disadvantage. When they're not blaming the civil rights movement, they blame welfare, for causing their former help to become lazy and not want to work.

Welfare was not a cause of cotton's downfall; it was a result. Continued dependence on welfare could have been minimized. The time to act was after the 1965 farm bill was passed that cut subsidies.

Paul Good said of that bill, in a 1966 article in the *Atlantic,*

Farmers, brokers, merchants, textile mills, and even the U.S. taxpayers are expected to benefit. Mississippi officials project a figure of 30,000 persons displaced in 1966. Yet in all the multibillion-dollar cotton legislation, not one cent was earmarked for worker relief, relocation, or retraining!

Welfare was not easily accepted by southern bureaucrats. *New York Times* reporter Walter Rugaber found in 1967 that Mississippi failed to take advantage of $75 million in federal welfare aid. Rugaber reported the situation the same across most of the cotton states. The commissioner of welfare in Alabama said he was opposed to welfare because it tended to make people "irresponsible."

Many former cotton tenants could have benefited from training or otherwise been helped through a transition to a better life, to be made productive in modern America. Instead, they were cast off and ignored.

Of course, for the poorest and most backward of the families still on or near the land, no government program could have done much to change things. It's hard to imagine how any program could have altered the fate of Margaret and Garvrin Arlo. The government could not have forced Garvrin Arlo and Margaret into a lifestyle they did not want. In the 1960s, the goal was to end poverty for all time. It was a noble goal, but some people just don't want to be saved. At any rate, the Rickettses would not take anything that smacked of charity. No one in the Ricketts family is on welfare or, as far as has been determined, ever was on welfare. It's a common mistake to assume that those who live in shacks must be on the dole. However poorly they may be living, some people, such as the Rickettses, find welfare repugnant. If any job at all is made available to them, they will take the job and perform its duties with blind fervor, no matter how they may be exploited in the job.

On first impression, it would be easy to laugh off people like Margaret and Garvrin Arlo. It is even easier to be repulsed by them. But after visiting them over three years, one can plainly see they were forced to devise their own survival plan in the face of mortal threats, and who really has a right to say that they ought to have devised some more elegant way to save themselves? The antics of Garvrin Arlo are a defense. He calms down after he becomes familiar with people, and he is a genuinely honest man who would do any favor asked of him.

In absolute contradiction to what one would expect, the Rickettses are probably happier than those in the Woods or Gudger families and than many upscale young Americans. When it is mentioned that they have not attained the "good life"—that is, the material trappings of well-being—it must be considered that they also lack the pressures of maintaining such a lifestyle. When Margaret says she is "rich-poor," who can argue with her statement?

WOODS

. i .

It was raining hard the night of January 27, 1976, and Emma was afraid, because lightning flashes filled her room, and thunder shook the house. It was very late, but she could not sleep, because of the storm and because it was a special day. So she put a pen to her diary.

> Well to day is my birthday. I am 60 years old. How about that. Now that seems like a long time ago. But sometimes I get to thinking back and it dont seem long at all. I can soon get on the old aged pension. That is if I live long enough. And I am just lonsom and I just write to have something to think about. I read the Bible a long time. I am lying across the bed all by my little self the Bible on one side and my diary on the other. Damon gave it to me for Christmas. He didnt know it would mean so mutch to me when my heart is heavy and when I am so lonsom and feel so all alone.

The time before Emma wrote this had been one of mixed for-
tunes. Six months earlier, she'd suffered a crushing personal loss, the
death of her only son. On the bright side, her long journey from the
cotton fields was about to yield a dream she'd dearly held for many
years—the purchase of her very own home. It was a little house on
the east side of Cherokee City, its age about equal to hers, and she
was going to buy it with her son-in-law, Warren, who was married
to Ruby, the daughter whose heart condition had long worried
Emma. Warren was a long-distance truck driver, often on the road,
and Emma worried about Ruby's being alone. The three had lived
together for many years. The plan was that they would all continue
living together.

Emma had long since adjusted to city life and much preferred
it to the hard existence that had to be coaxed and scratched off the
land. With the help of a state employee charged with the rehabilitation of people whose poor health no longer enabled them to do their
former work, Emma had moved to the city about fifteen years earlier
and found work in a nursing home, her first nonfarm job ever.

From the beginning, Lonnie had little patience for the idea that
Emma might be happier off the farm than on it and expressed his
outrage at her giving up cotton. Whatever it was that Emma learned
about herself when she went to the city and got away from sharecropping, her husband neither liked nor understood.

This man whom James Agee loathed had turned out to be just
the kind of husband the writer had predicted he would be, and
Emma had indeed spent years of cold and hopeless nights with him.
In these later years, when he felt he was finally losing his grip on
"his" woman, the level of his anger rose.

As he became more furious, Lonnie actually started making
threats on Emma's life. He even went so far as to put his threats in
a letter to the police, apparently believing that they would be sym-
pathetic to a man so driven to distraction by the refusal of his wife
to mind him that he was contemplating killing her. Emma says that
she had never considered divorce, but now, with the police
confirming for her what others had told her, she had no choice. And
she believes that he continued to keep a girlfriend through this
period.

The last straw may have been his suggestion that she feign inability to work in her new job, so that she could get full disability
pay and still be available for whatever Lonnie wanted her to do with

her time. When Emma vetoed the scheme, Lonnie became abusive. The way she looks at it, it was he who abandoned the marriage, not she.

Quite naturally, Lonnie saw it differently. He blamed all their troubles on the move to the city and the new influences on Emma. Cotton enabled him to control his wife. In this new and strange environment, free of bondage to a crop, Emma gained new strength, and Lonnie was unable to stop what he viewed as her insolence. In letters he wrote to the judge hearing his case, he hints that it is people like Mrs. Clayton, Emma's employer through this period, who must share the blame for what has happened to his marriage. On May 27, 1965, he wrote,

> To the honorable judge in equaty Circuit Court Cherokee City Ala——
>
> Your honor. I want to state to you my side of the devorce suit against me. My wife Emma was a good and faithfull wife and mother up untill she went to work at Oak Knoll Nursing Home. She gave all of her time, all of her talant, all of her love and devotion to the home. She gave me a devorce then. She neglected her children. And me. She had not time for home, husband, or children. Mrs. Clayton assured her of a home, a job, and security if she would get rid of me. And she began to make my life just as miserable as could be. She did not drive me away in so many words, but by her actions toward me. . . . The woman that is now seeking to destroy me is a different woman than is the mother of five children. . . . I have been treated about as dirty as a man could be treated. She posed as a friend to the wife of the man she is devorcing me to marry. She is two faced a cheat and a liear. God pity the man when he gets down and disable as I did to satisfye her.

On June 5, 1965, Lonnie wrote,

> Judge: your honor,
>
> I am makeing a plea and praying that your honor will consider my status as is now existing and has been in existence for some four years or more. Due to an accident while employed by State Highway Department as a carpenter, I was in Stonehedge City Hospital for some 45 days or more and underwent surgery. I was totaly disable to do any work for a year or more . . . and was solely dependent upon my wife Emma for support. But she fell in love with another man who she is devorceing me to marry. I am

asking your honor to make some provision for my welfare in granting the divorce which she is asking on false accusation.

Like many abusive husbands, Lonnie saw those who counseled
his wife to stand up for her rights as provocateurs, and he could not
pass up the opportunity to excoriate Mrs. Clayton for her role in
this:

All of this deal I am getting Mrs. J.C. Clayton, supervisor of the
Oak Knoll Nursing Home was well aware of, and was very much
in favor of my wife getting rid of me in some way.

He closed his letter:

I thank you your honor for reading my plea. I will soon be 69 years
of age looseing my wife to another man. Alone. Throwed away
forsaken.

Emma's divorce was granted on June 22, 1965.

This apparently freed her to make a life with someone else. She
was not yet fifty years old, but still haunted by her old guilty feelings. The man Lonnie claimed was her lover was nothing more than
a friend at the time of the divorce; he later came around asking for
marriage, but Emma refused, because, like Lonnie, he had been married before.

You see I lived 33 years with a man that had a living wife.
But he told me that he had that reson to put her away but I have
wondered about that a lot. I have never said this before but the one
time I married I married a man that had a living wife. And I have
thought so many times is that why we never prospered.

As for Lonnie after the divorce, Emma says, "He stayed mad
for a while. But after a while he came back arond and we was the
best of friends. He ask me to take him back a few times."

Several years later, Lonnie was admitted to Stonehedge City
hospital, suffering from heart disease, which was exacerbated by
asthma, bronchitis, and emphysema. Emma was not a hard person
and helped make his last days easier.

I was taking care of an old Lady and she fell and got hurt 2
weeks befor Lonnie died so they was on the same floor at the hospitle. So I got to be arond him them 2 weeks. I would go and feed
him. The day befor he died he laughed and said we should go back

together. We cant live with out each other. So we laughed and I made him set up in bed and I rub his back.

The next day every chance I got I would go and see about him. . . . I know he was going away. So I call his mama and he looked at me. I ran after a nurce. She said Lonnie will pull out. I said not this time. . . . I hurryed back to him and tuck his hand in mine. He looked at me. I just prayed that the children would get there. Sister just made it and I think Missy was a few minutes late and the others came as soon as they got the word. I fed him last and I held his hand until he was gone. Fed him about 4 and he died at 6.45.

Lonnie died on November 17, 1972. He was seventy-six. Emma says,

After all I was with him at the end. We had lots of up and downs. I loved him but I always look up to him kindly like a Dady I think.

. *ii* .

Emma's children had grown and prospered. Judith and her husband became the most successful, running their own auto repair shop a few blocks from Emma's house. Sonny had two children and was working as a riverboatman on the Mississippi. He worked with Judith's son, who was just entering the trade. Riverboats pushed cargo down to the gulf ports—barges of ore and timber, and coal that had been strip-mined from the hills, the products of highest value coming out of the rural South. These jobs pay well and are difficult to get. They do require being away from home for two and three weeks at a time, and they involve some danger.

On September 20, 1975, a boiler exploded on Sonny's boat, killing him.

Again, Emma wondered if God was punishing her. She had just visited Sonny in Greenville, Mississippi.

We cant understand why these things has to happen so quick. He was so big and healthy we thought and he went away like a candle blowed out or at least that is what we was told. But as for knowing we dont. I ask my self what did he think about last. . . . And then he lay on the floor of that old boat burnt up and me here sleeping in my bed of ease. I wont never get over that. He had to die all by his self. And the way he had to go is killing me. He was so afraid of fire. He never liked for me to even burn trash in the yard. He was a sweet old boy to his mama and he knew that. My heart is broke in a way that it will never heal. A part of it is in the grave with my Sonny. God have mercy on us.

Emma wrote this a few months after Sonny's death, during Christmas of 1975. Then she remained silent about Sonny in her diary until the following September. The loss of Sonny was particularly painful for Emma, and she had to rely on her faith to get her through the ordeal, her only consolation being the hope that they would all eventually be reunited:

Sonny I read in a book the other day that when we wake up from the dead that we will look like we did when we went to sleep and have the same tone of voice and if we do what you going to say? Good morning Mama—ore will you say hi Emma. What you doing there, now that is what I am looking for you to say to me the very first thing and I will be so glad to see you. I can allmost see us now. I want to be right close to him and put my arms arond him and say Hi Sonny. Of corse I want all the rest of them to be there to and I want us all to set down and just have a happy reunion. And Lonnie will say Hi Baby. All 4 girls be there. All the son in laws. And the Grand children and Mama and Dady. And Dawn be there to. Oh ever body. Not just mine. Then we all will be hapy holding hands. I just want to take my little bunch and run down to the river and gather arond them every green trees and just sing and prase God for ever and ever and then we wont have a broken heart. And there wont be no more tears.

In a poem, she expresses her desires for this place:

Just sing and play
And be so happy
Just see all them
Smiles We wont get
Tird we wont hurt
Any more we can
Get out breath good
And clear
Thank God for
The hope he has
Given us

> Thank you God
> Thank you God

> When I get to thinking about it I cant hardly waite. This life has
> ben kindly rugged here. I have never seen to mutch happines. My
> road has ben pretty bumpy. The happyest part was when I was
> trying to bring my children up and I thought I done the best I
> could. I dont know. But Mama tried.

The forty years since Emma had left the tall, dark stranger from
the North standing in front of her brother's house and gone off to
raise cotton and a family with Lonnie had not been easy ones for
her. There had been Lonnie's periodic absences, and the many seasons she had been forced to work the cotton alone, with only the
help of the little ones. There had been sickness, Ruby's, hers, and
Lonnie's. And now, when the family had finally broken free of cotton and she looked forward to her last years surrounded by her
loving children, one had been torn from her in an ugly and seemingly senseless accident. But the human spirit is indomitable, and
Emma was a survivor if nothing else. Over time, her diaries came to
introduce a new feeling:

> Now I feel kindly alone. For a long time I looked for some
> thing real good to happen to me. Like a little home. A pretty yard
> of flowers and a garden. Even some chickens. And a good some
> one to be with to laugh and talk with. When things was good and
> when these trubles and heart akes come about some one to under
> stand me and help me throu them. And let me be the same way to
> that some one.
> I found a some one that I love so very mutch. Some one that
> understands me. We see so mutch alike. I belive we would be
> happy. Of corse it wouldnt be for such a long time for natchur tells
> us so for now I am 60 years old. He is 67. But for some reson we
> dont have the chance we need.

Emma was in love again. Her man's name was Bill.

. *iii* .

In 1986, Emma lived in the house she'd bought with Ruby and Warren. They'd been there about ten years.

The house has one story, with a foundation of brick, narrow
sideboards painted white, windows trimmed in blue. It has no gut-
ters but wide overhangs at the roof.

There is the obligatory porch and a screen door that opens into a small living room, but not all the way, because it strikes an over-stuffed chair where Emma often sits. Across the room is a couch where Ruby always sits. Both will sit wordless in this room for hours, often doing nothing more than reclining with hands clasped at the waist, but one is uncomfortable if the other is absent. At three o'clock, one will rise to turn on the television, the large console type popular in the 1960s, to a favorite soap opera. Unlike many others in the three families, Emma and Ruby have not embraced video tapes, stereos, or microwaves.

It's a house that deceives. At first, it appears wealthier than it really is because of the care put into it. It's clean and organized; everything has a place. It takes several visits and a close eye to notice the torn linoleum hidden by a strategically placed couch and the frayed couch arms veiled by crocheted doilies.

In the center of a shelf is a heavily geared clock that goes about its business loudly, flanked by two dancing horses. The bedroom contains family pictures—Emma with her sister, Annie Mae Gudger; the Walker Evans portrait of their father, Bud Woods. The largest picture, a color photograph so faded that the skin is now blue, is of Sonny. It is in a frame of gold that stands alone on the dresser. It is the picture they placed on the casket at his funeral.

James Agee devoted much of his book to the houses of these people he was studying. The dwellings had something to say about them then, and their homes have something to say about them today.

The old-time slope-roof shacks of the tenant variety are vanishing. One day soon, the last of them will be gone. As they burn or are pushed over, the preferred dwelling to replace them has been the house trailer. Trailers are more popular in the South than in other regions and have been gaining in the total share of its housing stock, according to the U.S. Census Bureau. In the 1980 census, 8 percent of the total number of the one and a half million Alabama homes were trailers, compared with 4 percent in California and 2 percent in Illinois.

A slight majority of the descendants of the three families Agee wrote about live in trailers. A small minority still live in shacks; a few more than this, in fine suburban homes. In quality and market value, the house Emma lives in lies between the house trailers and modern city homes.

The most impressive middle-class home among those associated with the families belongs to Emma's daughter Judith. Sonny Gudger, the youngest boy of George and Annie Mae, the one who is now in the jewelry business, must also be said to have a fine home, judging by the value of its contents.

The prize for the worst dwelling does not go to Margaret and her son Garvrin Arlo. It falls instead to Ethel, the wife of the late Buddy Woods, who was the three-year-old naked little boy in the 1936 Walker Evans photograph of the Woods family. Ethel lives in a shack that rents for ten dollars a month and has no electricity, no running water. In thousands of miles of travel across the rural South, blacks were often found occupying such dwellings; it's rare to find whites in such "little country homes," the preferred euphemism when whites occupy them.

Poor to middle-poor whites prefer mobile homes. These mobile homes come in many kinds and styles, but they are generally defined as "single-wide" or "double-wide." As one would guess, the double-wides are twice as wide as the single-wides. These homes are anything but mobile—they are intended to be moved only occasionally and in practice are as immobile as a sharecropper shack or tract house.

As they age, they become tight little boxes of pitted aluminum that burn hot in the sun. As families have grown, some have built verandas supported on poles; others have tacked on porches on which to sit out and rock; others yet, wooden lean-tos.

The daughter of Emma's stepsister, Ellen Woods, lives in a single-wide bought secondhand for $3,500. A new single-wide goes for something like $10,000, only a fraction of the cost of a new frame home, and therein lies the practical attraction of trailers. It's a dream among many to get themselves a nice double-wide some day, cash paid out.

Some of the double-wides, such as the one lived in by Gretchen, are nicer than a person who has never been inside one might imagine. They feature pressed foam made to look like carved wood, carpeting, air-conditioning, and good heat, but are far less durable than even the old shacks. Some floors shake with the burden of heavy steps. They are easily victimized by storms. It is a joke in newsrooms that trailers attract tornadoes—the proof is that when a twister strikes, news photographers run to the trailer parks for the best pictures after the storm. Some who know the vulnerability of these structures have storm pits nearby. The trailer-dwelling Gudgers have one of these pits. They learned about them in their youth, when they lived in a sharecropper shack, but the pits are even more necessary when one lives in a trailer.

. *iv* .

Work centered on cotton and ruled the lives of all within the three families in 1936. Today, the jobs held by the descendants old enough to work are varied. Though none have jobs as grueling as that of growing cotton, most work at jobs that require hard work and long hours. Debbie, Maggie Louise's daughter, is a manager, and Nancy Ann, the Ricketts grandchild, is a secretary, but the few among the descendants who have such managerial or white-collar positions are outnumbered by those who have jobs that still require back power, long hours behind the steering wheels of trucks, on the decks of ships, on factory assembly lines, in textile mills. These are a people built for working, and they have adjusted to the new labor patterns of the rural South.

Warren, the husband of Ruby, is seldom home with Ruby and Emma, for he is on the road about three out of every four weeks. In several years of visits, we never found him home, and he soon seemed suspiciously like a creation of Emma and Ruby. Then one day we found him in the living room of the house he had bought with Emma, sitting in the overstuffed chair. His right black cowboy boot had a quarter-size hole worn through on the side, where the leather of the boot must rest against the gas pedal. He has eyes that are recessed, as if they have evolved in that certain way to allow him to watch the road for hours on end with a minimum of strain.

Warren, who started in cotton with his father, talked about work and about his journey from being a cotton farmer to being a trucker:

> I was in cotton with my daddy. My daddy worked on halves. I always said when I was a kid that I wasn't going to be no farmer. I was going to drive a truck. I'd make my own trucks out of pieces of wood. Farming was a good life but it was hard work. You didn't have no time off. All you did was work. The man you worked for got one-half of you.
>
> I was a farmer until 1951, down in Cookstown, when I went

into the service. I got out in 1953. I applied for a job. The man
asked if I could drive a truck. I never did. I didn't know it had
more than one gear. I said yes. He said I had the job. Then I had
to drive the truck out of there, and you shoulda seen me. But I
didn't get fired.

There wasn't too much trucking then. It was just local haul-
ing. Two years later, I went on the road. I have been to thirty-eight
states.

His first truck, he recalls, was a KB7 1947 International, a "gas
burner." He remembers every truck he has ever driven for pay. He
no longer does the local runs; most of the miles he puts in now are
in the Midwest and the East. The week before, he had been to Cin-
cinnati and Chicago. The next day he was to leave for Florida. He's
not entirely happy with how things have worked out for him as a
trucker, but he has too much time invested to be able to change
things now:

> Truckers used to be real respectable. Now, I hate to tell any-
> body I drive a truck. People now think truckers are low-class.
> People think of dope when they think of truckers. Go sit at most
> truck stops for fifteen minutes, and watch what goes on. You turn
> your radio on, and hear guys asking for dope, coke, hot parts,
> hollering for women. People think all truckers is that way. We got
> some nasty people out there. There's more people now. The roads
> are bigger. Freight is cheaper. There ain't much money in it. More
> people is saying I'm hanging it up. It's a bad life, being out there
> by yourself. Times come when you don't want to go. It's not a life
> for a married man. I don't think I could do anything else. I got nine
> more years to go.

. *v* .

The road south from Cherokee City is not a modern freeway, for the
needs of commerce and a sparse population in this part of Alabama
have not created a demand for one. The road tramps for two hours
through forests and occasional towns, finally arriving in Jefferson, a
city with fifty storefronts, six gas stations, a hamburger joint. This
is where most of the descendants of Bud Woods's family by his second wife have settled.

Lulla, the first wife of Bud Woods, seems to have been responsible for instilling a special kindliness, sensitivity, and hope into her

children. These traits were passed on to Annie Mae Gudger and Emma, then to their children, especially to Annie Mae's Maggie Louise, and then to the next generation, including her Debbie and the others. A comparison of these descendants of Bud Woods and Lulla with those who came out of his later marriage to Ivy is startling.

Ivy died at one in the morning, on June 16, 1971, of a heart attack. She was sixty-five. The boys from her marriage with Bud Woods were wastrels. Marion reached adulthood and lived off odd jobs. He married a heavy woman-child with a disease that ate her skeleton. They had a son, but Marion left wife and child early to become a wino roaming the streets of Mobile. He died homeless in the summer of 1986, suffering from both tuberculosis and cancer. Marion's son hates his father and plans to change his name from Woods when he turns eighteen.

Buddy, who was three in 1936, worked dairy farms for twenty-eight years. He lived above honky-tonks and died one year before Marion, of a heart attack. He was an alcoholic who beat his children on his frequent binges and forced them to drink, says his wife, Ethel, so the county took the children away and put them in foster homes. The two oldest sons have just moved back home to Cherokee City. They are in their twenties, one a mechanic and the other a laborer.

In *The Human Geography of the South*, Rupert B. Vance sums up the attitude of many toward those whose worst sin was being born to the wrong parents: "In mountain parlance the poverty stricken fall into three classes. There are the Lord's poor, destitute by misfortune; the devil's poor, stranded by their own follies; and poor devils from worthless stock who never were nor could be otherwise."

In terms of these categories, Ellen, the infant child of Bud and Ivy Woods in 1936, must be classified as someone destitute by misfortune.

It was an evening when we first visited her, and she looked that night the same as she did on another evening several years later, when we bid her a final good-bye. She is on the porch of her single-wide, where she is always found, in a rocker, the timeless image of a southern woman on her porch. One eye is fallen and her face is soft, lost to the senses of this world in the magic that is Alabama porch evenings. Her good eye moves on the approach of visitors.

"Are you Ellen?" we ask.
"What's left of her."

. *vi* .

Ellen does not live far from her stepsister Pearl, who is a child not of Bud Woods, but of Ivy from an earlier relationship. When Bud Woods died, Ivy decided to come live closer to Pearl and persuaded Ellen to come along with her. Ellen, between husbands at that time, had young children to care for and came along with her mother. She never did get along with Pearl, however. When Pearl changed her name to Ruth Ann, Ellen was the sister who enjoyed teasing her by persisting in calling her Pearl.

Ellen is a pleasant woman, whose children lead lives that stand in contrast to those lived by Ivy's other grandchildren. Everyone speaks kindly of Ellen. Neighborhood children call her aunt. Ellen loves the world and finds fault with no one but Pearl.

Ellen was married four times. Perhaps she was looking for her father in her men. But the children of these men, as well as her own children, loved her, and in them she found her role, somehow saving them from the terrible influences to which they were subjected. She married her second husband because she fell in love with his children. She had two girls of her own and three boys. One died long ago in a car wreck, and she wishes God had taken her instead.

At the time we first interviewed Ellen, she was with her fourth husband. The man had moved in his stepson and the stepson's wife. During that first visit, this son's wife came home, moving her obese body up the stairs of the porch. Her puppy was in front of the door, and this woman kicked it broadside out of the way, slamming the door behind her. She often screamed at Ellen. On a later visit, we learned Ellen had finally decided it was better to be alone than put up with that and had divorced the man. She is alone now but the happiest she has ever been.

Pearl, by the accounts of Ellen and other family members, tried to assume a new identity after she fled Cherokee City. She changed her name after arriving in Jefferson, afraid that the man with the knife and salami might come down to Jefferson asking after her.

Pearl's son, Bobby, has had several marriages. He has left the area and no one I talked to in the family knows where he is.

I approached Pearl for an interview. She answered the door of her home, filling the entry with her six-foot-two frame. Her face had turned from the soft beauty of youth to something that would have been unrecognizable from Walker Evans's picture—tight, full of emotion. It was a tense conversation.

Mere mention of the 1940s caused her to fly into an awesome fit, nearly shouting, so it seemed unwise if not inappropriate to press for details about her life.

"You don't see no disgrace," she said. "There's no scandal. I think you better leave it alone!"

A year later, when we again approached for another interview, she screamed, slamming the door. So her side of what happened was not heard.

In most matters, Ellen tries to be a forgiving woman who looks forward, not back, trying to find the best in any situation. The road to her hatred of Pearl came in late 1976, on an afternoon when Ellen and her daughter Diane were coming up the highway south of Jefferson. It's a stretch of blacktop flanked by a swamp and trees hung heavy with Spanish moss. Ellen was driving. The car was bobbing in the many dips at a smart speed. At the top of one hill, a logging truck dodged a dog that came into its driver's path and crossed over into their lane. There was nowhere for them to go. The impact crushed the side of Ellen's car, pinning her in the rush of sparks and metal. The car landed in the swamp. The medics who arrived looked at Ellen, bloody and motionless, and gave her up for dead. They pulled Diane from the wreckage. Then they detected life in Ellen and worked her free. Doctors told the family she would not live, but Ellen found some way to hang on. She remained in intensive care for months, in a coma, her life precarious the whole time. During this period, Pearl called Ellen's half sister Emma in Cherokee City and said Ellen was bleeding on the inside.

When Ellen overcame that, the same doctors said she would be paralyzed and have no brain function left. She again proved them wrong. First, she regained her mind. She began crawling, later walking. It took years to reclaim the use of her body. She is limp on her left side, but otherwise seems to show few effects. She has an occasional seizure, but the last one was several years ago. The settlement money from the accident paid for a trailer for her to live in. There was a little left over, which her last two husbands tried to take, but they were thwarted by court orders obtained by her daughter Diane.

At the time of the accident, Ellen's youngest daughter, Mary

Lee, was still a minor. Mary Lee had been born premature and weighed only two pounds, fourteen ounces. She had to undergo many operations to repair her underformed bones, so her childhood was one of pain. Ellen doted on and sheltered this daughter, thereby extending her childhood. Mary Lee was in her teens when the accident occurred, but was like a small child.

At the time of the accident, Ellen's third husband had left, and Mary Lee had no one to care for her. Diane was too young in this period to help and had her arms full with a new baby. Aunt Pearl seemed a likely choice.

Pearl stepped in, taking guardianship of Mary Lee. For almost the next decade, Mary Lee lived with her. Little is known about those years except that Mary Lee remembers doing a lot of housework and many of the tedious chores; it also appears that during that time she almost never saw her relatives or boys. Pearl was given the support money for Mary Lee and essentially raised her.

Inside Pearl's house, Mary Lee sat nearby, mistrustful but curious. Other family members in the north of Alabama had mentioned this "retarded" daughter, but the girl we saw responded in ways that suggested she was not retarded; indeed, she seemed brighter than Pearl.

Even after Ellen's survival became first a possibility and then a likelihood, Ellen, it seems didn't reclaim Mary Lee from Pearl. At first she remained in the hospital, undergoing therapy, and could not physically reassert control over Mary Lee's life. Indeed, for more than half a dozen years, Ellen was simply in no position to intervene, and by the time she was well enough to do so, Mary Lee was an adult.

About a year after we had first seen Mary Lee, she decided on her own to leave Pearl. As Mary Lee describes it, Pearl either suggested or in some more direct way communicated to her that she should not attend her own father's funeral. She rebelled, running away to her sister Diane's. A week later, she was in the living room of Diane's trailer, chain-smoking cigarettes. Pearl, she commented, had not allowed her to smoke.

Away from Pearl, Mary Lee seemed a different person. Clearly, Diane had been right all along, in insisting that Mary Lee was not retarded. Although Mary Lee spoke of the authoritarian rule she had lived under in Pearl's house, she clearly was looking forward and not back. She talked with real excitement about life and its future possibilities. In one area, however, Mary Lee clung stubbornly to a view from her past. She said she would never marry.

A year later, however, Mary Lee was both married and making up handsomely for the missing decade in her life. She had wed a truck-driver of Indian descent and was living in a nearby town. They had first met as teenagers. He is gentle and understands the events in her life.

Ellen is content, knowing that her daughter is now away from Pearl.

. *vii* .

Forty years after Emma's flirtation with Agee, she was still looking for love. About to enter her seventh decade, she thought 1976 might be the last year she was going to have a real chance of finding it. She was dating her Bill, scratching for moments they could go out for supper together and have long talks.

Her diary records the tensions in the relationship in this period when she was grieving the loss of her son, as well as the joys the relationship brought her:

> He tells me he loves me and I believe he does. And I know I love him. He has asked me to marrie him more than once. We have so many times have wanted to get married but . . . we cant see how we can do it. He loves my children. I dont know his. I have seen one of his girls a lot. I like her.
>
> So Dear Aby what do you think will ever happen to us.
>
> Signed Allice in Wonder Land.

By 1976, they had been seeing each other for three years. By her account, it was a tumultuous relationship—Bill's long work hours and Ruby's sickness, which kept Emma home many nights, made it difficult for them to see each other. Bill wanted marriage. But Emma's old tensions about religion made her stop short of saying yes—she believed God had punished her for marrying the divorced Lonnie, and she felt that her wedding the twice-married Bill would incur even greater wrath.

> I realy dont think that God wants me to love Bill, for you see he has already ben married twice and both of his wifes is still living now. I have prayed hard for God to lead me the right way. . . .
>
> I believe that is one of the bigest sin going on today is

ADULTER. So many people gets married and dont really love each other and the way I see it they are not married. They are by the law of the people but they are not in the sight of God. For God is love.

I had a chance with him and I wanted very mutch to take it. But I was afraid to. And now I can and will tell the reson. I didnt want to live the rest of my life in Adultry for I just couldnt belive that both of his wives comited fornication. But now he did not say that they did. But any way the Bible tells us if we put them away for other reson and marry again that we do commit adultry and he comanded us not to do that. Now you might say that is old fogy but it is in the Bible.

This late in life, Emma was more uncertain of what love was, anyway. It is the curse of each generation to agonize, to remember the excitement of first love, that feeling of being unable to live without someone; that first pain is like no other to follow. By the second, third, and fourth love and beyond, the calluses grow; we are dulled, we wonder if it exists, if it has eluded us, and why. Many of us in our youth think we have the answer, only to find new realities as we age. Emma thought she was in love with Fred Bungy, a good-looking boy from her youth. He was a navy man whom all the girls wanted. She confesses that she dreamed about him through thirty-three years of her marriage to Lonnie, until one day she finally ran into him. It was a shock.

And I would have never known him any more. He looked aful. I still cant belive he is the man I thought I loved so dearly.

And so Emma found the answer, that for some childhood deprivations, for some lives lived in hope, a quest for love is not the answer; maybe there is no answer. This truth was really at the heart of so many of her problems:

I am going to stop writing now. I may never write any more about this. But good people I just want to say this. I think what I have missed has ben a mothers tender love. I think that is the reson that I have looked for something that I have never ben able to find.

The summer of 1976 wore on, and Emma's relationship with Bill continued at the same pace. Ruby was frequently in the hospital that summer, and Emma felt she had to spend a lot of time with her daughter. This added to the tension with Bill and made it impossible for her to see him on weekends. There was another falling out, and Emma did not see Bill most of August, though her entries tell us she thought about him more often than she might have wanted to.

> With all my heart I have tried real hard to stop loving him but that is one love I cant shack a loose. But I am better than I was the first time he showed his ass with me. The first time it liked to have run me nuts. You see he wont just go and get out of my life. He will always call me. Tell me he knows he has done wrong but he loves me. If he loved me he wouldnt do these things that he knows hurts me. I havent done him wrong. But every time he does me wrong I catch him. . . .
>
> We have ask one another just why couldnt we have met a long time ago. We have set and talked about God and we have set and talked about dieing so many times. We have went to church together not just once. We have laughed and we have cryed together. There was nothing I wouldnt tell him and he would tell me anything. We was just to close not to be man and wife. Now it is hard to give all these thing up. But I still say God will be done not mine. But I am lonly. . . .

The next entry in Emma's diary shows a resolution of sorts between the couple:

> Well I have got my book messed up. So today is the 30 day of Aug but I have to write this. I have wrote a lot about Bill and my self. But tonight we have talked a long time. He told me I was the best woman he ever went with. He told me he wanted me for his own. Yess we have wanted to get married. We have talked about it so many times. But he said that he know that Ruby need me to and that he just couldnt ask me to leve her and he just couldnt see a house big enough for 2 famlys.
>
> He told me that he tryed to find another woman to take my place but he could not find one. He said know matter how hard he tryed I was always there in his face and before he new it he would have the phone up calling me for he was afraid of loosing me. We talked a long time. We both even cryed. It is bad to love some one so mutch.

One of Emma's entries after this date treats the reality that they will never be married. She now devotes her time to Ruby and to reading her Bible and praying. Her entries reveal her solitude:

I am alone, and still I dont feel so lonly. I know it is my nearves but I have felt Sonny so close to me. I have just set so timed tonight just looking for him to open the door and walking in smiling. Now this is true. I have realy ben looking for him for I feel him so close. I cant hardly waite for him to open that door. I wonder why I feel him so close. I havent had this feeling before. I wish some body would come and brake this spell. I dont feel like I can waite mutch longer.

As the holidays come around, Emma starts to think less about building a new life than about taking satisfaction from what she has managed to accumulate over the course of her sixty years. It is all in the love of her children and grandchildren.

To day is Christmas Day. Me my radio and little dog is spending the day together. Now I dont have to but all the children has things to do and I dont. I dont know why I havent done any thing. Didnt even get up untill one oclock. It is raining and so dark and gloomy, just such a good day to think. I have got so mutch to be thankful for and I am. I thank God for all my blessing and my children and my grand children is so wonderful and butful and loving and they all are so good to me. I am one of the riches women in the world and I know it and I thank my God for all of this but to my sorrow part of me is gone.

I cant explan this to you. I gess the best way to explan is this. I feel like a big bird with one of my wings broke. Can you understand. I might fly a little ways but then I fall.

We went and put flowers on Sonny + Lonnies grave. I wasnt happy at the way Sonnys looked. As for Lonnie he wouldnt care. But Sonny would want his to be pretty. Very pretty. He has ben gone 15 months today.

And then the year ends, as does her diary. She will not keep a diary in the coming years, because the arthritis in her hands makes it painful to write.

This is the 29th day of Dec. It has been cold all this week. Kate and Damon is here tonight. They are asleep for it is after 12 oclock. Warren has got home. I came in my room and I just stoped and looked at Kate sleeping. I looked over on my dresser at Sonnys pitcher. She looks so mutch like him across her mouth. It sad. I just look at her and think.

I feel so bad. My breath is so short. The house is nasty. The water pipe froze and bursted. Of corse every thing will be alright when the new year comes. I just know every thing is going to be alright. After all I have a lot to be thankful for.

. *viii* .

The middle 1980s found Ruby increasingly ill. Two-month stays in Cherokee City Hospital were not uncommon.

In 1987, Ruby suffered a heart attack. After many weeks in the hospital, she became pale and weak. When she simply stood to go to the bathroom, her heart rate jumped to 140 beats per minute. She ran a fever for months from an infection in her chest.

Ruby had lived with this bad heart all her life, yet she endured the misery of her illnesses with an acceptance that was fearful in its power. She is bitter about nothing.

Ruby's room was in an old wing of the hospital, and the odor revealed the great age of the building and a greater sense of sickness than is found in most hospitals. Cancer can be smelled, coroners say, when you enter the home of someone who has just died of the disease. It gives off a special taste to the air as it eats flesh. If you have known this odor, sweet and half-rotting, you can imagine this ward. The cinder block walls were spiritless. The window was shuttered, and Ruby's skin was like chalk in the half-light. Ruby couldn't afford the three dollars a day it cost to rent a television set to distract herself from all this.

Sonny and Ruby were Emma's favorite children back in the 1940s, she wrote in her diary. The closeness to Ruby solidified with years of living together; Emma became even more attached to Ruby than she ever was to Sonny.

Of course, Emma was ruined over Ruby's failing health. Warren was, too, but his boss man was tough, and he was afraid to ask for much time off. He couldn't afford to lose his job now that he was so close to retirement. His income was badly needed by Ruby and Emma. He was in Chicago when Ruby had the first attack, and today he was somewhere in Tennessee.

Ruby went home from the hospital. A year passed. She was again stricken, this time worse than before. Doctors operated and placed a pacemaker in her chest. In the spring of 1988, she spent a lot of time in the hospital. The second time she was admitted, she stayed for eleven weeks. In the eleventh week, Emma, nervous and worried, suffered a diabetes attack and blood pressure that soared off the chart. She was admitted to the hospital one floor below Ruby. She spent two weeks there.

Emma was sobbing one day in the hospital. "I took care of her forty years," she said, "and now it's out of my hands. There's nothing I can do." She went over her old guilt again. If she had just picked up the girl and walked all those miles from their cotton farm to the doctor when Ruby fell ill at the age of nine, maybe the rheumatic fever would not have damaged her heart as it has.

They gave Ruby three options: a transplant, life support, or a trip home to spend whatever time she had left with her husband and mother. She said no to the first two.

Emma got better the day after Ruby was released, and she in turn left the hospital. During all this, Debbie heard about her cousin Ruby's condition. Debbie had not seen her aunt Emma and kin since Maggie Louise drank the rat poison. Debbie had withdrawn from the family after her mother's death, but things had changed enough that she could come to Ruby's bed. She felt she *had* to come. Ruby's head was turned, and she was asleep. Debbie simply said hello. Without looking, Ruby awoke and said, "It is you, Debbie." After seventeen years, she knew her lost cousin by one word, and this caused Debbie's eyes to well with tears. Ruby turned her head and smiled. They hugged. Emma was happy Debbie had finally come home.

It was another day when I visited. The living room clock was ticking loudly at Emma's house. Warren was home from the road this time. He came to the door and was silent. He walked back to their room, past the twenty-four-hour home-hospice nurse sitting at the kitchen table, and Ruby labored to open her eyes to see me. Her face was paperlike, lacking contour, every muscle fallen. Warren stared at his shattered wife. Ruby tried to smile, but met with failure.

"It's over," Ruby announced. Then she was again sleeping.

Soon afterward, with Warren holding her in his arms, Ruby died.

. *ix* .

Let us now praise famous men, and our fathers that begat us.

The Lord hath wrought great glory by them through his great power from the beginning.

Such as did bear rule in their kingdoms, men renowned for

their power, giving counsel by their understanding, and declaring prophecies:

Leaders of the people by their counsels, and by their knowledge of learning meet for the people, wise and eloquent in their instructions:

Such as found out musical tunes, and recited verses in writing.

Rich men furnished with ability, living peaceably in their habitations:

All these were honoured in their generations, and were the glory of their times.

There be of them, that have left a name behind them, that their praises might be reported.

And some there be which have no memorial; who perished, as though they had never been; and are become as though they had never been born; and their children after them.

But these were merciful men, whose righteousness hath not been forgotten.

With their seed shall continually remain a good inheritance, and their children are within the covenant.

Their seed standeth fast, and their children for their sakes. Their seed shall remain for ever, and their glory shall not be blotted out.

Their bodies are buried in peace; but their name liveth for evermore.

—Ecclesiasticus 44:1–14

BRIDGES

. i .

It's a late summer afternoon, and a group consisting of Joe Bridges's family and neighbors sit in the shade of a fruit stand constructed of chicken wire and rotted planks, down by the main highway in front of the Bridges house, waiting for customers who never seem to stop to buy the produce they try to sell. The thermometer reads well over ninety degrees, and a waist-high industrial fan fails to soften the impact of that temperature. It ruffles a rack of dusty out-of-fashion dresses Kate hopes to sell to the people who don't stop to buy their eggs or vegetables.

Twenty hands furiously labor at unzippering peas. Tiny orbs rain into pails. Shelling peas has been a way of life for these people. Their parents grew peas and shelled them just like this in August, to dry and be eaten in the winter. They freeze most of the crop now, but otherwise little in the practice has changed.

In this circle are the Bridgeses—Kate, her husband, Joe, their son Huey, Kate's mother, an octogenarian who lives in a trailer by the pond down the road, a neighbor couple, a few others, Joe's brother, who lives across the highway. Barney is the one who had three ships blown out from under him in World War II and who has never been the same since. He is laughing, mouth agape, chewing tobacco, drooling on the whiteness of his shirt, the spot growing to resemble a map of Australia.

Beyond the shade of this stand, the land reclines, auburn, crisp, at the base of Hobe's Hill, beneath the August sun in this year of drought, "drawth," as Joe says.

Joe's farm is showing the ill effects of the lack of rain. It's too hot to walk the rows of soybeans Joe planted in the spring, when it seemed he might get the rain the crop needed. Now that the beans are so brown, Joe wonders how he could have had such hope back in April. It's so warm, it's even too hot to fuck, confides Huey, Joe's thirty-year-old son, who works for the county and still lives at home. It's even too hot for fucking down by the swimming hole, beneath the shade of that big oak tree, Huey adds. It has been a long time since Huey has engaged in that pastime. He says that he likes to think of sex with his last fling, a woman now lost to marriage with another man.

Barney overhears Huey whispering about sex and starts talking about butt-fucking in the barn. He loudly repeats his contribution to the conversation, but no one pays any attention.

To turn the talk in a new direction, Joe begins telling stories about the old days.

"It was hard times in the Depression," Joe says.

> We had to raise just about everythang. I mean, there just wasn't nothin' branging nothin'. When Roosevelt took office in thirty-three, thangs started pickin' up. Before then, it was awful bad. I was just a kid, but Lord God, we was poor. Oh Lord yeah, hell, everybody come up from where they was back there.

The conversation inevitably finds its way to the families on Hobe's Hill and the book published by James Agee and Walker Evans. The book is well known by just about everyone in this county.

One seventy-eight-year-old woman in the Cookstown City Hall jumped to her feet at the mere sight of *Let Us Now Praise Famous Men* held in hand. "That book! We knew what he was up to! Come down here to low-rate the South. I just resent it to death, him picking those people! People up North are still eating that garbage up!"

It also upsets Joe's neighbors. The man and woman put down fistfuls of peas.

"You have to remember those were very special people, and it would not be fair to use them to represent what people in the South are like in general," says the man. His wife says the New Yorkers chose the strangest people, and now the outside world retains an image of their county based upon the Rickettses. She advises it would be better to look at all the nice homes, as fine as those seen in any suburb, that dot the county today.

When reminded of all the shacks between those fine homes, she replies, "But it's not fair to look just at them."

In 1932, Holland Thompson was quoted by Rupert B. Vance in *The Human Geography of the South* as saying of the antebellum South,

> There was a South of the plantation, and of the upland farm; . . .
> the South with lands almost incredibly fertile and the barren South
> where living was hard; the civilized South, and nearby the South,
> ignorant and rude; the austere Calvinist South, and the South of
> romance; the haughty aristocratic South and the democratic South.

Today, a visitor can still find any South he or she desires. There is the South of shacks, of fine restored antebellum homes, tract homes, ghettos, shopping malls; the bastard un-south South of Atlanta, the frozen charms of Selma; the redneck South, yet ignorant, yet rude, alongside the mint-julep South of refined cordiality; the Styron South, the Faulkner South, the Hurston South.

Unlike his neighbors, Joe takes no offense at the Agee-Evans book or even at the Rickettses. He says the book was about a time long ago. He says there's a reason for everything. A reason for the book. A reason for the Rickettses. A reason for the bedbugs that infested their house.

> You know what a bedbug is? It's a bug that gets along on filth. Ya
> know, when body bacteria come off a person on a sheet that ain't
> washed and cleaned. It's somethang God put there and had to be.

Let me tell ya somethang people don't thank about. You look at it as being a bad bug. But if it weren't for that bug, what do you thank woulda happened to that bed? God wanted somethang to eat up the filth. It's just like the salt in the ocean. The salt in the ocean purifies all the waste. All of the creeks, all of the branches, all of the rivers, all of the water that all goes into the ground, it goes down streams back into the ocean into salt. The salt purifies. The sun pulls it out and recycles the water, brangs it back over the land in the form of rain. That water we drank today was maybe drunk a million years ago, by the people, the animals. You can't throw water away. See, it's a reason for everythang. Everythang out there, God's put there for a reason to make the world survive.

. *ii* .

Across the paved road from the fruit stand where the Bridgeses and their friends have congregated this afternoon, a dirt road enters the main highway, the road that leads to the top of Hobe's Hill. Up that road five hundred feet, on the right, is the now abandoned frame house where the Woods family lived for seven years after Joe's dad took pity and brought them down off the hill that day in 1937 when they were starving.

A little farther up the road are some shacks; two black cotton men of old sit in weather-bleached rockers with wood as white as their hair. They announce matter-of-factly they have nothing to do and are just waiting to die. There is a house trailer nearby where a divorced woman lives. Up around the bend, a suburban-style brick home. It's the last inhabited home on this road. Streamers of red dust rise behind the rare vehicle that passes beyond this point. The road enters a forest, thick with vines, whose fingers creep into the roadway and strike the fenders of passing cars. The vines are kudzu, which infests all the South, an exotic visitor imported from Japan. It was planted in the 1930s to end erosion caused by improper cotton cultivation. It was also supposed to feed cows. Kudzu can grow one foot a day—the southern poet and author James Dickey calls it a "vegetable form of cancer." It now is considered useless, out of control, covering some six million acres of the South. It relentlessly climbs billboards, poles, and empty buildings, until they resemble giant Halloween figures cloaked in acres of green blankets.

Two miles from the Bridges fruit stand, a hemlock tree grows next to the dirt track. This is where the Ricketts home stood in

1936. Hidden beneath a tangle of kudzu is the cistern hole, a few chimney rocks, charred boards. It was eventually handed down to a black family. In the 1970s it burned.

Across the lane, a quarter mile distant, are the remains of the Woodses' 1936 home. That shack was abandoned in the 1950s. By the late 1960s, it simply got tired of standing and fell down. It's a well-hidden pile of lumber, the worm-eaten wood smelling of great age.

No one lives on Hobe's Hill today. Only a few abandoned shacks remain. The land has greatly changed. When Walker Evans took his pictures, it was a grand, open place, full of cotton. Now forest has reclaimed the land. There is still some field, planted in soybeans, and this provides some sense of how things once were. These soybeans, as well as those down by the main highway, were planted by Joe Bridges and his son Huey.

Amid the soybeans, the ground is stony, and the water-starved beans grow with more courage than success. This same dust was breathed by Fred Ricketts as he plowed behind the sweaty rump of a mule fifty years ago. He and his children stared at this ground as they chopped weeds and, later, hunched over the long rows to pick. They knew this same sun, this silence, the awful loneliness of this red plateau.

The heat dulls the senses. Even sulfur butterflies, those neurotic field strutters, are slothful. The whole South seems under a hot Augustan pause—all the highways blurry beneath the burden of heat, be they four-lane marchers, two-lane winders, single-track dirt poems. From this hill, it's hard to imagine life going on in this heat anywhere across the six hundred miles of the South, in any of those terrible little towns: in Fort Adams, McComb, or Newburn or even in the biggest one, Atlanta—that Los Angeles of the "new" South, with its two million citizens populating suburbs and ghettos without hope of redemption.

It takes faith to believe men and women once trod and worked this land. It seems some terrible holocaust must have claimed them. Two abandoned houses at the end of the soybeans stand like ruins from a war. The distant porch of one has long been silent of footsteps, its chambers quiet of human utterance. The dwellings are the only signs that men and women ever called this place home. All else is gone, save for the road, the beans dying beneath the whiteness of the afternoon sky.

Those homes were the "negro houses" described by Agee. They were owned by Mr. Foster, the black landowner who farmed a small part of Hobe's Hill just down from the Rickettses. Agee described having to pass the buildings on his night walks from the Gudger house to the Ricketts house. In the dark, dogs would bark, men would stir, and he'd hurry on.

The porch of one of the kudzu-laden Foster homes leans on a bended knee, collapsed to a forty-five-degree angle, with floorboards that break away and swallow feet.

After the end of cotton, it didn't take long for this home to die. When a house like this is abandoned, first to go are the windows, broken by a fusillade of rocks hurled shortly after the last occupants move on. All local kids are suspect, but no one sees the little guerrillas—they kick in doors, getting an excited chill from their fear of being caught at their mischief, piss in the kitchen, vanish. And then through the jagged open frames enter the rain and wind, which for years gnawed at the house's hide until it was left hoary gray, and rusted the tin roof the color of sun tea. Now homes like this are under an occupation of rattlesnakes, and squadrons of violin wasps swarm when surprised by visitors.

Ever since people began fleeing the land, rumors have circulated about old farmhouses. The rumors have it that money and valuables are stashed behind fireplace mantels, which in days of old were used as safes. Treasure hunters have combed Alabama, ripping open fireplace fronts in empty homes in search of forgotten treasures. The fireplaces of this home have been so ravaged, but left behind as worthless are hidden letters and objects that reveal its history, most eaten beyond recognition by whatever creatures now inhabit the house.

Among the objects is a picture, vague from age, of a black man and woman, presumably Mr. and Mrs. Foster, she standing respectfully behind. They are dignified, serious, perhaps too much so, as if trying hard to look better than other nonlandowning farmers. He wears a wool coat and tie. A mustache stands out under a receding hairline. His eyes make it uncomfortable to gaze at him. She has hair parted in the center, hand on his buttocks, looking away and not at you. Her ample bosom brushes his back.

The following letter is in the handwriting of a woman.

Cherokee City Ala
Oct 1st 1901

Dear Mr. Foster:

I arrived home safely yesterday morning. I found all well and glad to see me. They took my being hurt very well so I think you can come to Cherokee City when ever you get ready with out any fear. My arm is much better to day. It is still badly swoolen but pains very little. My school opened this morning I was able to go myself by keeping my arm in a sling. I don't feel at all at home seemingly I am visting. Convention is going on and oh how I wish I had some of those turnip greens butter milk and "taters" to give the "dele go ats." Love to each one of the family and all the friends that inquire of me. All sends love.

As ever your friend,

Annie

This letter is difficult to read, with uncrossed *t*'s and no periods (which have been supplied for clarity's sake), full of rat bites and insect holes.

Sept. 15, 1902

My dear Brother with such pleasure take to writting you. I am well and hope that you are the Same. I am at work & am ———— I hope that you had a good rain last week. We had a good one. Everything is getting along. There is some strang girls ———— and the boys is bout to go crazy about them. There are foor of them. I was out last night with one of them alone ———— is about to go crazy with them. They is all right. Give my love to Miss Annie and all the familey. Tell Mama that grand mama is well and send love to her. Write and tell me all the news. Tell Miss annie that I often thinks of her while I am in the mines By my Self ———— I am on the night shift. It is shure lonesome around there ———— is getting a long with his cotton. Tel me all the news. Write me soon. From your devoted brother.

J.S.

Then there is this letter dated July 5, 1905, from the cousin of Mrs. Foster.

Miss Viola Foster
Madrid, Ala.

My Dear Cousin

I have often thought of writing to you. And if I did would I even hear from you. Or would it be like the other time I wrote? I am glad to say this leave me well and haveing a very pleasant time. Truely. Hope you are enjoying the same sweet blessing of life. What are you going to do for a good time on the fourth? I received an invitation to ———— picnic. I have made a smile on a northern peach. He is very gay. I wish you could meet some of the Indiana people. When we were coming we stayed in Chattanooga and spent the after noon on the Look Out mt. Its qui— a beautiful— —co——ed see in ———— different states. When you are in the north the white and colord are just the same. All eat at the same table. Some time I think am I white or col, from the way I am treated. How are you and ———— Lee? give my best regards to all the neighbors. Viola write me 12 pages and tell me all the home news. I hope I won't get ———— will come south in September. I am coming home Xmas if nothing happen. You must be a sweet girl and as soon as you get this letter, give my love to Lee when you see him. I guess it's miss Foster yes. Is it?

With this I'll close, hoping to hear from you soon.

Your loving Cousin
Lucy D. Ephus
192 West Broadway
Shelbyville, Indiana

The following letter, dated February 22, 1922, is from the H. E. Powell Lumber Company in Cookstown.

Mr. Foster:

You owe me the amount of $17.25 that has to be settled. I have waited on you as long as possible. You had better come up quick and do something. I will give you until Saturday to settle this. If something is not done, I am going to turn this over to Mr. Wiggerly Saturday night. I am hoping you will do something though.

H. E. Powell

And the final letter, from a brother to the one who took over the Foster farm, is dated December 3, 1941.

Dear Joe

How are you all getting alone?

How is Papa does he seems to be getting any better?

Did you get the box that I sent him? If so write and let me know so that I can send him something else.

Listen Joe, I have enclosed in this letter a card addressed to myself. All that you'll have to do is to write on the front of it and it's already addressed so that I'll get it. Please let me hear from Papa.

Love to all.
R. W.

The postcard remains unanswered in the envelope, never returned to R.W.

There is also a much newer photo, of a black couple being married outdoors, from the late 1960s. The bride's face is veiled and the groom's serious. Were they related to the original owners? Did they end up living here after the owners died, on rent and welfare, as check stubs indicate, the last to occupy this home?

Behind these two homes is a barn with an open middle, the one Agee described having to walk through to reach the trail leading to the home of George and Annie Mae Gudger, about half a mile south of here.

Nothing remains of the Gudger house on the twenty acres of hill where it stood. What was then open pasture is now chigger-infested jungle concealed by a fog of brush that limits vision to a few feet. All that indicates the homesite is an old dump of tin cans that crunch beneath feet passing over the thick blanket of pine needles. Pretty Boy, the black man who in 1939 was struck and killed by the car at the base of Hobe's Hill, was the last man to occupy the house. His was the final challenge to the futility of trying to grow cotton at the end of that dwindling, muddy branch road that has long since melted into the landscape.

After Pretty Boy's death, Chester Boles sold the ground to a timber company, which planted pine trees, maybe the best use for this mineral soil. The home either fell or was pushed over, and the trees have done well, growing thick.

. iii .

Trees are everywhere. The only untreed land around Hobe's Hill is the fields planted by Joe Bridges. For two miles north of his fruit stand, all the wilted soybeans are his. The fields exist as patches of openness about to be swallowed by marching columns of expanding woodlands. Four miles south of his fruit stand—all the way to Madrid and the dirt turnoff leading to the old Burgandy place, where

Maggie Louise's children were born—all the soybeans on either side of the highway are also his.

Fair quantities of beans are scattered along these six miles of highway and on top of Hobe's Hill, with some occasional fields of wheat, raised to feed thirty-one brood sows. The Bridgeses sell a few pigs to make money, keep the rest to eat. A small bit of corn grown for a few cows is planted down in the riverbottom, where Indian arrowheads can be found amid the rows.

The county agriculture extension agent is no fan of Bridges. He cautions that Bridges isn't the type of farmer anyone should hold up as an example. The agent says that he's not good at farming. Joe blames forces beyond his control—the weather, equipment trouble. That Bridges has filed for bankruptcy would seem to confirm the agent's views, but he is trying to reorganize to save his farm.

The agent tries to direct outsiders to "better" farmers, but they are wealthy weekend tractor men who own hundreds of acres and work them more as a hobby than as a way of life. Like so many people around here, the agent is conscious of the image that the Agee-Evans book presents to the outside world. He wants to steer outsiders to the "good" people of the county.

In spite of the agent's derogations, Joe Bridges can make one claim to distinction: he is the last farmer left on this six-mile stretch of road.

It's unclear just how many once farmed this same swath of highway, but they numbered in the dozens. When Joe's father was going strong, this farm alone supported six to seven sharecropping families. A dozen surrounding farms were populated the same way. It was a community.

They all left or died, and Bridges outlasted them all. His reward, if it can be called that, will be to become the last man ever to break ground on Hobe's Hill. He'll be the last to see its earth freshly turned and smell its tired breath; the last to harvest a crop that rises from that clay; the last to watch the sky and hope for rain that never comes or to curse when too much falls.

He farms the remaining two hundred acres he owns. He leases more land than this, but the term "lease" is a misnomer. No one other than Joe wants to farm, so there is no market for the land and he gets to farm for nothing or next to nothing all the combined acreage once worked by the tenant farmers written about by Agee.

For reasons of sentiment, the sons and daughters of the onetime cotton lords do not want the land grown in trees. They now plead with Joe to farm, a sharp turnaround from the days when their parents coveted every square foot of soil, extracting so high a price in dollars and dignity from those who with their own blood and sweat, and that of their children, squeezed the South's cotton crop out of the land.

It takes a lot of work to keep wild trees off this land. They're eager immigrants, arriving on airborne seeds. Joe provides a protective service with his planting, plowing back the saplings that emerge each spring.

The daughter of the Burgandy woman, the one-time landlady of Maggie Louise and Floyd Franks, gives Bridges seventy acres; the grandson of Boles, the Gudgers' master, thirty acres.

On top of Hobe's Hill itself, Joe actually pays a nominal fee of five hundred dollars for the land still owned by the descendants of T. Hudson Margraves, the much-despised landlord of Ricketts and Woods in 1936. Margraves's nephew, T. Wilson Margraves, inherited a 240-acre remnant of the vast spread once controlled by his uncle, who died on June 25, 1958, at the age of eighty-nine. Until 1970 or so, Margraves leased it to those two white-haired, just-waiting-to-die rockers. They were the last to plant cotton on Hobe's Hill. After they quit, the land sprouted sumacs, oaks, renegade pines. Margraves worried he'd lose the land to overgrowth, so he contacted Joe and offered it at a pittance just to keep it open. If bankruptcy forces Joe out of farming, Margraves will have no one to turn the soil, keep the land alive, as if cleared farmland here still has any value.

To rid himself of this worry, Margraves once put the land up for sale, but no one wanted to buy, not even at a giveaway price. The land, once a grand measure of wealth, has now become a terrible bother.

Margraves has plans to plant the field in pine trees. When he is old, he can then sell the timber, perhaps making a profit. That has been the pattern all over Alabama. As cotton was phased out and replacement crops like corn and soybeans failed, field after field has succumbed to pines. Nowadays, weeks of searching in central Alabama will uncover just occasional cotton patches. Few want to grow it any longer in this place, which was once the geographic heart of the Cotton Belt. Pine trees are the last crop that will ever be planted in much of Alabama.

Joe says of the Hobe's Hill fields,

> It would be grown up now if it wasn't for me. It laid out for ten years, and trees got as tall as that door there. We went up there and bushed it all out. When I was a boy, I used to haul pickers up there to pick cotton. It was as big as the fields I plow down here. Now it's all woods. A lot of this land will be planted in pines, off the road, up there on the Margraves place. Well, what it is, when I quit, there won't be no one else to farm that land. I ain't gonna farm. I won't be sorry. If you don't make money, how the hell can you miss it? Of course, we tried to hold out. I've done everything I can do. All my land 'round here was paid for at one time. Now, I got it all mortgaged up to my dick on account of bad years and high prices I pay out. We just ha'n't made any money on the farm in the last five year.

In 1973, Joe's father died. He was eighty-three. Joe gained title to two hundred acres, and his brothers and sisters got the rest of the original six hundred acres. Joe raised cotton one season after the death of his father. In the 1960s, the Bridgeses had invested in a used cotton picking machine that cost $2,500. They still had to hire chopping hands, but the machine enabled them to farm cotton through the decade. But the price continued falling. That last season, they grew one and a half bales to the acre and made eighteen bales. Small farmers couldn't do that any more. So 1974 was the last year the Bridgeses grew cotton, ending 150 years of family tradition.

Soybeans were going up in price. Joe had to make a decision.

The next season, he turned heavily to soybeans. Joe invested in machinery, buying on credit. Those were the years when it seemed American farmers were destined to feed the world. He was caught, like many other American farmers, when the bottom fell out. Soybeans and not cotton led to Joe's current crisis.

The golden era of farming was over. Joe talks about his father and how it was better back then:

> He died before all this depression came on. Up to his death, you could make it. My father, when he died, had over eighty-some thousand dollars in the bank, and he never did nothin' in his life

but farm here. Back then, the money he got, he could buy somethang with it. He raised wheat. He got two dollars a bushel for it.
Wheat is two dollars sixty now. Remember this: he was payin'
seventeen cents a gallon for tractor fuel. Today, diesel fuel is a dollar twenty-nine. Back then, fertilizer was twenty-five dollars a ton.
Now it's two hunnert a ton. Everythang went seven or eight times
as high, except the price you got. That son of a bitch went down
lower. I don't know where you can make it. I was gettin' seven or
eight dollars a bushel for soybeans. It went down to four somethang. You can't make money there. Of course, in the Depression
days, it was real tough. But Lord knows about now.

Time is running out for Joe.

His doctor tells him the outlook for his health is grim. His lungs
are seared from farm chemicals sprayed on the crops and from toxic
materials in the tire factory in Cherokee City where he worked for
thirty years.

His lawyer tells him court protection from the bankers will last
only so long. Joe would quit now, but he believes if he has one more
good year, he can pay off the credit and keep his two hundred acres.
Soybeans are his only real cash crop.

Each year, however, has been worse for soybeans. He keeps
planting them, like a gambler pulling more money out of his pocket
to lay on the table, hoping to break out and get back at least some
of what he's already lost.

See, last year, if I could have saved my crop, I would have been in
no trouble. I would have come out and caught everythang up. I
figure I lost at least twelve thousand dollars. So they call me and
threaten me. I wanna quit now. But I got to farm to pay on the
land. If I can manage to pay for it, and they let me sell it, I could
make some money on it, sell it to people to put homes on. That's
what the man would do who would buy it from the bank. I gotta
put a hold on them and let me work it. The other way I don't have
a durn option. They'd buy it cheap and make a big profit.

But he has been playing with ever-losing hands.

. *iv* .

For the younger members of the Margraves family, the land holds
little value, sentimental or monetary. At least, that is how T. Wilson
Margraves III feels. The son of T. Wilson Margraves, the nephew
who inherited the Hobe's Hill land from the childless T. Hudson

Margraves, he is twenty-six and lives in California with his wife and new baby. He was just transferred to Sacramento by the food conglomerate for which he works.

He visited the Hobe's Hill land only once, as a boy, when his father went to check property lines. He remembers little of the land and does not care about it. He is not a man of the land, but a suit-and-tie man, educated to fear office problems, not the vagaries of weather. He deals in flow sheets and performance evaluations. When visited in Sacramento Margraves comes to the door of his rented condominium, starched shirt freshly unbuttoned, physically a youthful version of his granduncle T. Hudson, a high melon forehead with small ears like airplane wings pinned to it. He knows little of his granduncle, who was hated by the Woods and Ricketts families for robbing them of a fair return on their labors.

He's found himself in a high-powered career as a director of personnel, which fits into the pattern set by his ancestors in the sense that he controls the opportunities of others to obtain work and the conditions under which they will work, but he doesn't feel wealthy or powerful. He says California is like a fast-paced foreign land. There are many differences between where he is now living and where his people came from. He says,

> Another thing in Alabama you don't see out here are all the shanties. You'll be driving along on a two-lane and all of a sudden, you'll see a shack. Go a bit further, you see another shack. In some towns, it's the 1960s. We're still trying to catch up. They can accept change, but they want change slow.
>
> Alabama is different. You had—still have—dirt-poor people, but they think they have it made. You got a lot of simple-type, good-natured folks who just don't understand a lot of things. They're happy. They got their family, they got a roof overhead, they can put food on the table. Some of those people believe "the man" still exists—"the man" being the plantation owner. If I work for "the man," "the man" never lets me down, gives me food on my plate, provides me a job, a place for my kids, all that. There's some of them who still believe in the way it used to be, the way they were raised, that "the man" has been good to me, so why should I get out and try to make it any differently?
>
> Poverty? Will it change? That's the way they was raised, that's the way their fathers was raised, that's the way their grandfathers was raised. Again, the Old South. Maybe sometime down the road. Probably not.

. *v* .

The Bridgeses grow most of their own food and work hard at it.

During one spring visit, on a motionless April evening, the Bridges house is found empty.

Lying recessed in a grove of red oak, the house looks much better because of a new coat of paint. The usual tractor implements are strewn across the deep-set yard. There's the fruit stand out front, shuttered this time of year, the weeds, already out of control, the crimson slash of harsh clay next to the road ditch.

Kate is found across the highway, partway up the Hobe's Hill road, in the garden plot near the empty house where the Woods family lived after 1937. Kate is in charge of the gardens. It is no small job. Part of the Bridgeses' religion is the faith they have in themselves, nature, and hard work.

Three large gardens are scattered across their spread: one by the main house; another, this one, at the base of Hobe's Hill; yet another by the pond down the road. These are not gardens, in the usual sense of backyard plots, but patches that cover many acres, critical to their food supply, especially since Joe retired from the tire factory. Another source of food is the pond, which contains large bass and catfish.

Kate is on the small tractor, drinking a beer and driving hard. She has tight muscles for a woman in her fifties, a voice stronger than the tractor engine. In a way, she is handsome, though not in any city sense. Kate seems to enjoy flirting, and her sense of humor at times takes on a robust, even crude, sexual aspect. She delights in announcing when a visitor's fly is down.

Kate is all business this evening as she jumps off the tractor and takes up her shovel. Darkness is nearing, and storm clouds climb the western horizon, discharging serious bolts of lightning. The last precipitation fell over a month ago, as a few inches of uncommon snow. The past five dry summers have devastated both the Bridgeses' soybeans and their gardens.

Kate wants a good garden this year. She is rushing to get in as many tomato plants as possible before the hoped-for rain arrives and darkness halts their efforts. Helping are her mother and her other son, his two blond girls watching from the cab of a rusted pickup. The work is a furious, beautiful act. The son follows Kate, dropping the plants into the holes she has made. The old woman crawls behind, on her knees, pressing soil in place. Kate's mother worries that she has to get back and skin the five catfish she caught this morning. She cannot work in the sun any longer, because of her pacemaker, but she is good at fishing, pea shelling, helping out with jobs like this. The thunder grows and voids most words; lightning flashes on forms hurrying down the rows. The air smells of earth—sharp, tasting of ozone.

There are those people who, in the 1960s, went "back to the land." They bought farms in places like Vermont and the foothills of California, subscribed to magazines that told them how to make windmills, waterwheels, solar panels. In time, many of them sold out and went back to the city. They were from a different culture, raised in the prosperous 1950s and 1960s. Some who had rejected their parents' world found they couldn't live without it.

People like the Bridgeses never have to go back—they've always been there. Unlike some modern back-to-the-land people, they have the cadence of spirit and style needed for this kind of life. Their lives never attained the obscene speed of city people's. When Joe went to his factory job in the city, he worked the second shift. The factory job was his "public job," as he calls it, and he never identified himself by it. Joe always called himself a farmer. Mornings, before the sun came up, belonged to him. He did all his tractor work before noon, when he drove north and vanished inside the tire factory.

When Joe was a boy, nearly half of all Americans lived like his family. Now, about 2 percent of all Americans do. The Bridgeses are holdouts in a world that has gone on without them. Unlike Margaret Ricketts, they did not reject the new world out of hand—they chose to try and accommodate themselves to it, while retaining the values of their early years. Now they, like the tenants who had once worked this farm, must face the reality of defeat. It appears the farm might be sold. The man who buys it would break it up into house plots near the road and plant the back land in pine trees.

What will happen if our country ever again plunges into economic chaos as it did after 1929? Many people like the Bridgeses were able to raise their own food. They hurt, but did not starve. Now that 98 percent of all Americans are off the farm, any repeat of the past could result in scenes of starvation similar to those we are accustomed to seeing in other countries. Already, there is this difference between our time's urban poor and farm poor, even with food stamps and welfare. The farm poor do not have to go through other people's garbage to find their meals. If the country were ever again to go broke, the army of people looking in garbage cans for their daily bread would turn our urban centers into a string of North American Calcuttas. The irony will be that some of our best farmland will be planted in trees. The Bridgeses may have something to teach modern Americans. But for now, they have their own storm clouds to think about.

The garden is a little over one acre, a square of dark brown surrounded by bright green. The son who helps Kate push tomatoes into the earth asks why his mother is planting so much ground. He has a city job and buys most of his food from the store. Kate is planting about a third more than in previous years. Kate reckons if the drought continues, they'll need the extra ground to make up for any loss in production. Last year, for the first time in their lives, she says, they had to buy greens at the store.

"I don't want to do that again," she adds.

In this patch are tomatoes, peppers, eggplant, squash of all types, beans, peas, peanuts, corn. Finally, it is not rain but darkness that halts the work. Kate stands back and stares. They have planted ninety-two tomato plants, dozens of peppers.

The rain does not arrive, passing far to the north, over the distant city. Kate goes back to wait for Joe, who is out plowing the Burgandy land. He is on the tractor in the middle of seventy acres where Maggie Louise and her family used to pick cotton, plowing by headlights, oblivious to the reports of farmers killed by lightning. He wants to get in another hour of breaking ground.

Joe always seems to be atop that old tractor. He starts in the morning and doesn't stop until evening in peak season. His six-foot body, topped by a cresting wave of full whiteness rising owl-like above his forehead, appears to have grown up on the back of that tractor, but his early work was behind mules. He is sixty-two, though his body looks young, with a waist snipped in the middle and strong arms. His tight lips release words with precision, though they often remain unclear because of his soft Alabama voice and a wad of tobacco always held in his mouth.

Frequent bursts of lightning illuminate the crude beauty of some abandoned shacks on the dirt road leading back to the main highway. A rain falls, spotty, without lust, and soon ends. On the main paved highway, steam rises in wisps. Stars come out.

They may not be the best farmers, but they are honest and work hard.

They occupy just a niche in the sweep of mostly unpeopled vastness that has come to characterize modern rural Alabama. The land has grown more frightening in its solitude over the past five decades. Each generation in time becomes the older generation, and soon these people will be forgotten. Our generation will pass. Another dozen generations will walk this planet, be forgotten; more beyond. If the planet is not killed off with poisons, the land of Hobe's Hill will still be there after all this passage, waiting, beneath the forest canopy, dripping in the wetness of winter, brittle under the yellow monotony of summer, ready for men and women who will again need to grow food and fiber.

They will not recall what happened with cotton and the decades that followed. They will cut back the trees and introduce the soil once again to the sun, and will not know of the struggles of the tenant families or the final desperation of Joe Bridges.

By 1988, Joe had restructured his loan, selling off fifty acres, still trying to stave off the bankers, living on fifteen hundred dollars a month in retirement income. He had stopped planting Hobe's Hill, but was again hoping to make a crop on the bottomland to pay off his debt. A drought far worse than any he'd ever seen was killing that chance.

. *vi* .

And what of the towns? For now, they remain basically unchanged from 1936, and they are likely to stay that way.

The downtown strip of Centerboro, a dozen miles south of the Bridges farm, is just as it was before Walker Evans's camera. A picture taken from the same angle today reveals the alteration of only a few signs and the style of cars. Waynesville, the seat of the neighboring county, was also photographed by Evans, and his pictures, never published in *Let Us Now Praise Famous Men,* show that this town is also essentially unchanged.

The death of king cotton has left these towns bypassed. But they have two major points of distinction they did not have half a century ago.

Waynesville is now largely controlled by blacks. Centerboro is mainly controlled by whites. Therein lies the basis for a tension that has existed since the 1960s civil rights days.

White leaders of Centerboro describe local blacks as satisfied with their lot and well behaved, and they point to Waynesville as an example of what happens when whites drop their guard.

Though in a slight majority, Centerboro blacks are disorganized, and whites want them to keep them that way. To retain power, whites are working to gerrymander voting districts. A town councilman explained this quite openly. He was working with other leaders to disincorporate black housing areas on the city's edge so that blacks would be excluded from voting in town elections. In the more conservative environment twenty years after the 1960s, white leaders felt they could get away with this scheme, but it has been learned since that the federal government ultimately put a halt to it.

"We've been able to maintain the white majority so far," says the town librarian. Federal regulators are empowered under the 1965 Voting Rights Act to monitor these small towns to ensure that no electoral fraud takes place. It will be a long time before the federal regulators can stop this oversight in many small southern towns.

In Waynesville, a few leaders, many behind Haskew, a longtime black activist, have led a 60 percent black majority in wresting a measure of control away from whites. Most of the county commissioners and school board trustees are black, as is the sheriff, though the council is still mostly white, as is the mayor. The white mayor felt uncomfortable talking. He describes one of the two black councilmen as "a good one," meaning he often gives in to the wishes of his white brethren. It also means he is called "Tom" by Haskew and some other blacks. All this should change, because the system of voting for the town's city council was altered by a federal court order after local blacks complained. Officials will now be elected not at-large but by district. Whites used the at-large system to retain power on the city level—they could dilute the vote in districts with low voter turnout so that no blacks were elected. Now even those voting blacks in districts with low voter turnout will be able to elect councilmen who represent them, rather than have their votes thrown in with those of all the other districts, where the whites, who vote in greater numbers, can be counted on to elect only their own.

But one liberal southern white newspaper editor says conservatives have actually gained from this, at least in larger cities. Before the change, white officials elected at-large had to pay attention to blacks, who could not vote in blocks but could make a difference in which whites were elected. Now, with the district basis, officials from all-white districts—and these are often the most powerful officials—do not have to court black votes. As a consequence, more hard-line whites are being elected than before, polarizing towns and worsening conditions. A few districts, each drawn so as to include almost only blacks, mean only a few token elected black lawmakers who cannot buck the powerful white politicians. It seems blacks cannot come out ahead in most towns no matter what is done.

Since blacks took control at a county level, Waynesville's downtown has been largely abandoned by white businessmen. The desertion of downtown also reflects the death of farming. There are many empty storefronts and a sense of gloom. The departure of whites has been hastened by blacks who gather each Saturday, led by Haskew, to picket the remaining white-owned stores to protest white control of money in the county.

Whites, as might be suspected, are naturally upset by this. Not long ago, Haskew's house burned. Though the evidence is inconclusive, the cause of the blaze seems suspicious. At the urging of local whites, Haskew was also arrested on federal charges of more than two dozen counts of tampering with the ballots that gave blacks control. Haskew was later found not guilty of any of the charges against him. He proclaimed his innocence vigorously, both in court and to us, and, to prove his point, produced some of the voters he was accused of coercing. He took us to a blind woman, so old that she was the daughter of a slave. The woman was barely able to recognize that she had visitors. It's hard to imagine, taking the point of view of the other side, that she would be able to vote without guidance in filling out the absentee ballot. But there's no other way she could vote, without Haskew's help. It is a bitter fight.

Still, Haskew may be as power hungry as some whites to the west in Centerboro. "We make the laws now," he says, and he is smug about it. Some blacks not involved in the fray dislike what he has done. They fear he is unwilling to compromise. At the least, they worry there will be no place to shop. Concern over this has erupted in warfare between him and other black leaders. One black politician says just putting black faces in office will not solve the problems of the county. Whites, who happen to have most of the money, are choking the town off.

Haskew says whites began planting the land in pines, switched to raising cattle or soybeans, and refused to create employment, in the hope of driving out young blacks, leaving a county of aged ex-sharecroppers who would soon die off. After this, he says, whites planned to regain control.

"Soybeans and white-faced cows was supposed to replace the niggers," says Haskew. But their plans after the disappearance of cotton were foiled by the decline of black outmigration that coincided with the decline of northern industry.

"If the North was still absorbing all these people," he says, "it would be a ghost place now. But nobody's going north anymore."

While Waynesville is being destroyed, Centerboro is a museum of the past, not decaying like its nearby sister, but not moving forward either. Local whites in power loathe change of any sort. Some of the biggest controversies occur when someone wishes to repaint a store sign. Ruling whites have regulated out fast-food chains and any business that competes with the monied men who run the politics of the town. They seem to disdain poor whites along with poor blacks. Their policies have led to a closed marketplace where prices are dictated and power is carefully handed down.

It's doubtful these towns will do anything but continue a slide into oblivion. Centerboro will probably look the same in another fifty years. Waynesville will be a populated ghost town, divided along white-black and black-black lines.

. *vii* .

At night in the end of a summer, Waynesville's streets, quiet by day, are simply dead. The streets extend into the blackness from the courthouse, which, as in all southern towns of any distinction, is the center of attention in the downtown district.

The courthouse stands bright in the night, pure in its whiteness, the painted brick chalky to the touch. The building is obscured by three dripping magnolias. Beneath their darkness is a Civil War cannon, and it may not be an accident that it points north.

Near it is a knee-high wall that at noon hosts a row of aged blacks. Many wait for their friends visiting the welfare office in an old bank across the street. Welfare provides the largest means of income in this county. On the welfare office door are several announcements. "Job Corps is the key to the door of opportunity."

The words are printed in faded marker pen inside a crudely drawn key. Below them is the following:

> Job Corps . . . Provides job training. GED preparation. Medical and dental care. Travel. Earnings. Job Corps gives young men and women 17 thru 21 the opportunity to find a brighter future. Help yourself by letting Job Corps help you.

Half a dozen pay phones surround the square. All are well used, for many people cannot afford phones in their own homes. A woman is arguing with someone on the phone at the corner of the welfare office. She implores the person on the other end to tell her the truth. Her husband sleeps in an old car. The argument continues, the best parts indecipherable, spoken in hushed tones.

At the hardware store, the window is filled with old-time goods such as washboards. The owner once said many local people still clean clothes by hand with them. At City Drug, there is a back-to-school sale. This is one of the stores picketed by Haskew, the black leader.

Last year, when being picketed, the owner refused to comment. He peered over the prescription counter and said outsiders should mind their own problems; Alabamians will mind theirs. He turned back to his pills. It is sad he did not choose to share his views. He assumed that anyone from out of town who asked about such things was a northern troublemaker who would make him look bad, no matter what he said. His is a common reaction.

Just outside of town, a country store photographed by Walker Evans is still run by one of the three large Depression-era plantation families, who now, if combined, own about 75 percent of this county. None of this family's land is in cotton, and the gin across the road from the store is rusted and falling down. Next to the gin is a shack still home to somebody. It lacks a door, and the porch leans like the brim of an old straw hat. Nearly naked black children with distended bellies sit on that porch. The man who runs the store is asked about poverty in this county.

"There ain't no poor people 'round here," he says. When the blacks across the street are pointed out, he shrugs. The faces of the blacks remain unchanged in the distance.

"I ain't seen one ever go into the welfare office that wasn't fat," he says. "I wouldn't say they was starvin'. They have it better now than they ever had it in their whole lives. They don't gotta work no more."

He goes on to say it was civil rights that poisoned their minds and made them want to stop working. That is what killed cotton, he says. If they had just kept on picking and kept their mouths shut, they'd be working today.

Then his friend nudges him, and it is like a switch has been thrown, with the realization that these words spoken to strangers might somehow be used against him.

Without missing a breath, he says, "I ain't gonna answer another question."

It is impossible to be an outsider and get honest views from whites. And most black officials are simply afraid. Some whites, when approached casually, say all the usual racist things one might expect. One white says that blacks are just as corrupt as whites were, but that whites at least kept the roads in good shape. Of course, there are whites who aren't racist, but they seem a minority in this town.

This night, there is no sign of conflict, just the faces of eighteen empty stores that surround the square of the courthouse. One is a monument to the 1960s. Shirts on racks rot on hangers, everything thick with dust. The seed store is permanently shuttered, reflecting the state of farming. There are no restaurants in the downtown district, just two on the outskirts. Few can afford to dine out.

Around the corner from the courthouse is the only tavern. The black owner once said he hates not only white leaders but most local blacks as well. He says he started hating fellow blacks after they started hating him for doing whatever it was they figured he must have done to get the bar permit. The way he sees it, they became jealous of his fortune. He's angry that many refuse to patronize him. Groups of blacks will stand outside his tavern door, drinking booze bought up the street in the package store, laughing wickedly when he tries to chase them away.

It seems everyone in this town is full of some sort of hate. It is not hard to understand, in a sorry place like this.

Tonight, the bar is closed, the inside dark. In the window is a hand-lettered sign, next to a drawing of a robot:

Welcome Lincolnites. City Lounge presents Friday-nite—9:00 p.m. August 1, 1986, "Dr. Throwdown and Johnny Jive"

Nearby, a church has located in an old storefront. On its window is a rough drawing of a dead man, hands crossed on his chest, and a warning:

> The living know they shall die. Regardless to race. Repent or perish.

Inside the outline of a tombstone, scrawled in blood-red watercolor, are the words:

> Rest in Peace
> Born 19____
> ?
> Died 19____
> Put yourself here

A church bell tolls a dozen times. Back in the square, the woman on the phone is still emotional, and her husband sleeps on. At the jail, prisoners jeer at passersby in the night. The parking lot near the jail—next to the church—was the site of a civil rights riot in 1965. Haskew was there. He and other demonstrators had been protesting county voting laws that excluded blacks, when some whites showed up. Whites smashed newsmen's cameras, police marched on the crowd, and no one is certain what happened in the confusion, but a shot was fired and everyone ran, leaving a young black man dead in a pool of blood at the center of the parking lot.

Waynesville—and Centerboro, to a degree—still lives with that day.

GAINES

.i.

No one knows when the people of Parson's Cove started using the spring. Sherman Parson is eighty-seven, and as a little boy he fetched its water. His grandfather told him that when he was a child, he too had filled his buckets at it. Sherman Parson and his kin are descended from slaves. They are named after the white family who owned them and who also gave their name to the Cove. The white Parson family is forgotten, but the black Parsons have been here a long time, predating the road next to the spring whose water they still drink. The spring is steady and has never gone dry, even in the worst droughts.

The spring lies several miles south of the crossroads stores and about a mile up the road from the Gaines home, at the bottom of a swale, about ten feet east of the road. Its water emerges from a low bank of earth that sprouts box elders and sassafras, red oaks that rise far above lesser trees.

The water emerges not from a single hole but from a series of seeps oozing faint hints bled from the length of the bank, and they merge and merge again until collecting about five feet below in a solid rivulet thick as a strong man's wrist, dammed by a bank of mud into a shallow pool, where many residents of Parson's Cove come to dip their buckets—still the sole source of water for them. Below the dam, rebuilt after each heavy rain, the water runs parallel with the road, until it joins a nearby creek of no consequence.

At the edge of the pool, the mud is tightly packed from the imprints of many feet. The water is used not only by the men and women of the Cove but also by dragonflies that light upon its surface, crayfish that inhabit the bottom and keep it clean of insects and debris lost by careless bucket dippers, and opossums that have left tracks. It is cold water that burns the lips. It absolutely lacks taste, unless the bottom is riled when a cupped hand is dipped too deeply, and then it has the flavor of bark.

One evening during a conversation on the porch of Frank Gaines and his wife, Urline, a group of residents decided that, after all these years, the spring needed some improvement. Frank Gaines, Sherman Parson, his son Herman, and two other men took it upon themselves to do something. Frank has a well, but he got caught up in the spirit to help his neighbors who don't. Much serious discussion ensued. A week or so later, someone found a length of concrete sewer pipe, four feet high, two and a half across. The pipe supplier never said where it came from, and no one asked.

Their idea became this: they'd punch a hole in the pipe wall and dig the pipe into the mud of the spring. The pipe would fill, and water would gush from the hole.

Sherman Parson envisions getting all the cold water he'll be able to draw by simply placing his jugs at the base of a spigot, rather than by the cumbersome process of transferring it with pans, a chore he's endured the past eight decades.

. *ii* .

It is morning, and five men are gathered at the spring. Herman Parson is the youngest, at fifty-six. He's also the tallest, with shoulders as broad as the pipe that lies next to the truck. His face is like a box, squared off by a flattop haircut. He has much lighter skin than the others, except for his father, whose skin is the same tone, blending perfectly with the earthen bank. Old man Gaines's shirt is spotted with holes, missing many buttons, open the length of his chest, held together in a knot tied like a bone joint at the waist. His pants are rolled to the knees. He has a face hardened from a scar earned at a pulp mill, when a chain licked him, leaving a lightning bolt across his forehead. It seems the oversize bones of these men's bodies are ill fitted to match their tight skins, and the skeletons protrude at the joints.

Sherman Parson goes to the bed of the truck, a 1966 Chevrolet with eight cracks in the windshield. He finds a hammer, handle splintered, taped together, and a chisel. He strokes the concrete grain. Each man has an opinion of where the hole should be bored. Some want it in the middle and some right at the edge. The men stand back. There is talk. It cannot be described as an argument, because each man lets minutes pass before replying. The words are said with a slowness that gives the impression that no conversation is going on.

"'Bout here?"

The heat of day has already matured into sweat on their faces, and the long gaps are filled with the sound of locusts somewhere in the treetops.

"Best put it there."

"No, there."

"There."

"There."

At noon, chips have been flying off the pipe for well over an hour, stinging flesh, propelled by carefully driven blows. Sherman Parson will hammer for ten minutes, stop, feel, resume. A thermometer in the cab indicates it's one hundred degrees.

The men decided to bore two holes in the pipe. On one side, a hole about an inch wide has been chopped about a foot below the lip. On the other, Gaines is finishing one of the same diameter eighteen inches down. They believe that the water will enter the lower hole and the force fill the pipe, driving it out the opposite and higher hole. It appears this theory defies the law of gravity, but it seems proper not to mention anything.

The pipe chopping finished, Gaines wades into the pool, shovel slung over a shoulder. The tool is as old as the bearer, handle worn to a pinpoint from years of rot and the abrasion of use. The steel blade is so unevenly worn that it seems to have teeth. Gaines wields the frail instrument with power, driving it into the water and thrusting mud on the bank. It doesn't take much to imagine him as a strong young man of six foot two some fifty years ago, standing firm behind a team of mules, riding steel across the earth. His back is now curved to a C from those early days behind a mule. It's easy to see why his landlord, Charles Gumbay, sold him the two acres before he died. Gaines must have been a tremendous worker. He moves fast, defying the pace of the day for ten minutes, until a hole is sunk in the base of the pool so that water reaches his knees. He slows, showing his age, and the scoops come only after long rests of leaning on the pointed end of the shovel. The other four men stand in the shade and watch. Gaines wipes his mouth.

"You sit there on yo' ass," he calls out. The men smile in response. Gaines goes back to digging.

Sherman Parson takes a turn, doing about as well as Gaines.

"Oh, things have changed," says the elder Parson of the Cove. "Cotton? What you talkin' 'bout? Used to be nothin' but cotton roun' here. Ain' no cotton here now. They planted cotton year before last. Jus' a patch. They planted pine trees there last year. I asked them, I said, 'You ain' gonna eat no pine biscuits.' They didn' have nothin' to say 'bout not eatin' no pine trees."

The day is advancing, but all the work seems as if it could have been compressed into half an hour. The sun has journeyed to the top of the trees on the west side of the road; it now invades the shade of the red oaks that shielded the spring during the morning hours. The waist-deep hole is at last ready to receive the great pipe. It takes all five men to roll it through the mud at the edge, now gelatin because of all the water being slogged over it. The bank swallows feet. The pipe falls in, water welling around the outside, heading downstream, refusing to enter the center. The men recognize the flaw in their theory. To correct matters, they try damming the flow in an effort to build some pressure and convince the water to rise inside. It does not oblige.

The men stand back and contemplate. Herman takes an old mayonnaise jar found in the mud. He rinses it with a slurry of gravel, and the men use it to drink water taken from the head of the pool, where it is still relatively clear. The water tightens the throat and satisfies better than any soda. They'll have to try and fix it some other day.

The men are frustrated—not only by their failure but also because none of the other residents who drove by have stopped and helped. It seems the younger generation is not interested in giving a hand to the old men, that its work ethic is not as strong as theirs. Of course, the young men lucky enough to have jobs were away at them, such as Gaines's son-in-law, who works at a distant lumber mill. But the half dozen young men who passed merely stopped to talk, not to help.

"They shore gonna use this," says Gaines, shaking his head.

The men pack the tools and head home to their shacks lost in the forest.

. *iii* .

The Gaines home is a mile away. Ten youths dribble a basketball in the dust near the road, shooting for a hoop hooked to a crudely planted log pole. Their bodies, bright with sweat, are shirtless and sleek ebony, like muskrats swimming in a pond. They seem taller than ordinary young men, with elongated arms bent in exaggerated arcs, atlatls of flesh and bone. They are intent on the game, timed by the setting of the sun.

Two homes stand behind the hoop.

The crude house on the right is the newer one, a simple square of three rooms, set across from the older house. This ancient home is of the classic tenant style, with a steep-sloped roof of rusted tin, a rock fireplace leaning away from the north wall at a queer angle. On the front and side of the old house are two porches. One is the morning porch. The other is for the evening, located to escape the shifting sun. The floor planks of both porches are rotted, and where the boards have broken through, they're patched with tin skins nailed in place.

The yard between the two houses is unfamiliar with the growth of grass. Whatever hasn't been trampled by the shuffle of many feet has been scratched raw by free-roaming chickens. Exactly in the middle is a large pecan tree, leaves soiled with dust kicked by three cars now parked at its base. Behind the tree is the Gaineses' well, the old hand-dip variety with a wooden bucket dangling from a rope crank. A low growth of pears and peaches rises behind the well, where a garden of shriveled corn, sugarcane, and peas is lost amid a tangle of weeds and pig pens made of half-sawed logs. Off to the right is a black mule. Near the barn is the rusted and rotten skeleton of a mule-drawn cart, last parked sometime in 1965.

This late in the day, all members of the Gaines family are seated on the evening porch, in homemade chairs. Frank Gaines delicately balances his buttocks atop the four-inch handrailing, wrinkled hands clasped to mouth, eyes gazing over his peaked fingers. Toes hook the splintered wood, and his pants are still rolled and muddied from the spring. There is a young fat boy; a thin girl; an older woman, Frank's wife, Urline, who is in a rocker, slowly waving a cardboard hand fan with a picture of Jesus on it. Jesus is waving his hand and saying "Go to Church." A bald man sits in a wheelchair. This is Frank's son Joe, crippled at an early age by diabetes. His eyes are not on the game but on the sun, in the mist, lost in the treetops.

Joe Gaines sits tall in the wheelchair. The only hair on his body is the thin line of his mustache flowing around his mouth into the dark rim of a goatee. He talks about the cotton days as the ballplayers walk from sight. The night shadows darken the porch, extinguishing the sharpness of faces belonging to still bodies. The only movement comes from Joe, who assists his words with motions of his stout arms, as round as the thighs of a thin woman. It seems improbable that his forty-year-old body should be wilted in that chair. Frank comes off the railing to sit near his son.

"We get by," says Joe. "We raise 'taters, corn, peas, all that stuff. We kill hogs. We don' need to buy no sto' meat. Make our own syrup from sugarcane. We go to the mill and grind wheat, make our bread. The bread you get out of a sto'? That ain' bread. We don' need nobody, nothin'."

Frank and Urline are retired. Most of their ten children have moved on. The parents still live with one young daughter and with Joe, who, when he fell ill, came back from Chicago, the city to which he'd fled in 1963. One son who never left and his wife live next door in the other house. That son works in the plywood mill. Frank and Urline's income is from Social Security and disability payments.

Of the Gaineses' two acres, almost every square foot is planted in food. Bill, the mule out back, is used to plow each spring. They have to grow food so they can eat, says Frank. But they can't grow anything of value that could bring in money.

For this family, survival has an even keener edge than it does for the Bridges family. They must grow everything on a patch the size of just one of the Bridgeses' three gardens. Whereas bankruptcy is ruining Bridges, these people face an entirely different problem.

Frank points to twenty acres of tall grass across the road, an overgrown field between the pavement and the distant tree line. By squinting, one can faintly see finger pines poking through the matted blades in the fading light of dusk.

"You see that lan' over there? I was workin' it. Now it's 'n pine. They planted them a few years ago. That white woman won' sell it. And she won' rent it. She jus' planted it 'n pine. It's like that all roun' here. Them whites jus' won' rent the lan', let anyone farm."

They are landlocked by white landowners on all sides. Those landowners control vast holdings, and Gaines views them as their largest difficulty. That twenty-acre section is part of the cotton land he worked for Mr. Gumbay long ago. It is still owned by Mrs. Gumbay. He'd like to plow it again in order to raise food on it to feed his family. If he could plant corn there, he says, they'd be able to survive better. "Me and my fam'ly can do it, but it ain' 'nough," says Frank of the farming they do to supplement their scant income. Now, in summer, a plane descends and sprays that land with herbicides, to kill the weeds that might compete with the pines.

The Gaineses are trapped in this bend of the river, still affected by a plantation matriarch. In 1986, the cycle of change brought on by the collapse of the cotton empire is not complete. Rural blacks like Gaines are still trying to cope. The old ones are stuck here. Many of the young ones can no longer go north for jobs. That escape valve has been closed to them. The land, more and more of it now forested, is off-limits and unavailable as an instrument of support for them. There seems to be no easy solution in sight for people like the Gaineses.

Frank continues,

> I was plantin' corn over there, but she jus' stop me. She was
> takin' a fo'th. You know what a fo'th is. I's where you git three
> baskets of corn, she gits one. Well, in a way it was fair, in a way, it
> wun't. You know, you got to buy the fertilizer, do the work. Why

won' they let anyone farm? We'd pay them. They jus' don' want us roun'. They don' want colored folks farmin'. They puttin' all the land roun' here in pine. I got to have some corn, for feed. They can' make nothin' in trees. They think they can raise pines on it better'n you can farm it.

. *iv* .

Mrs. Gumbay lives some distance from the Gaines family, in a real town across a range of hilly ground from Parson's Cove. Her home is on the main highway north of Jefferson, where Pearl and Ellen Woods live. It is set far back from the road, at the end of a long paved drive, behind a grove of fourteen trees in a yard as large as a city park. The heavy oak door, in the center of the stretched brick home, cracks an inch with a knock. Mrs. Gumbay is wearing white tennis shoes and white slacks, her white hair freshly curled. She resembles the kind of woman who is a member of the library association. She is wary, but opens the door and makes tea. She sits in an air-conditioned room paneled with hardwood, next to a fireplace flanked by squatting stone Buddhas holding logs.

Now, I don't feel content to talk freely with you. You won't understand. You know as well as I that when the South is mentioned, people think of the nigger picking cotton for the rich plantation owner. There was so much talk about the black man picking his cotton for the white man. But the man who had the land had to have something for it. Back then, the owner didn't get anything much out of it. We farmed until 1970. The old way ended about 1970. We never owned a cotton picker. We had about thirty families over there on our land. They picked by hand.

What would they have done for jobs if they didn't have cotton? What would they do now if they didn't live off the government? It all goes back to integration. That integration problem hit and tore farming up. When the integration problem came on, they would not he'p you on the farm anymore. There's a resentment. The black people don't want to farm anymore. Well, they do, but they want to own the land.

You think I'm a segregationist? No. I believe in them having equal rights. I raised a little black boy. He now works in a paper mill, earning thirty-five thousand a year. He's doing well. He stays loyal. He's really better to me than my adopted daughter. He comes around and still mows my lawn. Integration has done so much for the blacks. But it's been hard for them to get jobs. They haven't been able to get up and go to work. They have outgrown share-cropping. Outgrown cotton-picking. But they haven't grown into anything else. Parson's Cove is really a hurting area. But there is no crime. People leave their doors open. A Nigra is afraid of authority.

They hate to be called nigger. But nigger comes from illiterate whites who couldn't say Negro. They made a bad term out of it. Just like they made a bad term out of picking cotton. But we all picked cotton. We all hoed. I didn't look down on people picking cotton. My husband worked day and night. He didn't ask them to do anything he wouldn't do.

Right now, I'm not doing much farming. We rent some to the government. Our taxes were real low. They upped the price of the land. Now, I can hardly pay taxes. They said all my land is worth six hundred an acre. It's not worth six hundred an acre for some of that land. Some of it is just holding the world together.

Would you want to live in Parson's Cove? Yes, I'm planting the land in pines. I put sixty acres in pine last year. This year, I am going to put a hundred and eight acres in pine. Let's reason. You see, I am seventy-five. I won't live to see any of those trees cut. I may have ten more good years left. I'm planting those trees for my grandchildren.

Frank Gaines? My husband sold him two acres before he died. He liked him. Charles sold several of them land. But now, Gaines couldn't pay me to rent twenty acres of my land. He wouldn't make anything sharecropping. What would I do with a few bushels of corn he would give me? Some of them want to buy some more land. But you don't want to sell them a little old two acres. They think the landowner is holding out. But it messes up your farm. They can't afford it, and it makes it harder for you to sell the land later if it's all broken up.

For the other ones, I rent them their little houses. They have lived there all their lives, and I could not run them off. It's the only home they know. I rent the homes to them for ten dollars a month. They don't keep them up. They're satisfied with those houses. They just let them run down. I fix the windows, and they break again. I don't get enough out of those houses. A lot of them have burned down over the years. They just keep burning. A poor old woman burned in one eight years ago on our place. It's a sad situation. I don't know what to do about it.

You know good and well I can't make anything on ten dollars a month. I don't get enough from those houses to pay the taxes. For ten dollars, they want hunting privileges. They want to go out and cut wood. They don't always pay the ten dollars. It is a pain in the neck. Yet I love them to death. They're just as sweet as can be. As long as I live, all of them will have a home. My adopted daughter doesn't feel as close to them as I do.

. *v* .

Mrs. Gumbay blames welfare and civil rights for destroying cotton.

In 1965, two professors were well ahead of their time when they advanced a theory that the quest for civil rights was led by a need for new jobs because of the mechanization of cotton.

Their theory was explained in a *New York Times* article by Austin C. Wehrwein:

> CHICAGO, April 24—Mechanical cotton pickers, tractors and chemical weed-killers that have driven hundreds of thousands of Southern Negroes off the farm were cited today as an explanation for the civil rights movement that has erupted in both South and North over the last decade.
>
> This explanation, advanced by Profs. Harry C. Dillingham and David F. Sly of Central Michigan University at the Population Association of America convention here, is a departure from the usual view.
>
> Many observers contend that the current racial crisis stems from the Negro's rising hopes that segregation and discrimination would soon be ended.
>
> According to the Dillingham-Sly theory, mechanization of cotton farming has displaced so many Negroes since 1950 that it has affected Negro job opportunities throughout the nation.

The article went on to quote Sidney M. Wilhelm and Edwin H. Powell's "Who Needs the Negro?" published in *Trans-Action:*

> The tendency to look upon the racial crisis as a struggle for equality between Negro and white is too narrow in scope. The crisis is caused not so much by the transition from slavery to equality as by a change from an economics of exploitation to an economics of uselessness.

The *Times* article ended by saying that blacks were being "pushed" off the land, not "pulled" by job opportunities, and that black political power did not seem strong enough to create new jobs for these former sharecroppers. It accurately predicted a grim employment future.

. *vi* .

Another evening on the porch:

Joe Gaines's wheelchair faces the setting sun.

"I'm gonna walk again," he affirms. "I will."

Joe does not do the therapy that might help him regain the use of his legs. He drinks many days, lost with his eyes to the west, as if looking for something to happen on the horizon. Joe asks to be wheeled down the plywood ramp.

Frank is across the road, somewhere on that twenty acres of Mrs. Gumbay's. He emerges from the weeds, leading Bill, the mule. Frank sometimes sneaks Bill over to graze on the grass amid the emerging pines, unbeknownst to Mrs. Gumbay.

Frank takes up his place on the porch railing. Joe settles his chair next to the trunk of the pecan tree. Sherman and Herman Parson are visiting. Herman straddles a waist-tall propane tank as if it were a horse, his mud-encrusted boots scratching slowly in the dust. Urline waves her Jesus fan. A parade of slow cars passes down the road paved just three years ago. Those in the cars are all residents.

Parson's Cove is at a point on the map that seems as far from anywhere as any visitor to Alabama should be. Few come. It is equidistant from the largest cities, at the terminus of a road that dead-ends at a bend in a large river. The road that leads here steadily shrinks into a forest, until it reaches the crossroads stores that mark the "center" of Parson's Cove, which is unlike anything that could be called a town. It has three stores, a church in a house trailer, a school, also in a house trailer, one mansion, numerous lesser homes scattered unseen and hidden over many square miles. It's one of the blackest places in Alabama, and none of the dozens of people seen walking on the road are white. One white woman remains living in all of the whole Cove, and she runs the store, a silver building twisted on its foundation; her husband is dead, and she is very old; she sits in the store, telling everyone who enters how lonely she is.

"There's a gang of people live roun' here, out back behind there," says Joe. "But you don' do nothin' roun' here hardly. If it wun't for the government givin' you a little somethin', this would be in terrible shape here. If the government wun't given them nothin', they couldn't live."

All those on the porch say many of their relatives and friends went north in the 1960s. Most of Frank and Urline's children moved on, one as far away as California. A daughter remains home, as does the son employed in the lumber mill who lives next door. Another son, James, lives in Montgomery.

"Used to be, you could leave," says Sherman Parson. "Lots of folks went no'th. Now, there ain' nowhere to go. Ain' no jobs up no'th. The kids, they're jus' stayin', workin' what they can. There'll be more livin' down here than there used to be. I don' know what folks is gonna do."

"They don' fix the houses," says Sherman of Mrs. Gumbay and some of the other landlords. "They jus' take the rent. The folks who got the money jus' run the sto'."

Joe wanted to stay when cotton went down in the 1960s, but couldn't find work. That's when he went to Chicago. He'd still be there, if he hadn't fallen ill from diabetes two years ago. He lived on the eleventh floor of a building with no elevator, and there was no one to take care of him. So he came home six months ago. His last job was on a warehouse loading dock.

"It's worse up north," says Joe of the violence he found. "Day and night somebody always gettin' killed, raped, shot. Here you have no problem with that. We can go away for a week and don' have to lock the house."

In some ways, even the racism Joe found up north was worse than what he says is now found in Alabama. But Urline still feels that nothing has changed in Parson's Cove.

"They go their way. I go mine," says Urline of the whites she sees when they journey to town. "They stay in their place. They don' come down here. I'm sure gonna stay in mine."

Herman Parson says there's a black sheriff in this county, but that doesn't mean anything regarding the rules of what a black man can or cannot do. "In the city, down in Mobile, it's okay. Roun' here, in these country places, it's different. You don' want to do things like go with a white woman roun' here."

"Back then," says Sherman of the tenant-farm days, "you never got out of debt. There were no cars. There was no place to go to be segregated out of, 'cause you couldn' get away. You ride mules, you go only to the grist mill, haul cotton."

It's gotten better, Sherman says, but the old ways endure in subtle ways.

"If you're a black man," Sherman says, "you don' look at a white man. They got an authority some of them want to use on you."

. vii .

For white men, blacks can be difficult to approach. Driving back roads lined with crumbling shacks at dusk, all eyes are on us, the residents' faces lined with mistrust, gazing from the dark of twisted doors, windows with pulled curtains. Our usual ruses that work well with whites often fail—Do you know how to get to such-and-such a place? Just how old is this town? and so on—questions whose answers are known. The eyes of blacks seldom meet those of inquisitors, feet shuffle, and the questions are answered politely, often concluding with "sir," but no conversations are started.

This kind of reaction was addressed long ago just after the Civil War in Robert Somers's book *The Southern States since the War, 1870–71:*

> A negro servant hereabouts, on approaching "Massa" to announce something . . . turns round on his heels in the awful presence, and with "bated breath and whispering humbleness" mumbles out his message in a jargon which nobody but a negro or a "Massa" can understand. The marks of servility are sometimes too deep to be wholesome betwixt one class of fellow-creatures and another.

This attitude of deference is a holdover from the cotton tenant days, which inherited it from slave days. Gaines and the Parson men say the way they got along was to play the game of subservience. Cotton is dead, but the game goes on.

Northern blacks don't act this way. Men like Joe Gaines who have gone north and come home act differently than do their brothers who never left. Joe took on the leadership role as spokesman for the family the first few days, because he was used to dealing with whites on a different level.

The cultlike brainwashing of the cotton system is slow to perish. It has been hard, ultimately fatal, for whites like Maggie Louise. But for the blacks, it seems even more intransigent. Racism against former black tenant farmers continues in the "new" South. But how does it compare with the treatment of those who fled to the more "liberal" North?

As Joe found, racism seems to be more violent and confrontational in the North. In some Chicago neighborhoods, such as Bridgeport, the Eleventh Ward district, whites emerge from their homes to throw stones or take baseball bats to a car of black men who just happen to be driving through. In Boston, a black foolish enough to walk alone through Southie will receive similar treatment. In Howard Beach in New York City, a group of blacks whose car had broken down were chased by a band of youths with baseball bats, one of them onto a nearby parkway and into the path of an oncoming car. In Cleveland, a white driving on East Fifty-fifth Street might find a brick sailing through his or her window. These kinds of incidents are relatively rare in the South. Few neighborhoods are this off-limits in southern urban centers, and certainly none are in rural areas.

In many ways, the North is now more racist than the South. Boston took a decade longer than much of the South to deal with school integration, and when it occurred, it was violent. It has taken Boston twenty-four years after the long, hot summer of 1964 to start integrating public housing. In some of these northern cities, blacks are more isolated by de facto segregation in ghettos than they ever were under the official segregation policies of Jim Crow.

The black-against-black crime of these urban northern ghettos is extreme. Drugs, murder, and a loss of hope are all too common. Black poverty can be traced to places like Parson's Cove. It is something that has been ill dealt with for decades. Yet many in the North still turn up their noses at the South for what they see as its primitive racial attitudes. What they hold up as evidence of southern racial hate are those images of state troopers bullwhipping marchers on the Edmund Pettus Bridge in Selma. But that South no longer exists. Its racism today is like the racism around the rest of the nation—clothed in other issues, rationalized in varied ways, much more subtle but ever present.

After spending so much time in Alabama with rural blacks, we found it interesting to have this perspective and be in Chicago just before the 1988 presidential election, doing a story based on the richest and the poorest suburbs in America, both of which happen to be in this city. Ford Heights, the poorest suburb, with an average annual family income of $4,523, was all black; this came as no surprise. The rich suburb, with an average annual family income of $48,950, was all white. They are at opposite ends of town, thirty-nine miles apart.

In Ford Heights, the only barber in town was sitting in front of his little shop, and it was also no surprise to learn he was an ex-sharecropper. Willie's story could be that of any one of thousands of other blacks.

Willie came north during what he calls the "flight" of the 1960s. It wasn't so bad then. He made enough money at a host of jobs to enable him to buy this barbershop in 1978; that year, he sometimes grossed as much as $300 a day. And then everything started retrenching. The day he was interviewed, he made just $17. Things for blacks have gone downhill, and no one has money to get a haircut any longer. Willie has tried to sell the shop so that he can go back to Tennessee, but banks have redlined and will not grant loans to buyers. Willie is trapped and angry. His story is not unique: we found blacks who feel just like this in Boston and other cities.

Up in the richest suburb, Kenilworth, on the North Shore of Chicago, everyone who came to the only barbershop was a Republican. The clients spoke glowingly of the Reagan tax cuts; they wanted to find more ways to keep even more of their money. It wasn't so much that they were against people like Willie; none wanted to openly hurt someone like him. It was their ignorance that was outrageous—they didn't even know he existed. They knew nothing about the Willies of this world, or of his problems, or of why he is the way he is, or how his problems might come back to bite them someday.

The first thing we noticed about Willie was that he talked about America in the second person. He kept talking about "your" president and "your" nation. He and his family have worked as hard as anyone can. He went from picking cotton, to trying everything else, to working hard to build his own business, and he wound up losing as if he'd never left the cotton patch. He could have just as well stayed home like some of the Gaineses and been better off. Now Willie feels removed from this society. This loss of hope has bred a bitterness this nation has not seen the last of yet. The rich Republicans in Kenilworth had better start thinking about these former sharecroppers and the way things remain stacked against them.

. viii .

Also in 1988, several years after the day the men were at the spring, on a return visit, we found the pipe in place and working, finally fixed so that jugs could be easily filled. The design, though originally flawed, was adjusted so the holes in the pipe were at the same level; it just had to be tinkered with.

Down the road, all the Gaineses were on the porch, sitting just as they had last been seen, with the company of Herman and Sherman Parson. Things happen slowly here. The only discernible difference from our earlier visits was that Joe was no longer saying that he would walk again. He still lived on that porch, slept in that hot room with a bare bulb dangling overhead, staring at the walls of the shack wallpapered with cardboard and newspaper.

The legacy of the cotton system that continues to haunt Willie in Chicago also still affects the people of Parson's Cove. In Alabama, it's the attitude of blacks that is the most scarring holdover of the cotton system. Even if a local man or woman can land one of the rare jobs, there is still the problem of "loyalty" to the boss man.

When Mrs. Gumbay talks about the black child she raised, and how he remains "loyal," she touches on the most important power the landlords had, the social contract of the South. You and "the man" (or the lady) have this deal. He will never let you starve and you will always remember that you're his boy. In the old days, the specifics of the deal were this: pick the cotton, don't complain or make waves, and the man will take care of you. Today, it's defined this way: The man has the only jobs, and if you want to be his boy he'll be happy to let you work in his factories. In exchange he asks that no matter how dangerous the conditions, or how poor the pay, you don't vote for a union.

The wage at most of the area jobs is the minimum or barely above. The Gaines son who works in the lumber mill and lives next door to Frank and Urline is one of those who has traded a cotton master for a lumber master. Many blacks still talk about "the man," believing he exists as an inevitable part of their lives, just as in days of old.

A few of the younger ones are somewhat freer of the effects of cotton and can escape the system of "the man" under which their older brothers and sisters grew up. It barely touched them. For the children under twenty, cotton picking is history told by the old ones, as it will be for the ones yet to be born.

It seems maybe half the children in Parson's Cove may yet make it, if the Gaines family is a fair example. Their youngest girl is in college in Montgomery, studying to become a social worker.

Then there is James Gaines, twenty-five. He is the last of the generation who picked Mrs. Gumbay's cotton, doing so around 1970, as a child. He went to Detroit, as did so many from the Cove, but he went to attend college, not to take a factory job. Now, he lives in Montgomery and is working while continuing his schooling. He is seeking a business degree. For now, says James,

> I work in a nursing home. But that won't be for long. Farming? It hasn't been that long ago. I picked cotton. I hoed. I dreamed about getting out of farming. Now, I work inside. When it's hot, I got air-conditioning. When it's cold, there's heat. It's my kind of work. The only cotton I will ever handle again is the shirt on my back. I'm saving my money. I drive a seventy-four Malibu. But I'm working for a Z-28. Who don't want to be rich?

James is going places. The days he spent in Parson's Cove are not a handicap. But many from the Cove have not been able to wrest themselves free of the old self-destructive mind-set.

In some ways, Mrs. Gumbay is right. Some of the black men and women of the Cove were not prepared for the death of cotton. James and his sister will prove her blanket generalization wrong, but the success ratio is not good.

For the half who break out financially, there will be liberation. But the half who "fail" will also be freed in a way. They will no longer be bonded to Mrs. Gumbay or her daughter in any way. The prison of psychological servitude will be destroyed as the cotton empire fades from memory. The young ones will grow out of Big Daddyism. The illusion that "the man" will always take care of them will seem archaic. It will be unfortunate, however, if they end up having wrenched themselves free of the old southern social contract only to pledge dependence on welfare benefits.

It may be a long time before all this plays out. Before it is over, the residents of Parson's Cove will pay more of a price. Mrs. Gumbay still owns ten shacks she rents out. Her largess encourages ten families to hang on to a system that is only a memory and to a future without hope. The shacks will soon fall down or burn, too worn to survive another generation. She will not improve the homes or let the former tenants buy them. As for the homes still standing when she dies, no one knows if her daughter will continue to rent them. The daughter may evict them all.

One way or the other, those ten families will have to move on. There is no place for them here. They will have to go into the slums of Selma, Montgomery, or perhaps, belatedly, Chicago, where they will join those who made that journey long before. Many of the landowners like the Gaineses will remain. Their young will be unaware of the price paid by their fathers and mothers. They don't vote, don't know why they came to be born in this wilderness.

Meanwhile, the pines will grow thick and tall, and this powerful land will retract under the encroachment of the forest's crushing silence. Men and women who pass down the roads carved through forests will not know what was.

For now, this night, the houses of Parson's Cove are quiet, the inhabitants inside ensconced in front of their television sets. In a window, the soft glow of an oil lamp burns across a distant field, the pane blurred from view by the heads of young pines coming of age. The pepper of wood smoke is in the air. A full moon arcs across the night. The vast tracts between the occasional houses seem extra dark, except down by the river, where it is still open, and the water flows swift and shiny in the moonlight.

CODA

. i .

Winter comes to central Alabama slowly and deliberately. Though the state is at the same latitude as northern Africa, winters there are not at all as universally kind as in the Mediterranean. Yet they are seldom as brutally harsh as those of the more northern regions of the United States. Alabama winters would be more honest if they went one way or the other.

Snow is rare. When it comes, it merely dusts remaining fields, filtering to the floor of growing forests. It soon retreats from the open places beneath the advance of day, lingering in the shade of vast linear tracts of pines, the needle-covered ground sealed by the crystalline brown frozen mat broken only by fresh exclamations that are the marks of deer that passed in secret.

More commonly, precipitation comes in the form of an in-between kind of rain, colder than snow but utterly unlike the region's summer showers, which are sharp, alive, quick.

During such onslaughts, the land is disoriented and silver: the leafless limbs of gum and oak stand naked and sharp against the sky; the fields, roads, the rooftops of the cities, all the same shiny gray. Colors do not exist. The sole movement is the crawl of water coursing this gorged land, rejected by the parking lots of shopping malls in Birmingham and Mobile, by the unchanged pavements of Centerboro. The creeks are swollen in arousal, awaiting their turn to feed the big rivers that themselves seem too gorged to accept the offerings.

Yet more comes.

The rain falls all over Alabama. At the cemetery where Maggie Louise is buried it buffets the unyielding granite of her stone, ravaging what is left of the map of Orlando, still held in place by the brick under which it was left.

Brown runoff rushes down the rutted dirt of the Hobe's Hill road, now seldom traveled. Some who journey this way go to the end at the brink of a hill to cast off unwanted bed springs, sinks, tin cans. Or they are lovers who park between the water-logged sofa and the television set with the smashed tube. They leave behind used condoms, now driven flat against the mud.

The rain-gorged air swallows the diesel horn of the train down in the valley that is working its way north through the drizzle. The sound is faint against the steady beat of water on the tin roofs of the Foster place, nearly rusted through. In places, it sneaks inside in precise streams that drill through rotting floors to seek out and use as a conduit back to the earth whatever remains of the structure's foundation, hastening the day when this shack, too, will succumb.

The barn behind this home is the one James Agee described having to pass through on his walks from the Gudgers to the Rickettses. It's a barn hollow through the center, with two large doors open at each end, smothered now by vines. At the west entrance, where a rotted mule collar hangs by a nail, water sheets down the two verticle jambs, framing the land, one of the last open fields. The brown stumps of soybeans are withered in death. Those beans are the remains of the second-to-last crop ever planted by Joe Bridges, and soon they will be replaced with young pines.

. *ii* .

Farther east, over the crest of Hobe's Hill, several miles through the land of unbroken trees and deep ravines, the Shady Grove church exists foursquare in the forest, against all probabilities, a sharpness of white against all that is wet and blurry, miles down a red dirt road.

It's not unlike thousands of houses of worship to be found all over rural Alabama, spindly structures cared for kindly when all else has been allowed to go to hell. It has a single bell tower, supported by a foundation of eight hunched pillars of unmortared brick. The exterior planks are buried beneath bonelike paint, a skin grown so much thicker since that summer of 1865.

The road flows fuller now, darker, almost the color of blood, promising that it will bring no surprise visitor to disturb our probing. It is easy to force a window and enter.

The chamber resonates the pelting of rain on the tin roof, and the interior is sweet, the walls and crude pews glowing with the deep richness found in century-old pine. It has a simple interior—a pulpit, rows of plain benches. There is an organ, and two brooms hang by nails next to the front door. The floor is carefully swept. Some people, probably the old ones who have memories of long-ago weddings and funerals, still journey the back roads occasionally to worship here, but they must be few in number now, judging by the scant number of hand fans kept in a box.

On the pulpit, a paper:

Prelude
Call to worship
Hymn 2
Pastoral prayer
Lords prayer
Responsive Reading "The Worth of Man"
Gloria
Announcements
Offering
Hymn 428
Scripture
Sermon
Hymn 287
Benediction

Postlude
Hand in hand
I need the prayers
Where could I go?
Lord I'm coming home
My Jesus

Behind the building: a cemetery of a few old stones, stout and powerful granite among trees that have grown to surround the building. The forest rises as high as the bell tower, with arms that arch in long sweeps over the road, dripping concentrations of rain. On the forest floor, among the black trunks, are depressions where water gathers, most six feet long, some shorter ones that represent the resting places of children. Some are so old that large trees have grown in the center of these pits. They are evenly spaced, and most are now unmarked, the names and dates of birth and death once noted on standing boards of pine that have long since rotted. These are the people whose families couldn't afford granite like some few of their cemetery mates, likely the landowners among the congregation.

It can be guessed, by proximity and description, that this is the same church broken into by Agee and Evans in 1936. Agee described a graveyard as one where both landlords and tenants were buried. Most of the plots were then new, the graves adorned with offerings—photographs pinned to the boards, china plates, light bulbs screwed into the earth, blue-green glass insulators, vases, a butter dish. All these objects are gone, but fragments of broken glass and china struggle against a permanent interment of their own in the mud.

The ones with the wooden headboards that have decayed, whose depressions are now filled with water, are as if they had never existed.

No one knows their names, ages—anything about them. Those grieving relatives who placed the articles on the grave sites are themselves likely all dead. It may be that the last children of these lost men and women are also dead. So no one remembers them. There is no longer anyone to ask about them. And so they are as if they never were.

The rain falls with increased fury. It soaks hair dripping wet, then washes over the body, seeking and finally discovering underclothes. It is a cold rain, soaking the earth; it can be imagined reaching into those crushed caskets, washing arm bones clutching rib cages, mandibles agape. How is it that people can put in three score and ten years on this planet, and some ten more, and then be buried, mourned for a while, only in so short a time to have their lives so completely erased, no monument left to mark the place or jog the memory?

Is this any indication of things to come for that other cemetery not so many miles distant, where Maggie Louise and Floyd Franks, George and Annie Mae Gudger are buried? Soon now children whose veins carry the blood of George Gudger will know nothing of the life of that man, nothing of the daily deeds that made up the record of his life, nothing of his habits, nothing of the way he believed that one redeemed oneself only by hard work, even if inevitably it would be others, not he and his own, who would most benefit by all his toil. They will have no cause to visit his grave site, for they will not know what it marks. So he, his wife Annie Mae, with all their hopes for her own children, his daughter Maggie Louise, who carried on the dream and shared it with a stranger from New York, and Maggie's husband Floyd, who filled his silent world with love for George and Annie Mae's grandchildren—all will be as if never born, anonymous names on granite, read only by those curious enough to visit old graveyards and stare at dates on stones and wonder. They will be as forgotten as those lying below the depressions in the churchyard of the forest. Their granite markers will not have saved them from oblivion.

Of the original twenty-two family members Agee recorded, a dozen still breathe, rocking on their porches, waiting their own day to be drawn into the earth. But though they live on, their time has passed. It is now the time belonging to the 116 others born of the 22, the youngest, the baby in the womb of Anna, the daughter-in-law of Debbie, the granddaughter of Maggie Louise and the great-granddaughter of Annie Mae and George Gudger, not yet born.

The child will be part of the fourth generation descended from the Hobe's Hill families, and will grow to walk this planet in the middle of the next century, 120 years after Agee was in Alabama. Agee discussed what a damaged, dangerous world the Gudgers faced back in 1936. What kind of world will their unborn heirs face? And what of the millions of others of this same generation who have inherited the legacy of cotton sharecropping? Will they be free of its effects by the time they reach adulthood? Will we as a nation have done the right thing by them? Will they themselves have done enough to purge their lives of the malignancy?

. *iii* .

Many members of these families were not ready to face the world that challenged them after the cotton tenant system went down. The urban middle-class belief system of hope and expectation that things will always be better had never been taught to them. The transition has been hard. The choice offered them—go forward or even further backward—seemed unreasonably harsh. Some insisted on barricading themselves in the past, living on back roads, avoiding the modern world. Some others did rise to the challenge, surmounting considerable obstacles to join the middle class of America. And most of the latter did it without abandoning the South for the industrialized urban centers of the North. Indeed, about half the descendants, no matter how well or poorly off they now find themselves, live within a thirty-minute drive of Hobe's Hill. All but one lived in the South as of 1986, and she hoped to return soon.

The best off among the families remember their roots well, and fear what their heritage says of their future. As Mort Jordan said, if another depression were to strike, most of these people would be the first to bear its brunt, just as their forebears had been the first affected by the Great Depression.

Agee, studying the economic stagnation of these families six years into the Depression, four and a half years into the bloodless American revolution we call the New Deal, with its many great hopes, its several false starts, its frequent successes, came to believe that the lives of these people could not, or at least would not, ever change. Agee was wrong about this. Many have changed for the better.

But what is success? And how does one measure it? There were reasons—political, economic, social—that the New Deal failed to provide for the sharecroppers of the cotton South even the marginal help it provided for so many others. Had Agee been able to look into the future and see his generation's second revolution, the postwar boom that created a wave of national prosperity never before imagined, would he have imagined that those people who had suffered the most during the Depression would now benefit the least from the national orgy of industrial and consumer growth? What lessons can be drawn from our national failure to assure that if all boats were not in fact raised by a rising tide, at least the lowest berthed would not be swamped? And have we made things better in this latest economic boom of the 1980s? In times past, portions of our society were left poor, but we felt guilty about it. Now it seems it is acceptable not only to ignore them but to flaunt our wealth, displaying an obscene national callousness to the suffering of others. There is no other word but obscene to describe a situation in which typical annual rents in the major cities are often double what a minimum-wage worker earns in a year. It is obscene when, in a city as short of housing as New York, an insider buys an apartment for eighty thousand dollars and sells it five years later for half a million dollars, while increasing masses of the hindmost are driven to hobo jungles, underpasses, doorways, train stations for shelter. It is obscene when you travel this nation in 1988 as a journalist and listen to people tell you they are going to vote for the party on whose watch a nation of homeless were recruited because, as one man said with blunt honesty, "I'm greedy." Greed, once a pejorative, has become the national credo.

Sonny Franks, the painting contractor who naively believed that his inherited commitment to working hard and honestly, often as many as sixty hours a week, would be enough to keep his family in their thirty-five-thousand-dollar tract home, can now sit in his rented apartment, looking back at a sixty-hour work week, and read in the paper that the top 20 percent of society gained more wealth than they had during the previous year, and that the same was true the year before that, and the year before that, and he can wonder why the 20 percent that have so much are getting more and why his 80 percent, in the middle and on the bottom, are stagnating or getting less. He can rightly ask just what the hell more he can do.

I began more than three years ago by driving up the Hobe's Hill road, seeking to learn all I possibly could about poverty through the families who lived there. I learned some things regarding the subject, but I cannot say I came to know these people as intimately as I would have liked. It was an impossible task to know—much less understand—128 lives, let alone make that understanding intelligible to others. About some, I understood virtually nothing. About others, so little. And even those I thought I knew best—do I really know them? I've had girlfriends I thought I knew well, only to realize after it was over that I knew nothing, that I'd been lying in intimate embrace with a stranger. Why should I expect to know any better people less close, unrelated by blood or marriage?

. *iv* .

All over Alabama, street lamps burn through the mist, illuminating an unpeopled night. There is no clear conclusion to this, nothing exact, abrupt, easy, just the road, rushing all its wet black miles into the void between midnight and that hour when the loneliness begs for the spiritual warmth of the rising sun, but the only glow on the horizon belongs to a Denny's.

The only ones out in the night are those who must be there, travelers journeying to distant cities, lone truckers working the highways. Warren, Ruby's husband, is on another run, the reach of his headlights weakened by water greeting the windshield. He misses his Ruby, his eyes lost on the rain coming at him, wondering how time passed so quickly.

But most beds are heavy with sleeping bodies lost in dreams. Joe Bridges is in that small white house behind the fruit stand, lying half awake listening to the rain, praying it will continue into the summer and be enough to make next year's soybeans grow and save him from bankruptcy.

Warren's mother-in-law, Emma, is also alone, without a man, without love, facing the faded blue portrait of Sonny, her son killed in the riverboat accident. She lies curled tight in fear of the storm, and her dreams are of meeting him and Ruby again in that place by the river, where she can find the love she was looking for that long-ago forgotten summer, from which she awoke one day so much later to realize it had never materialized, that she had been robbed and had never known it until that moment. When that day comes, and they are all reunited, Emma will finally be able to work it out with Lonnie and he will be a responsible husband. He will hug her. And she will smile and they will all be happy.

The water falls against the roof of the apartment where Emma's niece Debbie lives. Debbie lies alone, once again separated from her husband, Ron; she now knows that no one knows anybody anyway. She dreams—not of what she has lost, but of her second grandchild, the love she has found, the understanding she has gained from her mother, Maggie Louise.

And it is another dream, in another city, and Maggie Louise is there, looking, but it is impossible to see her face. She talks, but not in words. She doesn't need them. She conveys what she has come to say, and that is: "I understand."

And Debbie replies, "Mama, I love you."

ACKNOWLEDGMENTS

Many lives came together to make this work possible. We extend deep gratitude to Susan Rabiner, our editor at Pantheon who guided us to completion, her assistant, Akiko Takano, whose astute editorial comments were valued, and Gloria Loomis, our agent who stood by through the early days when this book was a most fragile idea. On another coast, we thank Gregory Favre, executive editor of the *Sacramento Bee,* along with its magazine's editor, Terry Dvorak. The *Bee* monetarily and otherwise supported much of the early research for what became this book. In Alabama, filmmaker Mort Jordan was a friend and confidant during our many visits, providing much insight on the region and the families.

Two journalist friends set aside much of their lives to transcribe my many tapes, and to Ronnie Cohen and Jan Haag I owe much; other friends were early editors and advisors. They include Eleanor Shaw, Howard Simons, Catherine Warren. Diane Alters, who first gave us a copy of *Let Us Now Praise Famous Men* in 1982, is the person responsible for setting us on our course. While I was at Harvard, Professor Theda Skocpol opened the door for much of the history of cotton and the invention of the cotton-picking machine included here.

Michael would like to thank Fearn Cutler, associate art director at Pantheon, and members of the *Bee*'s graphics department for their guidance—Ed Canale, George Wedding, and Rick Perry. A special indebtedness is owed editor Lisa Roberts, who was always encouraging and yet objective.

And finally, we'd like to say how much we appreciate the people who, if you get right down to it, were most responsible for this and our other work—our parents, Ray and Mary Ann Agee; Steve and Joan Maharidge.

MAIN CHARACTERS AND PLACES

These are the characters and places most often mentioned in the book. Most names of people and places have been changed. I have kept the names given the families by Agee, made new pseudonyms for those born after 1936. There were 22 members in the original three families in 1936. In the summer of 1986, 12 were still living. Those 22 men and women and their children gave birth to 116 offspring still alive, as accurate a number as we have been able to determine. All ages, dates, and numbers throughout this book are as of the summer of 1986, unless otherwise noted.

GUDGER CLAN

DEBBIE ....a grandmother, thirty-five, who has returned to school.

SONNY ....Debbie's brother, thirty-four, a painter in Mississippi.

PARVIN ....Debbie's sister, thirty-three, a bookkeeper, healing church member.

MAGGIE LOUISE ....their mother, who killed herself by drinking rat poison in 1971.

GRETCHEN ....Maggie Louise's sister, fifty, who was there when it happened.

ROLAND ....son of Debbie, twelve, who likes school.

WOODS CLAN

EMMA ....retired former cotton farmer, seventy.

RUBY ....Emma's daughter, who had rheumatic fever as a child.

ELLEN ....a stepsister of Emma, fifty-two, maimed in an auto wreck.

PEARL ....Ellen's sister, fifty-eight, who took in Ellen's daughter after the wreck.

MARY LEE ....Ellen's daughter taken in by Pearl, twenty-eight, now living on her own.

RICKETTS CLAN
MARGARET ....a holdout from the past, seventy.

GARVRIN ARLO ....Margaret's son, forty.

CLAIR BELL ....almost killed in an accident caused by Agee, fifty-four.

MARGRAVES CIRCLE
T. WILSON MARGRAVES III ...descendant of the wealthy cotton lord who ruled over the Ricketts and Woods families.

JOE BRIDGES ....a bankrupt farmer who leases the land from Margraves and will be the last to plow it.

GAINES CIRCLE
FRANK AND URLINE
GAINES ....aged black sharecroppers.

MRS. GUMBAY ....onetime landlord to the Gaineses.

OTHERS
JAMES AGEE AND
WALKER EVANS ....original spies and instigators.

MORT JORDAN ....amateur filmmaker in Cherokee City and friend of the families.

HASKEW ....black leader in Waynesville.

PLACES
BIRMINGHAM ....a large southern city of dying industries.

CHEROKEE CITY ....a medium-size Alabama city.

CENTERBORO ....a county seat, population 4,000.

COOKSTOWN ....the three families' town in days of old, still their town for many who remain, population 1,500.

MADRID ....a crossroads, near Cookstown, where Debbie and Parvin were born.

WAYNESVILLE ....a seat for the county east of Centerboro, population 4,000.

PARSON'S COVE ....the town of the Gaines family, population several hundred.

HOBE'S HILL ....the clay plateau where the three families lived in 1936, population now zero.

PHOTO CAPTIONS

. photo page number .

2. Centerboro, 1936; Centerboro, 1986. (*Top photo by Walker Evans.*)

3. Margaret Ricketts, 1936; Margaret Ricketts, 1986. (*Top photo by Walker Evans.*)

4. A crossroads store, 1936; the same store, 1986. (*Top photo by Walker Evans.*)

5. Maggie Louise, 1936; Parvin, a daughter of Maggie Louise, 1986. (*Top photo by Walker Evans.*)

6. Bud Woods's home, 1936; the ruins of the same home, 1986. (*Top photo by Walker Evans.*)

7. Annie Mae and George Gudger, in a 1953 photo by their son Burt Westly, made into a plaque that now hangs on the wall of one of their children's homes.

8. Margaret, a daughter of Fred and Sadie Ricketts, on a bed with her Bible.

9. Garvrin Arlo, Margaret's son.

10. Joe Bridges standing in his field of soybeans on Hobe's Hill, the same ground where Bud Woods planted cotton.

11. Pine trees have been planted in the scarred land near Cookstown where cotton once grew.

12. Ethel, the widow of Buddy Woods, washes clothes.

13. Family on the porch of their trailer near Cookstown.

14. Man at auto-repair shop, Mississippi.

15. Teenager turtle-hunting in a swamp near the Alabama-Mississippi border.

16. Pictures of Fred and Sadie Ricketts taken by Walker Evans, on the wall of the home of their daughter Margaret Ricketts.

17. Margaret Ricketts's feet.

18. Home near Centerboro.

19. Margaret Ricketts's living room.

20. Garvrin Arlo and his wife, Jeannie Kay.

21. Trailer near Cookstown.

22. Sonny Franks, the only son of Maggie Louise, at work.

23. Sonny, the youngest son of Annie Mae and George Gudger.

24. Emma, the daughter of Bud Woods.

25. Ellen, the youngest Woods daughter.

26. Debbie, a daughter of Maggie Louise, and her son, Roland.

27. Linda and Barbara, great-grandchildren of Annie Mae and George Gudger.

28. Dogs greet visitors at home next door to Margaret Ricketts's.

29. Taylor's Big City store, Cherokee City.

30. Child on motorbike, Cookstown.

31. Abandoned car, Alabama-Mississippi border.

32. Ruins of Foster family home, Hobe's Hill.

33. Mobile-home church, near Jefferson.

34. Frank Gaines on the porch of his home in Parson's Cove.

35. Urline Gaines, wife of Frank.

36. The daughter of Frank and Urline Gaines.

37. Man outside a roadside diner, Mississippi.

38. A one-hundred-year-old former sharecropper on the porch of his home near Parson's Cove.

39. Century-old former sharecropper.

40. Resident of Waynesville.

41. Child in Parson's Cove.

42. Basketball players, Parson's Cove.

43. Man plowing, Mississippi.

44. Church service, Mississippi.

45. Young boy after church service, Mississippi.

46. Men waiting for a ride near Parson's Cove.

47. Frank Gaines's work boots.

48. Spring from which many residents of Parson's Cove draw their water.

49. Sherman Parson draws a drink from the spring he and his neighbors decided to improve.

50. Store, Parson's Cove.

51. Interior of store, Parson's Cove.

52. Home near Waynesville.

53. Retirement home, Mississippi.

54. The river near Cookstown.

55. Former ferry crossing at the river in Parson's Cove.

56. Vicksburg, Mississippi.

57. Fisherman near remnants of a paddlewheel riverboat, Mississippi River.

58. Mississippi town.

59. A new mobile home being delivered, on a highway near Birmingham.

60. Cherokee City.

61. Church on the highway leading to Jefferson, Alabama.

62. Town square, Waynesville.

63. Window display, Waynesville.

64. Dusk, Temple City, west of Centerboro.

65. Convenience store in Cherokee City.

66. Night spot, Waynesville.

67. A dairy, Centerboro.

68. Church near Parson's Cove.

69. Church south of Centerboro.

70. Roadside sign north of Mobile.

71. Watermelon seller near Temple City.

72. Abandoned cotton gin, Madrid.

73. Interior of abandoned cotton gin in Madrid.

74. Roadside sign on the highway to Birmingham; abandoned store near Cookstown.

75. Used-car lot, west of Centerboro.

76. Chicken Mart, Cherokee City; plastic deer and trailers, near Centerboro.

77. Martin gourds, Cookstown.

78. Wobbly Hill, the road north from Centerboro to Cookstown.

79. Kudzu on the Hobe's Hill road leading to the original homes of the three tenant families.

80. Church and graveyard, near Shady Grove.

Dale Maharidge is an award-winning reporter for the *Sacramento Bee*. In 1988 he was a Nieman Fellow at Harvard University. Michael Williamson is an award-winning *Bee* photographer; his work has appeared in *Life, Newsweek, Sports Illustrated, Time,* and other major publications and has won numerous awards, including the World Press Photo and Nikon World Understanding Through Photography awards.

Both have traveled on assignment widely, including trips to Central America, the Philippines, and across the United States. Together they wrote *Journey to Nowhere: The Saga of the New Underclass.*

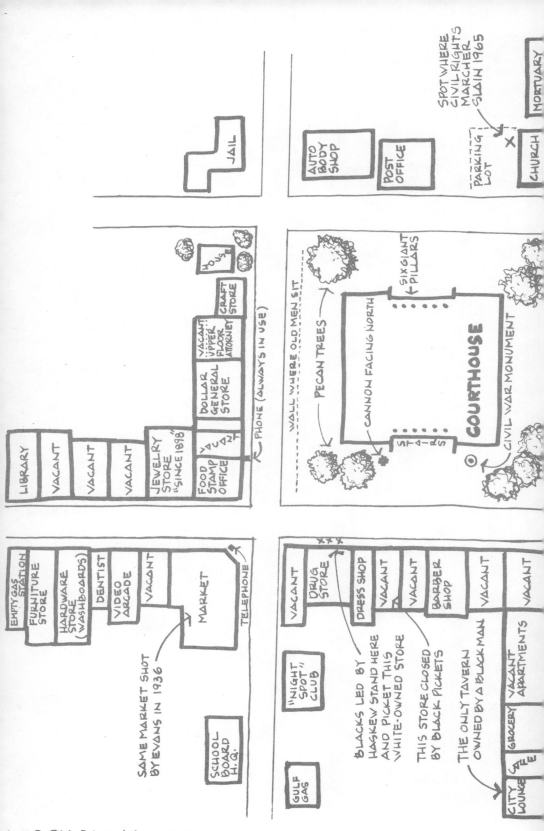

MAP BY BILL KILLMER